ACKNOWLEDGMENT

The author, editor and publishers are indebted
to Mr. Godfrey Thompson and The Architectural Press Ltd. for the use of material and
diagrams from Mr. Thompson's book "Planning and Design of Library Buildings"
(© Godfrey Thompson 1973), published by
The Architectural Press.

PLANNING

Buildings for Education, Culture and Science

PLANNING, Ninth edition

Other volume titles

Architects' technical reference data

Buildings for habitation, commerce and industry

Buildings for administration, entertainment and recreation

Buildings for health, welfare and religion

PLANNING

Buildings for Education, Culture and Science

Edited by
EDWARD D. MILLS, C.B.E., F.R.I.B.A., F.S.I.A.

ROBERT E. KRIEGER PUBLISHING COMPANY
HUNTINGTON, NEW YORK
1976

ENGLAND	Butterworth & Co (Publishers) Ltd London: 88 Kingsway, WC2B 6AB
AUSTRALIA	Butterworths Pty Ltd Sydney: 586 Pacific Highway, NSW 2067 Melbourne: 343 Little Collins Street, 3000 Brisbane: 240 Queen Street, 4000
NEW ZEALAND	Butterworths of New Zealand Ltd Wellington: 26–28 Waring Taylor Street, 1
SOUTH AFRICA	Butterworth & Co (South Africa) (Pty) Ltd Durban: 152–154 Gale Street
UNITED STATES	**Robert E. Krieger Publishing Co Inc** **645 New York Avenue, Huntington, NY 11743** **Exclusive Distributor — ISBN 0 88275 381 9**

First published in 1936 by Architect & Building News
Second edition 1937
Third edition 1938
Fourth edition 1939
Fifth edition published for Architect & Building News
by Gilbert Wood & Co Ltd 1947
Sixth edition 1949
Seventh edition published for Architect & Building News
by Iliffe & Sons Ltd 1953
Eighth edition published for Architect & Building News
by Iliffe Books Ltd 1959
Ninth edition published by Newnes-Butterworths 1976

© E. D. Mills, 1976

Filmset by Ramsay Typesetting (Crawley) Ltd

Printed in Scotland by Thomson Litho Ltd., East Kilbride

FOREWORD

By Gontran Goulden, O.B.E., T.D., F.R.I.B.A.
Deputy Chairman, The Building Centre Group

The construction industry becomes daily more complicated and to attempt to abstract the relevant information from the mass of literature available is no easy task. It is now almost impossible for one man to know even the main sources of technical information by heart.

For nearly forty years *Planning* has been a leader among the books that list, discuss and illustrate all those vital facts and figures that are not to be found in one place elsewhere. The man on the drawing board, whether a beginner, experienced in general or specialised practice, or about to burst into computerised building design will always need simple basic information of the kind that packs the pages of this entirely new edition of *Planning* which has been expanded and now comprises five volumes.

The whole question of information for the construction industry still awaits a satisfactory solution. It is doubtful even whether it is capable of being solved to meet everyone's demands. At one end of the scale there are those who demand comprehensive lists of manufacturers and products, corrected up to the minute and covering every conceivable detail of each item. Others require research information in the greatest depth with all available sources equally up to date and comprehensive. We know that this problem can be dealt with by computers, at a price. We know too that various attempts and exercises have been and are being made to turn this major undertaking into a financially possible service.

Only time will show whether the user can be trained to realise that time spent in his office on research costs money and that the answer could be available in less time, thereby saving him money. A small proportion of users are prepared to pay for information, most still think it should be free and paid for by the other fellow. Comprehensive information for the industry will require a nationally co-ordinated effort. So far there is little or no sign of this.

In the meantime the need for the right information continues in all branches of the industry. In addition to major outside-the-office sources each one of us has his own particular favourite reference books and catalogues. This personal preference will always be there wherever comprehensive systems develop.

Planning has filled many people's personal information needs for years. With a mass of useful data, and as a guide to the form of construction industry information generally, this new edition should, like its predecessors, prove invaluable and I wish it every success.

Gontran Goulden

ACKNOWLEDGEMENTS

The editor and publishers would like to acknowledge the following for their assistance in providing illustrations and information to the various contributors in the preparation of their sections.

Arup Associates

Crosby Lockwood & Son Ltd.

Delaney, McVeigh and Pike (Architects) Dublin

Department of Education & Science

F. W. Doidge Corporation

Educational Facilities Laboratories

H.M.S.O.

Laboratories Investigation Unit (sponsored by DES and UGC)

Wm. G. Lake, AFS, FIArb., Architects Co-Partnership

Nuffield Foundation, Division for Architectural Studies

Plint & Partners Ltd

Robert Matthew, Johnson-Marshall & Partners, Bath University Press

Sintacel Ltd.

UNESCO

University Grants Committee

University of Cambridge School of Architecture

University of London Computer Centre

CONTENTS

INTRODUCTION

Planning first appeared as a weekly feature in the Architect & Building News and was contributed by two architects under the pseudonym of E. & O.E. In 1936 the first bound volume was published and the authors were subsequently revealed as Roland Pierce and Patrick Cutbush, later to be joined by Anthony Williams. Since that date eight editions have appeared at frequent intervals and the general pattern has changed little over the years. Today, *Planning* is recognised throughout the world as one of the standard reference books for architects. There can be few architects offices in the UK which do not possess and constantly use at least one copy, and in many architects offices in the remote parts of the world a much used copy still holds pride of place on the bookshelf. Architectural students have always found this to be an essential work of reference and many have started their architectural libraries with *Planning* and one or two of the other well known books of reference.

The radical changes which are taking place in the world of building has led to a reappraisal of the place of *Planning* in the technical information field and in the way in which the valuable material it contained is presented. New techniques and disciplines are being developed in the building industry and these must be reflected in the technical information available. The building industry is becoming more closely integrated and *Planning* must inevitably reflect this. It has, therefore, been restructured so that it appeals to a wider cross-section of the industry including architects, builders, quantity surveyors, engineers, planners and students. With these considerations in mind, together with the change to metric in the building industry, the publishers Newnes-Butterworth and Building and Contract Journals who have taken over the publishing responsibilities of the Architect & Building News, decided that a completely new approach should be adopted and this volume is one of a series which reflect the new pattern.

The previous edition consisted of three sections; a general section dealing with information applicable to more than one type of building; a section dealing with information applicable to specific building types and metrication information to aid the conversion of imperial units to metric ones. In essence the new edition accepts this broad classification and although the work has been conceived in metric, the conversion material is retained in part.

The volume entitled *Planning—Architects' technical reference data* includes sections dealing with legislation, British Standards, materials etc. as well as basic planning data which concerns all types of building, such as landscaping, car parking, circulation, sanitary requirements, storage requirements etc., together with the metric conversion material originally in the eighth edition. All information contained in earlier editions that is still valid has been retained and a considerable amount of new material has been added. Other volumes deal with specific building types and cover a wide range of subjects, some of these building types have not been dealt with in previous editions.

The unique characteristic of this series of volumes is that it indicates how various types of buildings are planned by supplying information and data which are essential before planning can begin. It does not deal with the aesthetics of design, although in the volumes dealing with particular building types illustration is not only by means of diagrams but by plans and photographs of actual completed buildings, either in part of whole showing the way in which particular problems have been solved.

The endeavour throughout all sections of the new edition has been to provide a ready reference of basic information, or guidance as to where more detailed information can be obtained. One book can never hope to provide all the facts, and inevitably information will be omitted or given in part but it is hoped that readers will find this new method of presentation useful, and that it will carry on the long tradition of *Planning* as an essential publication for all concerned with building.

The volumes dealing with specific building types are sub-divided as follows: *Habitation, Commerce and Industry; Health, Welfare and Religion; Administration, Entertainment and Recreation; Education, Culture and Science.* Each building type is covered by the following subsections to ensure uniform treatment and to facilitate ease of reference. These are—Introduction; siting; planning; space requirements; data; accommodation; statutory requirements, legislation and Authorities; examples; bibliography.

Whenever possible diagrams and tables have been used and the bibliography lists the important books and publication that will aid further research. Unlike previous editions, the material for each specialist section has been prepared by architects with a special knowledge and experience in the particular category of building, and the range of building types has been considerably extended. By this means it is hoped that the 9th edition will be even more useful to architects and others than its predecessors.

The sources from which the material for the present edition has been gathered have been many and varied. The Editor greatly appreciates the willing co-operation of the various contributors and a biography of the author is given at the end of each section. Books, periodicals, people and associations have all contributed in a very practical way and because it is impossible to set out a complete list of those concerned, this general acknowledgement is addressed to all who have been associated with the preparation of the book and is an expression of the sincere thanks of both the Editor and publishers.

Finally, special thanks are due to Gontran Goulden who has contributed the foreword in his private and personal capacity. He has been intimately concerned with all aspects of building information in this country and abroad for the past twenty-five years and his continued interest is greatly appreciated.

The Editor would welcome any constructive criticism or comments, as the work will be constantly revised and kept up to date, and every effort will be made to take account of suggestions which may be made, so that they can be applied to future editions.

Edward D. Mills
Editor

1 SCHOOLS—PRIMARY

MARY MEDD, O.B.E., R.I.B.A.

INTRODUCTION

Compulsory state education begins at 5 years, but permissive legislation allows Local Education Authorities to build also for children of 3–5 years, either in separate buildings or in nursery groups attached to primary schools.

Until recently primary schools were divided into the following types:

		Children aged
(a)	Infants' schools	5–7 years
(b)	Junior schools	7–11 years
(c)	J.M.I. schools	5–11 years
	(Junior mixed and infants)	

Since the Plowden Report (1967) other types of school have been added, which include:

		Children aged
(d)	First schools	5–8 years
(e)	First schools	5–9 years

From these 'first schools' children can proceed to Middle schools, for the age ranges of 8–12, 9–13, or occasionally 10–13 years. Middle schools therefore cross over the legal boundary between primary and secondary education. Most Nursery and Primary schools are for both boys and girls.

SITING

Reference: The Standards for School Premises Regulations 1972, H.M.S.O.

Notes on Procedures for the Approval of School Building Projects in England, HMSO.

There are statutory requirements which relate to:

(i) The ground covered by the buildings, their immediate surrounds and the paved areas for play. (A paved area is defined as one having a hard, impervious surface constructed of materials such as tarmacadam or concrete).

(ii) Playing fields.

For a nursery school the minimum site area is based on the number of pupils, and this must include a garden playing space – again a minimum area is given – some of which is to be paved.

For a nursery class designed in conjunction with a primary school, a minimum area, based on the number of pupils in the nursery, must be added to the site area of the primary school. This must include a minimum area of garden playing space and paved area.

For a primary school there must be a minimum site area, including, as above, a paved area, to be laid on suitable foundations and properly graded and drained. In addition, every primary school except those for infants only, must have a minimum area of playing field, with certain modifications if provision for physical education and recreation is available either indoors or elsewhere.

The scale of provision for car-parking facilities is given in 'Notes on Procedures for the Approval of School Building Projects in England', Appendix 13.

There are, of course, many other factors to be taken into account, e.g. safety and ease of access, service approaches, treatment of boundaries, natural features and wild areas, sheltered gardens and courts, planting, contours and levels (see Fig. 1.1), seating etc. For these there are recommendations, but not statutory requirements.

PLANNING

In any discussion of planning trends, educational principles must always be the starting point. While a classroom/corridor basis of design, with formal rows of desks, may well have satisfied the educational needs of the past, it has lost its relevance today.

The richness and variety of primary education—variety in the activities, in the materials and equipment used, in the sizes of working groups—call for richness and variety. This also applies in the design of space and furniture, and the furniture is as important as the space. For most of the time the children work in small groups and individually, each taking his own time to find his own way, and becoming involved in many sources of information. Preconceived subject categories and a fixed timetable are largely irrelevant.

The problem is to provide space and equipment for such frequently changing patterns of work and materials and how to achieve a balance between small scale privacy for young children, and large scale exploration.

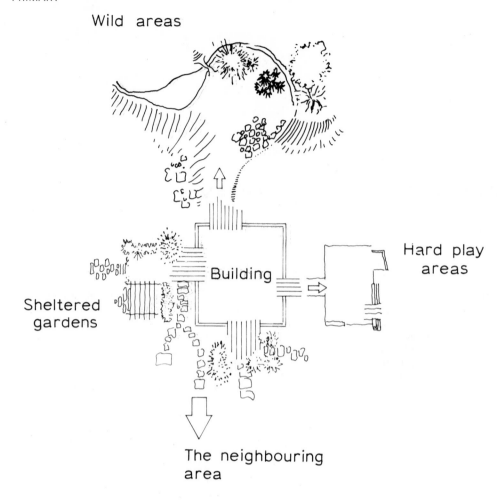

Wild areas

Building

Hard play areas

Sheltered gardens

The neighbouring area

Fig. 1.1   Some ingredients of planning. Outside

There are some fairly straightforward needs to be met for all children:

(i) A welcoming entrance, with somewhere to hang a coat and put one's things;

(ii) A place and a person to turn to easily for a sense of security;

(iii) A more general kind of studio-workshop area in which experiments, testing, painting, construction can be undertaken, with small bays or locations where this first hand experience can be used for recording, writing, calculating, discussing;

(iv) A small enclosed room, or rooms, where really quiet work can be done without disturbance, or where noisy work can go on without causing disturbance;

(v) A covered work area leading to a sheltered garden court where bigger apparatus can be handled, animals and plants cared for and studied.

Such planning ingredients as these are likely to be organised into centres in which two or more teachers can together be responsible for groups of children—perhaps 2-teacher centres for younger ones and 3- or 4-teacher centres for older ones. (Lavatories and coats areas are likely to be dispersed in small units in each centre.) See Fig. 1.2.

Other parts of the school, shared by all, e.g. a hall, a central books area (in addition to local provision), spaces for meals etc., are also likely to be more informally designed than in the past.

For very young children (under 5 years) the principles governing planning trends are fundamentally similar. The changing patterns are likely to be more extemporary, however, with variety achieved largely by means of furniture rather than by architectural definition. Parents may play an important part in the life of nursery schools, and this will affect the planning.

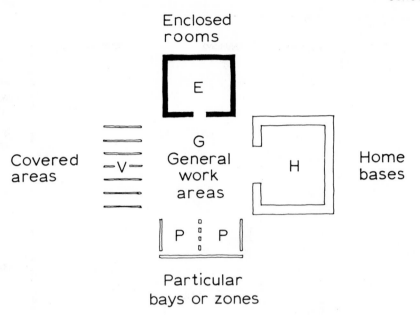

Enclosed rooms

Covered areas

G
General work areas

Home bases

Particular bays or zones

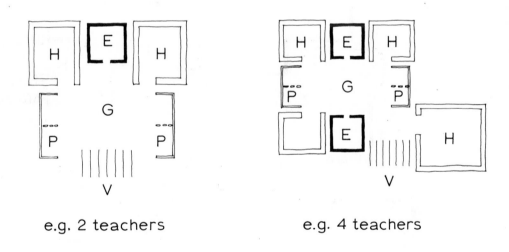

e.g. 2 teachers

e.g. 4 teachers

Fig. 1.2 Some ingredients of planning. Inside; local work areas

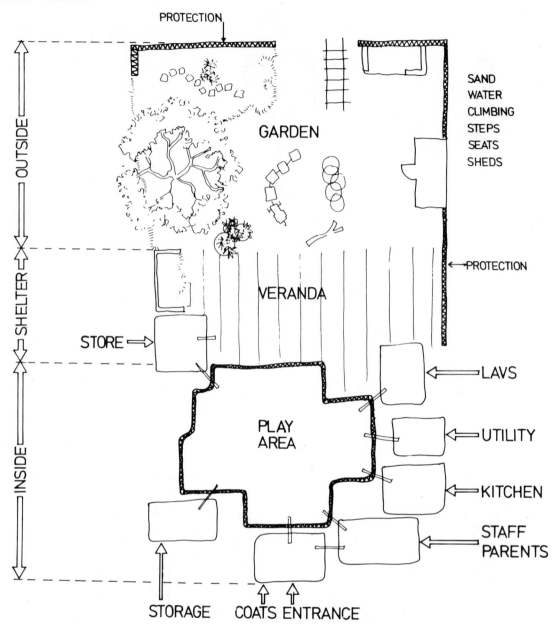

PROTECTION

GARDEN

SAND
WATER
CLIMBING
STEPS
SEATS
SHEDS

OUTSIDE

SHELTER

INSIDE

VERANDA

PROTECTION

STORE

LAVS

PLAY
AREA

UTILITY

KITCHEN

STAFF
PARENTS

STORAGE   COATS ENTRANCE

Many primary schools include a nursery group of under fives, either incorporated in the main school, or built as a separate unit.

There are three places for work and play:
(a) Inside
(b) Sheltered transition between inside and outside.
(c) Outside.

Fig. 1.3   Under fives. Main ingredients

Small rural schools are likely to have very small groups of under fives. These should always have a comfortable play area of statutory size to which they can all withdraw with those who are responsible for them. It will not be large enough for the full range of nursery activities, but will perhaps be more appropriate for the quieter and less energetic ones.

The under and over fives may or may not share sink, lavatory and coat areas, which must always however be very convenient for the youngest children. Movement between spaces for under and over fives must always be easy, to encourage sharing. The furnishing should provide for adults.

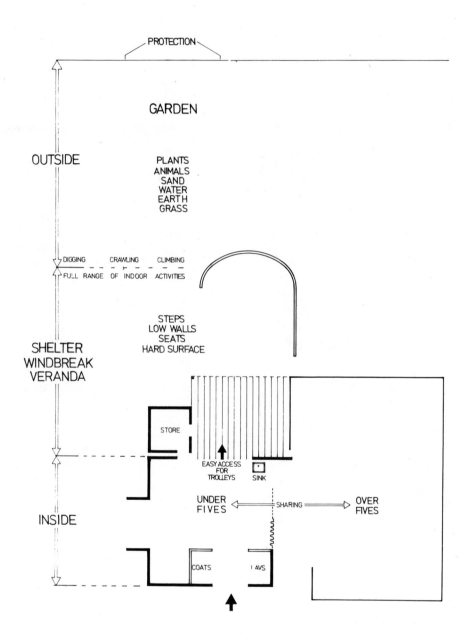

Fig. 1.4   Relationship between spaces for Under Fives and Over Fives

1
TABLE WORK   eg. using materials & objects - not making much mess - small scale.

2
ACTING   eg. home play - camping - shops - hospitals.

3
MUSIC   eg. exploring sounds individually, singing & dancing together.

4
MESSY   eg. using clay water sand etc.

5
QUIET WORK   eg. looking at books, writing, resting, story telling.

6
MOVING   eg. climbing, swinging, jumping, rolling.

7
CONSTRUCTION   eg. building with blocks, small & large scale, undertakings such as engines, buses, boats, houses, etc.

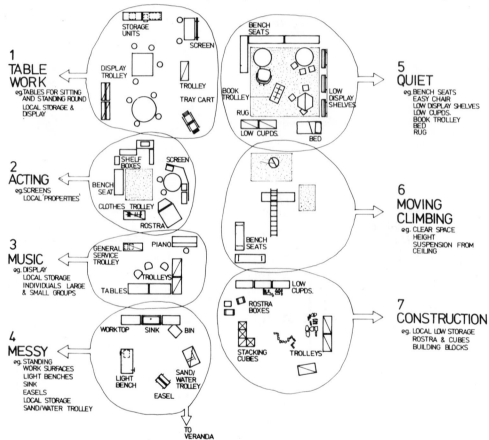

The activities outlined above are likely to be pursued by children both under and over five, and the degree of sharing is likely to be greater with smaller numbers.

Fig. 1.5   Main zones of activity—younger children

Years

12

11

10

9

8

7

6

5

4

3

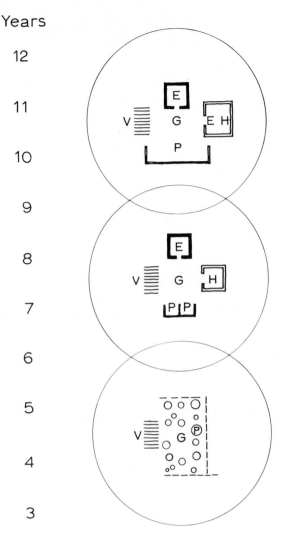

o Work still in small groups
   Greater range and depth
   of interests
   Developing provision for
   particular skills in general
   context

o Work in small groups
   More definition of different
   zones by planning as well
   as by furniture
   Less space available
   Fewer teachers

o Children working individually
   Many extemporary situations
   Changing patterns
   More variety through furniture:
   less through architectural
   definition
   Many adults

This diagram shows how the arrangement of planning ingredients is likely to vary as the children progress from 3 to 11 years.

Fig. 1.6   Continuity—transitions. Some ingredients of planning for local work areas.
H. Home bases.   E. Enclosed rooms. G. General work areas. P. Particular bays or zones. V. Covered areas.

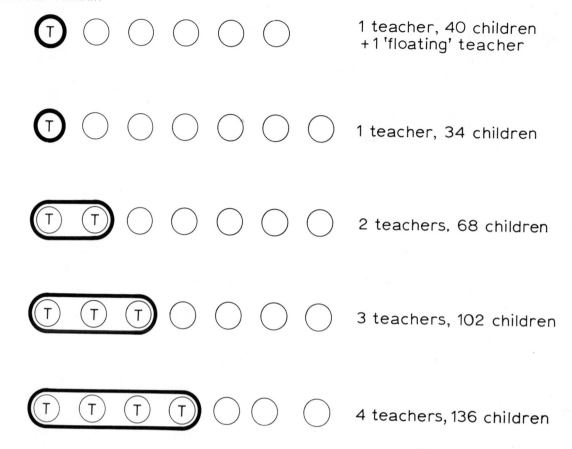

1 teacher, 40 children
+1 'floating' teacher

1 teacher, 34 children

2 teachers, 68 children

3 teachers, 102 children

4 teachers, 136 children

As teacher pupil ratios frequently change, it is necessary in each project to be clear on the number of teachers, and how they are likely to be grouped, before the building is designed.

Fig. 1.7   Changes in teacher-pupil ratios. Choices. Groups.
The example shown is for 240 children, school head and 7 teachers

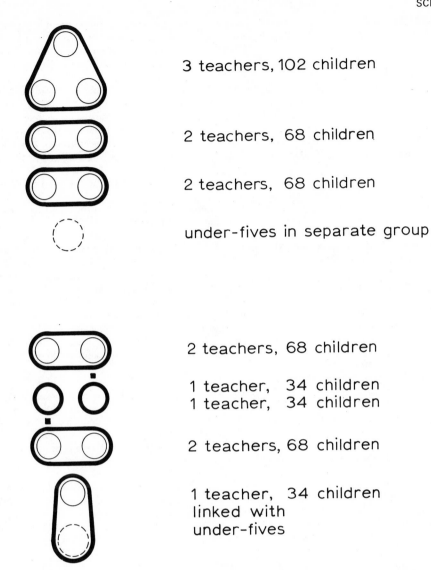

3 teachers, 102 children

2 teachers, 68 children

2 teachers, 68 children

under-fives in separate group

2 teachers, 68 children

1 teacher, 34 children
1 teacher, 34 children

2 teachers, 68 children

1 teacher, 34 children
linked with
under-fives

This diagram illustrates two of many possible groupings of teachers and pupils. In the top example it is the older pupils who are in a larger centre, with three teachers. In the second example the single teacher groups can either be independent, or be associated with the two-teacher centres.

Fig. 1.8 Changes in teacher-pupil ratios. Some relationships. Choices. Groups.
The example shown is for 240 children, school head and 7 teachers

SPACE REQUIREMENTS

Reference: The Standards for School Premises Regulations (1972)

(a) *Playroom and teaching space.* An overall minimum internal area per pupil is required for:

(I) Playroom accommodation for pupils of under 5 years.

(ii) Teaching accommodation in primary schools.

There are no specific requirements for the division and arrangement of these overall areas. Clients and designers have freedom to use their own discretion, and there are wide variations.

(b) *Storage Space*

(i) For teaching apparatus, equipment and materials.

(ii) For school stocks, maintenance equipment, furniture and fuel.

(iii) For pupils' outdoor clothing.

(c) *Pupils' sanitary and washing accommodation.* Minimum numbers of fittings are specified in the Regulations.

(d) *Staff rooms*, etc.

(i) In a nursery school one room is required for the 'superintendent' and one room for the remainder of the teaching staff. Cloakroom, sanitary and washing accommodation for adults must be provided.

(ii) In a primary school a common room is required for the teaching staff.

A separate room is required for:

The head teacher, in a school for more than 120 pupils;

The teacher in charge of the infants in a JMI school for 280 or more pupils;

The senior assistant teacher in a Junior school for 320 or more pupils.

Cloakroom, sanitary and washing accommodation for adults must be provided. Suitable accommodation for medical inspection and treatment must be available.

(e) *Accommodation for meals. For a nursery school* a kitchen must be provided for cooking a midday meal for full-time pupils; if all the pupils are only attending part time there need only be a sink and some means of heating drinks. For a nursery class, only a sink and heating for drinks are required. No separate dining room is required.

For a primary school there must be a kitchen, or (if meals are cooked off the premises) accommodation for receiving, serving meals and washing up. No separate dining room is required, but suitable space—or spaces—must be available, the area per person being related to the number of sittings.

(f) *Space requirements for Middle Schools.* For Middle schools, space requirements are similar, but minimum teaching areas are greater. These are listed for different sizes of school in 'Notes on Procedures for the Approval of School Building Projects in England': Appendix 5.

DATA: FURNITURE AND EQUIPMENT

Dimensional data for furniture and equipment can be summarised as follows:

(a) Dimensions of children.

(i) Relevant body dimensions. See Figs. 1.9 to 1.16.

(ii) Sitting furniture heights. See B.S. 3030.

(iii) Recommended standing furniture heights. See Building Bulletin No. 50 para 27.

(b) Distribution of sitting heights in schools. See B.S. 3030, from which Fig. 1.17 is taken.

(c) Recommended plan sizes of tables.

The diagram of plan sizes includes those for nursery, primary and secondary schools. Those for nursery and primary are tinted. See Fig. 1.18.

For recommended positioning of wall mounted furniture and equipment see Fig. 1.19.

The dado rails should be extended upwards by 100 mm where socket outlets are required above worktops.

The current trend is for storage of pupils' belongings to be separate from the workplace, i.e. in trays or lockers in trolleys or cupboards.

Reference to B.S. 3030 does not take into account the possible revision of the six recommended sitting sizes to five sizes. It is possible that there will be a simplification of the nursery and primary sizes, and the establishment of regular increments which will incorporate both sitting and standing heights.

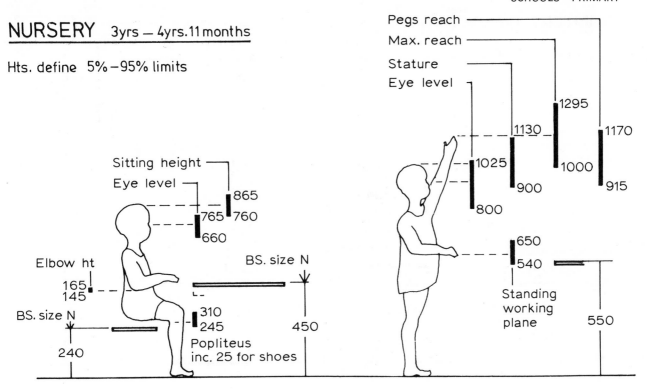

NURSERY 3yrs — 4yrs.11months

Hts. define 5% — 95% limits

Sitting height
Eye level
865
765 760
660

Elbow ht
165
145

BS. size N

BS. size N
310
245
Popliteus
inc. 25 for shoes

450

240

Pegs reach
Max. reach
Stature
Eye level

1295
1130
1025 1170
900 1000
800 915

650
540

Standing
working
plane

550

Fig. 1.9   Relevant body dimensions. Nursery. 3 yrs–4 yrs 11 months

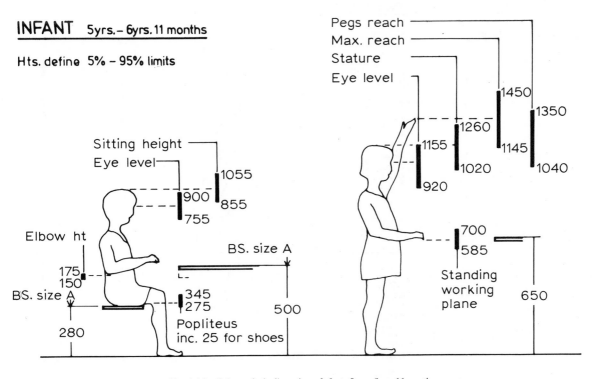

INFANT 5yrs.– 6yrs.11 months

Hts. define 5% – 95% limits

Sitting height
Eye level
1055
900 855
755

Elbow ht
175
150

BS. size A

BS. size A
345
275
Popliteus
inc. 25 for shoes

500

280

Pegs reach
Max. reach
Stature
Eye level

1450
1260 1350
1155 1145
1020 1040
920

700
585

Standing
working
plane

650

Fig. 1.10   Relevant body dimensions. Infant. 5 yrs–6 yrs 11 months

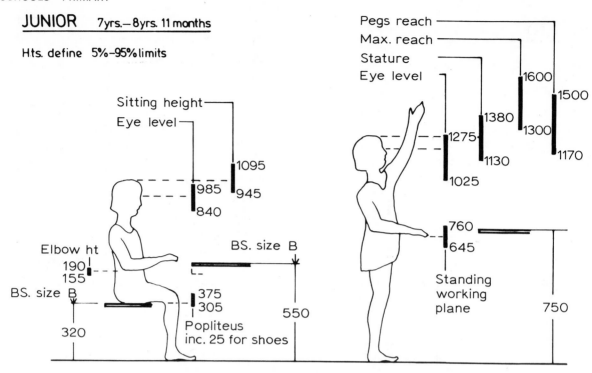

Fig. 1.11   Relevant body dimensions. Junior. 7 yrs–8 yrs 11 months

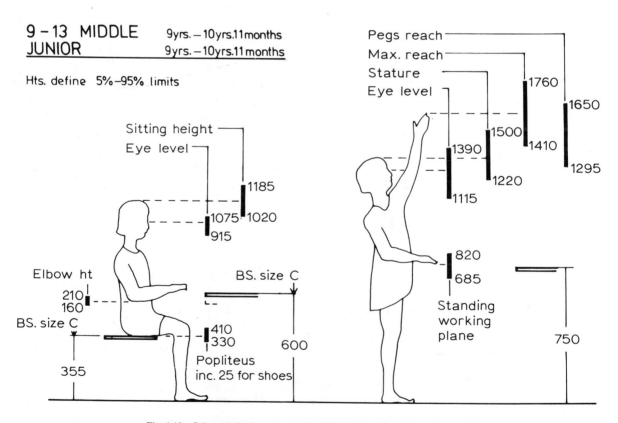

Fig. 1.12   Relevant body dimensions. 9–13 Middle Junior. 9 yrs–10 yrs 11 months

9–13 MIDDLE   11yrs.–12yrs.11months
SECONDARY   11yrs.–12yrs.11months

Hts. define 5%–95% limits

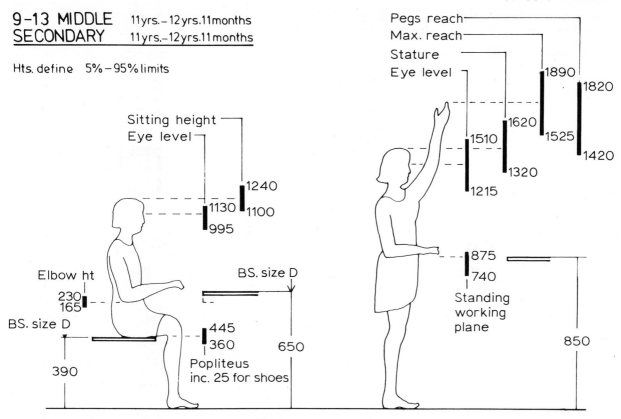

Pegs reach
Max. reach
Stature
Eye level

Sitting height
Eye level

1240
1130 1100
995

1890
1820
1620
1510 1525
1320 1420
1215

Elbow ht
230
165

BS. size D
445
360

BS. size D
650

390

Popliteus
inc. 25 for shoes

875
740

Standing
working
plane

850

Fig. 1.13   Relevant body dimensions. 9–13 Middle Secondary. 11 yrs–12 yrs 11 months

FIRST   5yrs. – 7yrs.11months

Hts. define 5%–95% limits

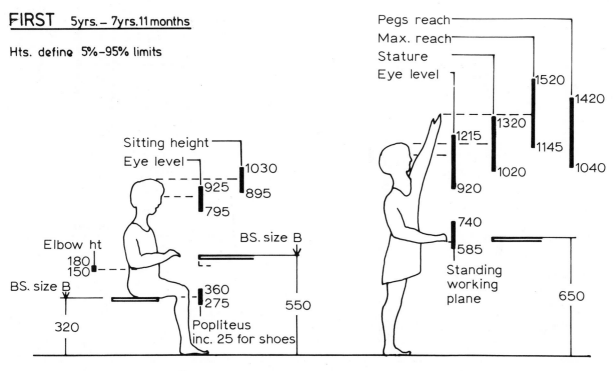

Pegs reach
Max. reach
Stature
Eye level

Sitting height
Eye level

1030
925 895
795

1520
1420
1320
1215 1145
1020 1040
920

Elbow ht
180
150

BS. size B
360
275

BS. size B
550

320

Popliteus
inc. 25 for shoes

740
585

Standing
working
plane

650

Fig. 1.14   Relevant body dimensions. First. 5 yrs–7 yrs 11 months

8–12 MIDDLE   8yrs. – 9yrs.11months

Hts. define 5%–95% limits

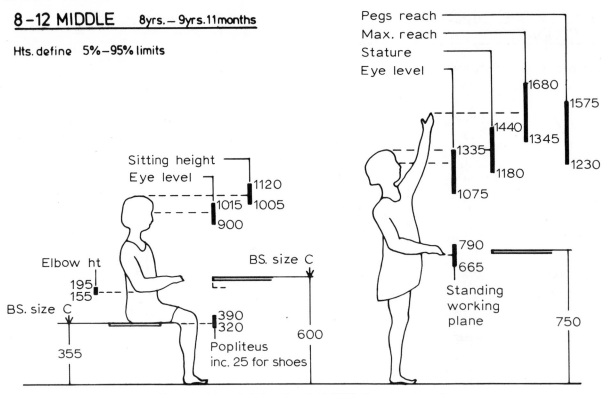

Fig. 1.15   Relevant body dimensions. 8–12 Middle. 8 yrs–9 yrs 11 months

8–12 MIDDLE   10yrs.–11yrs.11months

Hts. define 5%–95% limits

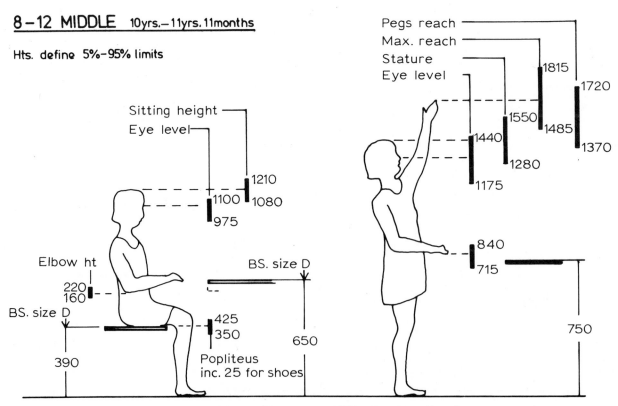

Fig. 1.16   Relevant body dimensions. 8–12 Middle. 10 yrs–11 yrs 11 months

Type of school	Age range	Furniture sizes					
		N	A	B	C	D	E
Nursery	3.5–5						
Primary	5–7						
	5–8						
	5–9						
	5–11						
	7–11						
Middle	8–12						
	9–13						
Secondary	11–13						
	11–14						
	11–16						
	11–18						
	16+						

Fig. 1.17   Distribution of sizes. Current recommendations. (From BS 3030; Part 3)

mm	800	900	1100	1100	1200	1200	1500	1800
450		Y						
550			R	R				
600	B				B	B	B	
800	W				G		G	Br
900		Y					G	Br
1100			R					
1200					W			

Fig. 1.18   Grid of plan sizes of tables. (From BS 3030; Part 3)

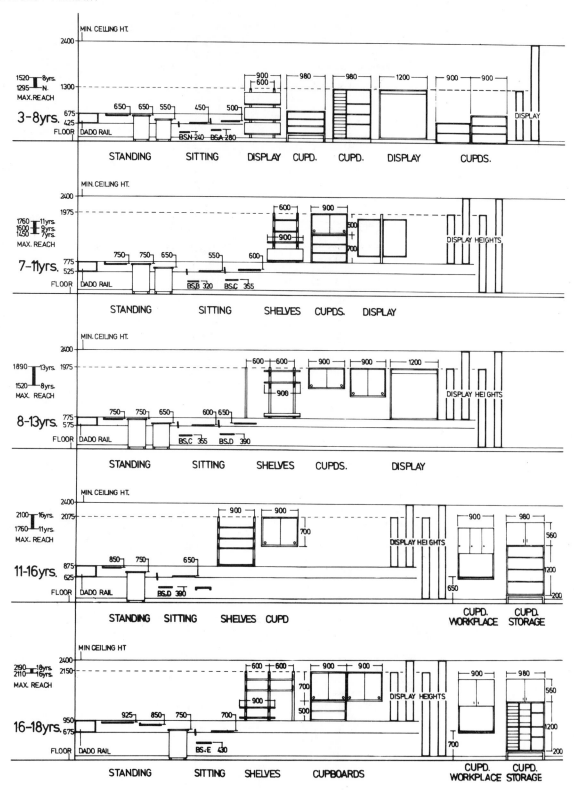

Fig. 1.19   Recommended positioning of wall mounted furniture and equipment

ACCOMMODATION

(a) *Some recommendations about the interior.* In addition to statutory requirements (e.g. precautions for health and safety, lighting, acoustics, ventilation and heating) recommendations are made in Building Bulletins and Design Notes. See also 'Guidelines on environmental design in educational buildings', DES August 1972 (available from Architects and Building Branch).

(i) The character of the interior depends to a considerable degree on lighting and colour. There needs to be a generous proportion of reflected light (i.e. avoid dark contrasts and silhouettes). The flooring in particular should be generally light in colour (40–50% reflectance value). Given generous reflected light, small areas of strong colour are often appropriate to achieve cheerfulness and richness.

(ii) Large areas of chalking surfaces for directional exposition are not now needed. Small areas, dispersed on walls and on furniture (e.g. movable screens and space divider units) are more useful.

For appropriate colours for chalk surfaces (using white chalk); see Building Bulletin No. 9 (4th edition).

References to B.S. 2660: 'Colours for building and decorative paints' are now superseded by B.S. DD/17: 1972 'Basic range for the coordination of colours for building purposes'. For a background to, and a technical description of this, see Building Research Establishment Digest No. 149 (1973) 'The coordination of building colours'.

(iii) All working areas should get sunshine for some part of the working day (generally 9 am–3.30 pm). There should be views out.

(iv) Windowsills should be generous in width, and their height should allow people, when sitting down, to see out, from all points of the interior.

Reference should be made to: sitting heights, sitting table heights, standing heights, and standing worktop heights. (See Data section earlier in this chapter).

(v) Generous provision of two- and three-dimensional display surfaces is important (e.g. surfaces for pinning into, shelves etc.). Much of the display should be within reaching height for the children.

(vi) Spaces should be easily and comfortably ventilated by natural means.

(b) *An example of a schedule of accommodation.* The range of sizes and kinds of Nursery and Primary schools is so great that it would not be possible to regard any one schedule of accommodation as typical. Each project is likely to have its particular requirements relating to size, organisation, arrangement of space etc. One example is given below. This is for a small rural school with provision for community use (for which an additional sum of money has been allocated).

Number of pupils: 120 pupils aged 3½–11 years.

Number of staff: Headteacher
Six full-time teachers.
One part-time assistant for nursery group.
Visiting teachers for instrumental music, remedial work etc.

General siting: The building to be sited near the road, to reduce drive lengths and service costs, and to allow the maximum area for a playing field.

It is suggested that the accommodation might be grouped around a sheltered garden court with access from the gate, and from which different parts of the building can be entered. A position is allocated for a caretaker's house.

Main grouping of teachers and pupils. (This determines the main grouping of the work areas.)

(i) A nursery group of 20 children of 3½–5 years under the care of one teacher and a part-time assistant.

(ii) A group of 50 children of 5–8 years, under the care of two teachers who are together responsible for the organisation of the work, but who are individually responsible for the general welfare of half the group (25 children each).

(iii) A group of 50 children of 8–11 years, under the care of two teachers with similar responsibilities.

Main grouping of work areas

(i) For the nursery group of 20 children:
Entrance lobby, with provision for outdoor clothes. Adjacent lavatory and small utility room with sink and services.
Playroom, possibly with carpeted bay window area (with books, seats, rocking chair etc.); a more general playroom area which can be rearranged easily; an area for wet and messy work with a door out to south-facing veranda and sheltered play garden.
A small room for parents and children, separated from playroom by glazed screen and door.

(ii) For the group of 50 children of 5–8 years and two teachers:
Entrance lobby from the garden court, with provision for coats etc., and lavatory.
Two home-base sitting rooms, carpeted and domestically furnished.
A general work area for experimental and constructional work with sink and a door out to small paved play area and garden.
Two small work bays (one with sink and cooker).
Walk-in store for materials and equipment.

(iii) For a group of 50 children of 8–11 years and two teachers:
Similar schedule, but the general work area may be used by parents and others in the evenings.

(iv) An enclosed room shared by these two groups and possibly used also for evening classes and discussions.

(v) A large, multi-purpose room to be shared by children and adults, with access to the garden, playground and playing field. Generous storage for furniture, apparatus, props, etc.

(vi) A meeting room for staff, parents and other local residents for socials, films, meetings etc. Adjacent pantry with sink and small cooker.

(vii) Office for the Headteacher/warden.

(viii) Small room for medical inspection and treatment, for sick pupils and first-aid etc. This may also be used for secretarial purposes.

(ix) Walk-in stores for school stock, cleaning materials, caretaker's equipment etc.

(x) Kitchen planned and equipped to produce approximately one hundred meals. Ancillary stores etc., and staff cloakroom and lavatory.

It is anticipated that lunches might be trolleyed from the kitchen, partly to located areas with window seats and tables in the circulation areas, partly to located window bays in the hall; but dispersed rather than served in a concentrated canteen atmosphere.

(xi) Lavatories and provision for coats for staff and other adults.

It may be possible to plan the accommodation, listed under (v)-(xi) above, as one wing surrounding the garden court. This wing should have a welcoming entrance for local residents, generous provision for displays, window and other seating and some tables. The room for the Headteacher/ warden should be near the entrance.

The different parts of the accommodation and gardens should be informally designed, to become an unostentatious, friendly small community which, with good planting and site design, will soon fit comfortably into the landscape.

STATUTORY REQUIREMENTS

Central control over the building of schools can be defined under two headings: (a) Cost control; (b) Statutory requirements: minimum standards.

(i) *Cost control.* The permitted cost of a school project is related to the number of full-time pupils and cost places as set out in 'Notes on Procedures for the Approval of School Building Projects in England,' HMSO. At the time of writing this section the cost limit procedure has been suspended. *Ad hoc* approvals are being given and this is likely to continue during the inflationary period.

(ii) *Statutory requirements, minimum standards.* The Statutory Requirements are set out in Statutory Instruments (1972), No 2051 Education, England and Wales. The Standards for School Premises Regulations 1972. The constructional requirements set out in this document are to be merged with the National Building Regulations. See 'Administrative Memorandum 11/73 (Department of Education and Science) and 7/73 (Welsh Education Office).

Fire Precautions. The requirements are specified in Building Bulletin No 7 (4th edition) 'Fire and the Design of Schools', HMSO.

Safety in Schools. The following three pamphlets may be relevant to primary schools although they refer mostly to secondary schools:

(a) Safety in school laboratories.   DES series No 2.
(b) Safety in practical departments   DES series No 3.
(c) Safety in physical education.   DES series No 4.

AUTHORITIES

The central authority for primary education in England is the Department of Education and Science, London, of which the Secretary of State for Education and Science is the political head, and which is staffed by civil servants.

The Welsh Education Office in Cardiff, part of the Welsh Office, is headed by the Secretary of State for Wales, is staffed also by civil servants, and operates similarly to the Department of Education and Science.

In Scotland the Scottish Education Department, Edinburgh, has as its head the Secretary of State for Scotland, and has an administrative staff and Inspectorate similar to those in England and Wales.

Control under the Education Act is exercised, and guidance is given by means of regulations, orders and circular letters, by pamphlets, handbooks etc. Minimum standards of educational provision are set, and the rate, distribution, nature and cost of educational buildings

controlled. The central authority itself does not provide, maintain or control any kind of school.

The provision of school buildings is the responsibility of Local Education Authorities. Under the reorganised system (operative from 1st April 1974) there are 101 local education authorities in England and Wales. A list of these can be found in 'Administrative Memorandum 2/73' (19.1.73); Addendum No 1 (2.5.73).

Education is the largest of the services provided by local authorities, the cost being met from rates and from the Rate Support Grant payable from the national exchequer.

The main bodies for establishing voluntary schools are:
Catholic Education Council for England and Wales, 41 Cromwell Road, London SW7.
Methodist Education Committee, 2 Chester House, Pages Lane, London N10.
National Society, Religious Education Office, 69 Great Peter Street, London SW1.

EXAMPLES

(a) NURSERY

(i) Beech Green Nursery School, Aylesbury, Bucks.
Designed for 50 places (10 of them for handicapped children).

(ii) Tilbury Nursery Centre, Essex.
Designed for 60 places. 3–5 years (See Fig. 1.20)

(b) PRIMARY

(i) Cobblers Lane Infants' School, Pontefract, Wakefield Borough Council.
Designed for 240 pupils 5–7 years. (See Fig. 1.21).

(ii) Montgomerie Infants' School, Thundersley, Essex.
Designed for 240 pupils 5–7 years. (See Fig. 1.22).

(iii) Millbrook Junior School, Grove, Berkshire.
Designed for 320 pupils 7–11 years. (See Figs 1.23 and 1.24).

(iv) Dalestorth Primary School, Sutton-in-Ashfield, Notts.
Designed for 320 pupils 5–11 years.

(v) Chaucer Infants and Nursery School, Ilkeston, Derbyshire.
Designed for 300 pupils 3½–7 years, also for community use (See Design Note No 11).

(vi) Llangybi Area School, Dyfed.
Designed for 120 pupils 3½–11 years, and also for community use. (See Figs. 1.25 and 1.26).

(c) MIDDLE

(i) Delf Hill Middle School, Bradford.
Designed for 420 pupils 9–13 years (1969). (See Fig. 1.27).

(ii) Heaton Middle School, Bradford.
Designed for 420 pupils 9–13 years (1973).

(iii) Woodside Middle School, Amersham, Bucks.
Originally designed as a Junior School (320 pupils 7–11 years) and converted into a Middle School for 320 pupils 8–12 years. (1974).

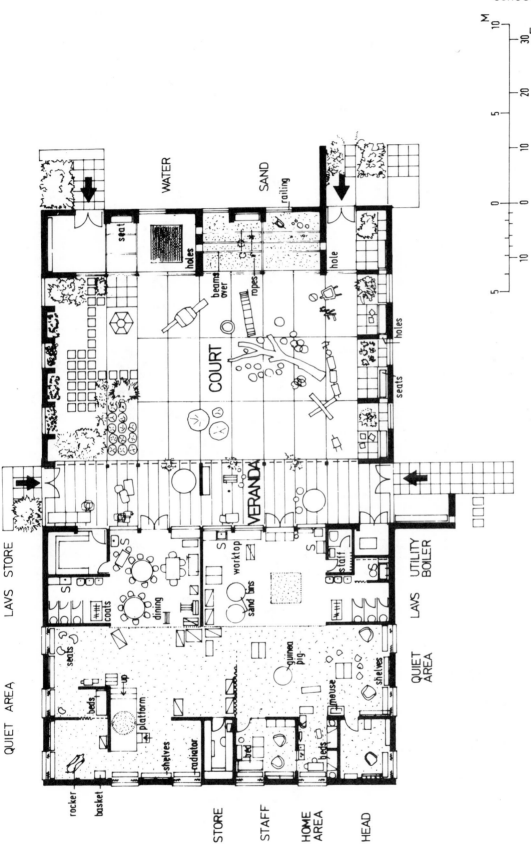

Fig. 1.20 Tilbury Nursery Centre, Essex. Designed for 60 places, 3–5 years

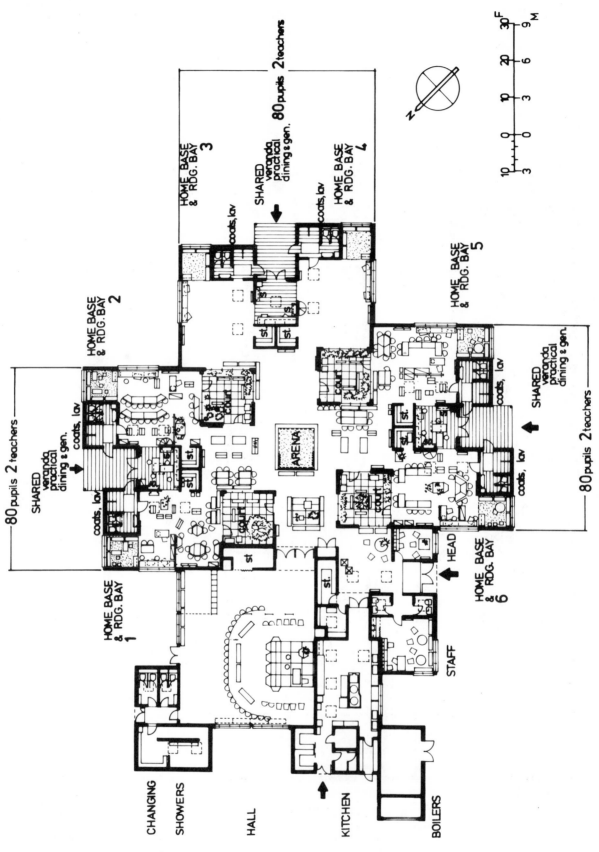

Fig. 1.21 Cobblers Lane Infants' School, Pontefract, West Riding, Yorkshire. Designed for 240 pupils, 5–7 years

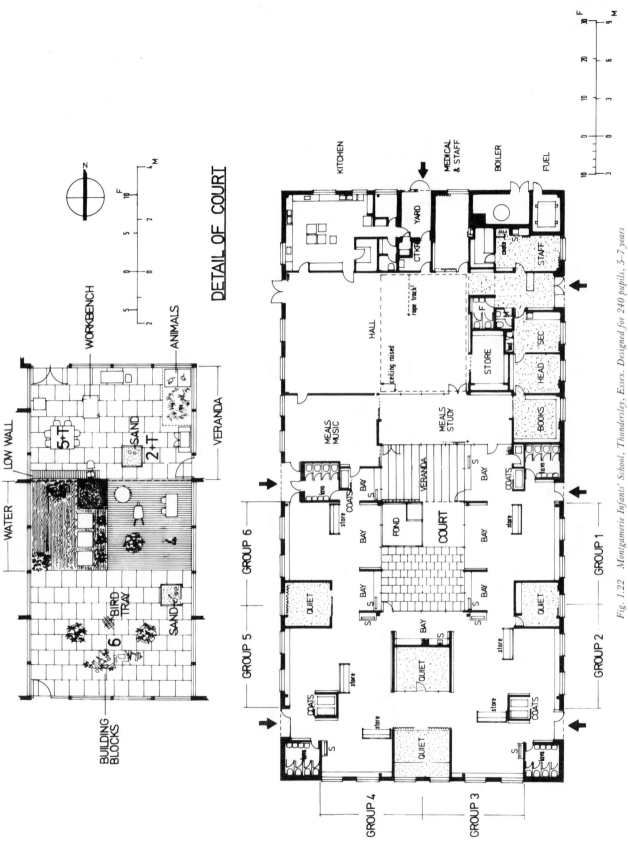

DETAIL OF COURT

WORKBENCH

LOW WALL

WATER

BUILDING BLOCKS

BIRD TRAY

SAND

ANIMALS

VERANDA

5+T

2+T

6

KITCHEN

CTKR

YARD

MEDICAL & STAFF

BOILER

FUEL

STAFF

HALL

rope track

ceiling raised

STORE

SEC

HEAD

BOOKS

MEALS MUSIC

MEALS STUDY

VERANDA

COURT

POND

BAY

BAY

BAY

BAY

BAY

BAY

BAY

QUIET

QUIET

QUIET

QUIET

QUIET

COATS

COATS

COATS

store

store

store

store

store

GROUP 6

GROUP 5

GROUP 4

GROUP 3

GROUP 2

GROUP 1

Fig. 1.22   Montgomerie Infants' School, Thundersley, Essex. Designed for 240 pupils, 5–7 years

1–21

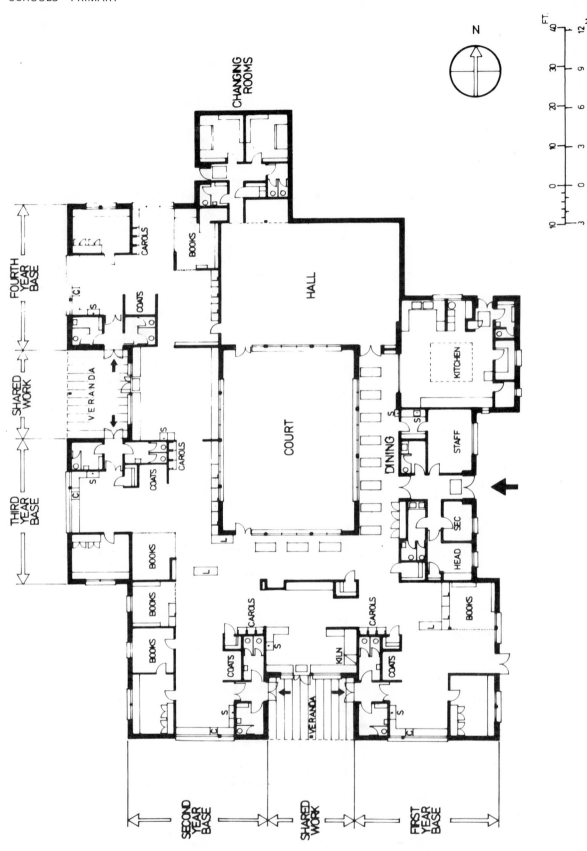

Fig. 1.23   Millbrook Junior School, Grove, Berkshire. Designed for 320 pupils, 7–11 years.

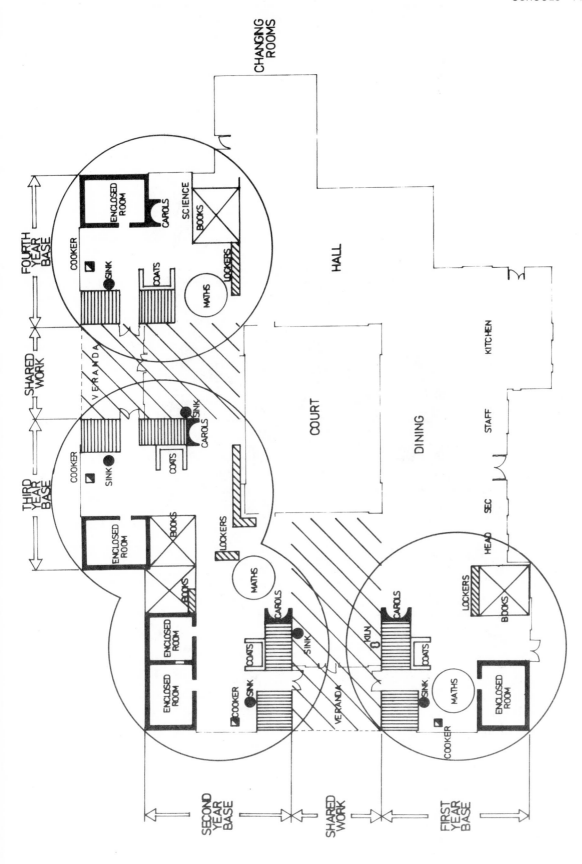

Fig. 1.24 Millbrook Junior School. Organisation

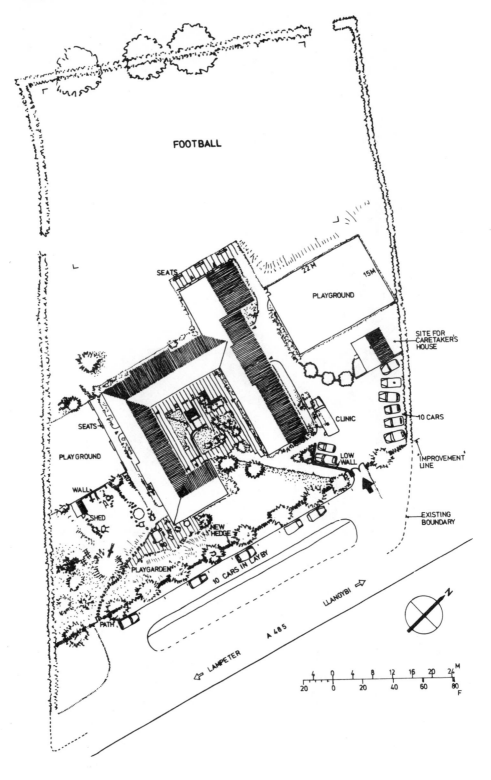

FOOTBALL

SEATS

22 M

15M

PLAYGROUND

SITE FOR
CARETAKER'S
HOUSE

CLINIC

10 CARS

SEATS

PLAYGROUND

LOW
WALL

IMPROVEMENT
LINE

WALL

EXISTING
BOUNDARY

SHED

NEW
HEDGE

PLAYGARDEN

10 CARS IN LAYBY

PATH

LLANGYBI

A 485

LAMPETER

N

20   4   0   4   8   12   16   20   24 M

20   0   20   40   60   80 F

Fig. 1.25   Site area of Llangybi Area School, Cardiganshire. Designed for 120 pupils, 3½–11 years, and also for community use.

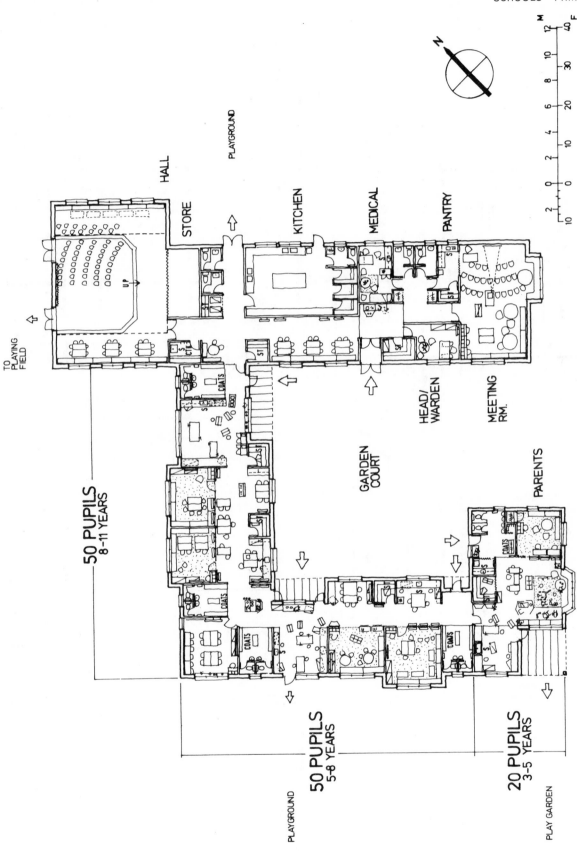

Fig. 1.26   Arrangement of Llangybi Area School

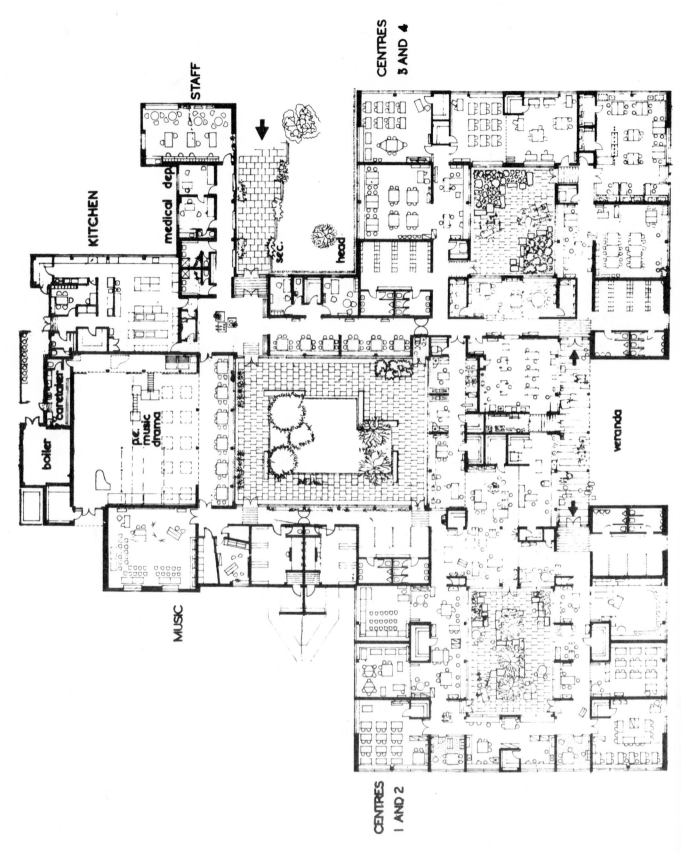

STAFF

KITCHEN

medical dep

CENTRES 3 AND 4

sec.

head

boiler

caretaker

p.e. music drama

veranda

MUSIC

CENTRES 1 AND 2

BIBLIOGRAPHY

Children and their primary schools, A report of the Central Advisory Council for Education (England), HMSO.

Marsh, L., *Alongside the child*, A. & C. Black Ltd.

Blackie, J., *Inside the primary school*, HMSO.

Lady Allen of Hurtwood, *Planning for play*, Jarrold and Sons Norwich.

The new nursery school, Nursery School Association.

Murrow, C. & L., *Children come first*, American Heritage Press.

Utzinger, R. C., *Some European nursery schools and playgrounds*, University of Michigan (1971).

Seabourne, M., *Primary school design*, Routledge & Kegan Paul.

People in schools—an attitude to design, RIBA Journal (June 1968).

Designing primary schools, Froebel Journal, No 19 (Spring 1971).

Building Bulletins and Design Notes; a number of these refer to Nursery and Primary Schools, Department of Education and Science, HMSO.

School Furniture 74, (obtainable from Pel Ltd.).

New ideas in furniture design. School Building & Design in the Commonwealth, The Commonwealth Secretariat, Marlborough House, London S.W.1.

Corbin, T. J., *Display in schools*, Pergamon Press (1970).

Clegg, Sir Alec, *Revolution in the British primary school*, National Association of Elementary School Principals USA.

Medd, Mary, *O.B.E., R.I.B.A. Since 1945, has been closely associated with leading educators and teachers in nursery, primary and secondary schools, and as an architect in the Hertfordshire County Architect's Department, and the Department of Education and Science. Independently, Mrs Medd, has been associated with many of the most influential developments in school design.*

2 SCHOOLS—SECONDARY AND COMPREHENSIVE

JOHN JORDAN, Dip. Arch (Birm.), R.I.B.A., and DIRK MOOIJ, M.Sc (Delft)
Architects Co-Partnership Inc.

INTRODUCTION

The Education Act 1944 is the basis of the current State controlled system in the U.K. and also provides for the control of independent schools. The Act led to very great changes in education which, in turn, reacted on the planning of school buildings. Educational changes continue, but the machinery of control has evolved from that established in the Act, which provided, under Section 10, for regulations prescribing standards for school premises. These have undergone various amplifications and amendments published by the old Ministry of Education, both as memoranda and as a series of Building Bulletins. The Department of Education and Science (DES) continues to issue and revise the Bulletins. The most important are:

(a) *Primary Level:*
   No. 1. New Primary Schools (2nd Edition) (1967).
   No. 36. Development Project; Eveline Lowe Primary School (1967).
   No. 47. Eveline Lowe School Appraisal (1972).
(b) *Secondary Level:*
   No. 48. Maiden Erleigh Secondary School (1973).
   No. 49. Abraham Moss Centre Manchester (1973).

The secondary level is also dealt with in a series of bulletins devoted to specialised aspects, all of which should be required reading for the architect (See Bibliography).

In addition, the DES publishes Design Notes on topics not meriting the full treatment of a Bulletin. Perhaps the most important of these to the secondary school designer is Design Note No. 5 'The School and the Community' (1970). The DES also publishes 'Notes on Procedure for the Approval of School Building Projects in England' (HMSO, 1972) which is updated from time to time on a loose leaf basis. This sets out procedures, standards and cost limits and, together with the 'Standards for School Premises Regulations' (No. 2051 HMSO, 1972) and the Building Bulletins, constitutes the main U.K. educational and planning references available to an architect.

The Education Act 1944 provides for changes in future education, and these changes are emphasised by the building regulations and the explanatory memorandum. The most important change is the progressive development of 'comprehensive' secondary education as a national policy; at the end of 1972 comprehensive school accounted for 40% of secondary education in the U.K. The compulsory school age is 5 years to 16 years and ultimately it is to be followed by compulsory part-time continued education for all young persons (under 18 years). The sizes of classes are to be reduced progressively from 50 to 40 children in primary schools, and from 40 to 30 children in secondary schools.

An important and overriding factor very seriously affecting the design of schools is the issue, from time to time, of DES circulars limiting the permitted cost per place. At the same time greater freedom is being permitted in planning, with a view to keeping reasonably within the 'cost per place' allowed as this cost has been progressively reduced.

These notes are prepared on the basis of encouraging good school planning and accommodation and may, therefore, depart from official recommendations arising temporarily from excessive economy measures.

The Act and the Regulations made under it provide for the requirements of all schools, whether administered by local education authorities or aided in some manner by local authorities. The terms used in the Act to differentiate between the two types of control are 'County Schools' for all those administered by the local authorities, and 'Voluntary Schools' for those administered by bodies other than local education authorities.

The accommodation and numbers in special schools vary according to the type and extent of the disabilities of the children for which each school is provided.

The classification of schools and those attending them has undergone several changes; schools, with a few exceptions, are no longer 'all-age-schools'.

Fig. 2.1 is an attempt to illustrate the classification of schools under each of the two types of education controlled by local authorities. It should, however, be borne in mind that there are many possible variations due to special circumstances, such as in villages where populations are small, or in crowded urban areas. The first divisions in schools controlled by local education authorities are nursery schools, or a nursery department of an infants' school for children of both sexes from the age of 2–5 years, and in some instances 2–7 years. Compulsory education commences at

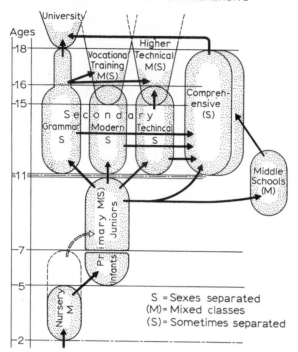

Fig. 2.1 *Classification of county and secondary schools*

the age of 5 years, and from that age until 7 years attendance would be in infants' classes or separate infants' schools, which usually accept children of both sexes. Primary schools deal with children from 5–11, which comprise infants and junior departments. Primary schools are usually mixed.

The main division is at the age of 11, when the transfer is made to secondary schools where the children remain until the leaving age of 16, or until passing on to university or to advanced vocational training at 17 or 18 years. A new type of school, the Middle School, is developing, which spans the age ranges from 8–13, after which children go to upper comprehensive schools.

It is the intention that comprehensive secondary education should increasingly absorb the historical pattern of different types of secondary schools. These were, as indicated in Fig. 2.1, divided into three main types, namely 'grammar', 'secondary modern' and 'technical'. It is suggested that the grammar type may be subdivided into:

(a) schools having a leaving age of 16, and

(b) schools, such as the existing high schools and grammar schools, having a leaving age up to 18, intended particularly for pupils passing on to higher education.

For the modern and technical schools, a leaving age of 16 is envisaged for the majority of pupils and those wishing to continue on to senior technical schools.

Secondary schools often provide for two or even three of the above categories; they are referred to as 'bilateral' if there are two of the three types, 'multi-lateral' if there are all three types in clearly defined sides, or 'comprehensive' if there are all three types without clearly defined separation, as is to become increasingly the pattern in the future.

There are also 'special schools' which care for children who need special educational treatment due to physical or mental defects, and the gradings referred to above do not necessarily apply.

The schools under private governing bodies tend to have rather different gradings and age groups. Fig. 2.2 illustrates the broad divisions in education controlled by the 'independent authorities' in relation to the age groups of the children. The kindergarten or infants school often keeps the child to the age of 8 years, after which it passes to a preparatory school, boarding school or junior section of a grammar school. The grammar schools and similar semi-public schools take children from 10–11 years up to 17 or 18 years.

Children going to preparatory schools pass to 'public schools' and similar schools at about the age of 13. From these schools, as well as from the secondary and technical schools previously mentioned, the universities are fed, as well as the main vocational training schools. Most independent schools accept pupils of one sex only after the age of 8 years. There are, however, a few co-educational schools for older children.

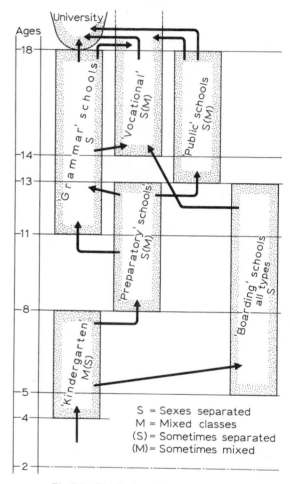

Fig. 2.2 *Classification of independent schools*

SITING

ASPECTS AND ENVIRONMENT

Insofar as it is within the control of the designer, sites will be selected and the buildings disposed on them in such a way as to optimise the comfort of the users and the efficiency of the development. Regard must be paid to the external environment and factors such as noise, prevailing wind, sun angles and intensity, direction of storms etc. will affect the preferred siting and aspects of buildings.

Previous thinking on the penetration of sunshine into teaching areas has been much modified and the relation between solar heat gain, daylighting, view out and the energy requirements of buildings must all be studied and balanced. The legislation which inevitably gave rise to overglazing and glare and heat discomfort in schools has now largely disappeared. The designer now has increased responsibility for decisions in this area. He will, therefore, need to take account of the microclimate of any site and use the techniques available for predictions of solar heat gain, sun shading, natural and artificial lighting and ventilation and both capital costs and cost in use to arrive at the optimum solution.

SITE SELECTION

The general considerations for the selection of sites for school building, the availability of services and provision of planting, have been outlined in Section 1 'Primary Schools'. Reference should also be made to the data given in 'Planning-Architects' Technical Reference Data.

In the case of buildings within the responsibility of the Department of Education and Science, school development will take place on sites selected by the LEA in agreement with the DES and the local planning authority, to whom reference should be made.

SPACE REQUIREMENTS

AREA OF SITES

Site area available will vary according to urban or rural locations, availability and cost of land. Site area will also depend on the size of the proposed school development and should take into account any foreseen extensions.

The Premises Regulations specify the areas of sites and these are set out in Table 2.1.

Table 2.1 AREAS OF SITES FOR SCHOOLS

Number of pupils	Area of site ha
Not more than 150	0·6
151–210	0·7
211–300	0·8
301–360	0·9
361–420	1·0
421–450	1·2
For every additional unit of 50 pupils the minimum area shall be increased by 0·1 ha.	

In addition to the buildings the following uses will have to be allowed for within the overall site areas.

PLAYGROUNDS

The regulations specify that a paved or hard porous area suitable for lawn tennis, netball, basketball or other appropriate games, properly graded and drained, shall be provided and the minimum area of such paving shall be 970 m² in the case of a school of not more than 180 pupils, or as set out in Table 2.2.

Table 2.2 MINIMUM AREA OF PLAYGROUNDS

Number of pupils	Area, m²
Not more than 420	1850
421–600	3180
More than 600	3180
For every additional unit of 150 pupils add 465 m².	

PLAYING FIELDS

The regulations specify that every school shall have a playing field either separately or jointly with another school or schools. In urban locations it may be that such playing fields are at a distance from the school buildings. The minimum area of playing field to be provided is as set out in Table 2.3.

Table 2.3 MINIMUM AREA OF PLAYING FIELDS

Number of pupils	Area, ha
Boys	
Not more than 150	1·8
151–300	3·0
For every additional unit of 150 pupils the area shall be increased by 0·6.	
Girls	
Not more than 150	1·6
151–300	2·6
301–450	3·4
For every additional unit of 150 pupils the area shall be increased by 0·4.	
Boys and Girls	
Not more than 150	1·8
151–300	2·8
301–600	4·0
For every additional unit of 300 pupils the area shall be increased by 1·2 ha.	

ACCESS TO THE SITE

A separate access is required for motor vehicles which should be reasonably segregated from pedestrian access routes. Provision may be necessary for school buses with appropriate setting down areas giving on to the pedestrian circulation routes.

ACCESS TO BUILDINGS AND CIRCULATION WITHIN THE SITE

Depending on the size of the school, several entrances may be necessary, arranged to give access to the divisions into which the school is organised, e.g. Lower School, Middle School, 6th Form. Pedestrian and service vehicle routes should be arranged in so far as is possible to be segregated from each other whilst giving access to all buildings.

It will be necessary for fire fighting appliances and ambulances to be able to approach all buildings and routes capable of carrying such vehicles must be provided.

CAR PARKING

The regulations require one car park space to be provided for Head Teachers and one space to three teachers for the remainder of the staff. It may, however, be necessary to provide more in rural areas by agreement with DES.

It should be possible for local community users to park in an organised manner for extra curricular activities. Allowance should be made at the rate of 23 m² per car space including access roads to and within car parks.

BICYCLE STORES

Allowance should be made at the rate of 1 m² per bicycle.

OUTSIDE ACTIVITY AREAS

These may comprise of the following:
Outdoor teaching areas.
Gardens and allotments.
Meteorological station.
Biological pond.
'Back-yard' area.
Special local community interests—which may extend to boat-building, horticulture, farming.

GENERAL REQUIREMENTS OF TEACHING SPACES

The Premises Regulations do not lay down dimensions for specific teaching spaces, but prescribe minimum areas of teaching space per pupil, see Table 2.4. A schedule of accommodation may be arrived at in detail by the client body, normally a Local Education Authority, and given as a brief to the designer; or the designer may be involved in the development of the detailed requirements. In the latter case these requirements will probably be developed from a proposed curriculum. The area of teaching space required by any teaching activity will depend on the teaching functions to be accommodated and the size of the pupil group using the space. The dimensions of any space will be generated by the need to provide viable proportions of space and to accommodate the units into which the space will be divided by the user's activities.

Examples are given in the form of planning diagrams which demonstrate commonly recurring teaching situations but which do not propose that these activities necessarily be accommodated in rigidly divided rooms. The requirements of specialised activities and teaching spaces are discussed in detail in later sections.

The Department of Education and Science has indicated in Building Bulletin 48, Appendix 3, Table 5, a notional net usable area required per pupil place for the range of subjects taught at secondary level based on the division of these

Table 2.4 MINIMUM AREA OF TEACHING ACCOMMODATION

Number of pupils under 16	Area per pupil in m²			
	Under 11	11 and 12	13 and 14	15 and over
Not more than 150		3·72	4·65	5·20
151– 300	2·14			
301– 450	2·04	3·62	4·55	5·11
451– 520	1·95			
521– 700	1·86	3·53	4·46	5·02
701– 800		3·48	4·41	4·97
801– 900		3·39	4·32	4·88
901–1050		3·25	4·18	4·74
1051–1200		3·21	4·13	4·69
1201–1350		3·16	4·09	4·65
1351–1500		3·10	4·02	4·58
1501–1650		3·07	3·99	4·55
1651–1800		3·04	3·97	4·52
1801–1950		2·99	3·92	4·48
1951–2100		2·97	3·90	4·46

subjects into one or more of four primary activity categories, see Table 2.5. By the application of proportions of time spent per subject per primary activity it is possible to generate an average area per place per subject and thus to build up a table of accommodation from an outline curriculum.

Table 2.5 ACTIVITY PATTERN AND AVERAGE AREA PER PLACE PER SUBJECT

	Proportions of time in subject spent in different activities (%)				
	Reading, Writing, Discussion, Exposition, 1·8 m² per place	Light Practical 3·2 m² per place	Heavy Practical 4·6 m² per place	Movement, or large projects 8·3 m² per place	Average m² per place
English	100				1·8
Drama	30			70	6·5
Languages	100				1·8
Science	30	70			2·7
Mathematics	75	25			2·2
History					
Geography					
Religion and Philosophy	75	25			2·2
Economics and Social Science					
Crafts and Technology			100		4·6
Home Economics		65	35		3·7
Art and craft		100			3·2
Music	30	70			2·7
P.E. (indoor)				100	8·3
Games (outdoor)					

Note. The dimensions in this table have been converted into SI equivalents (*From DES Bulletin No. 48, App. 3*).

A method of deriving teaching area allocation is shown in Fig. 2.3 taken from Appendix 3, Building Bulletin 48. This is reproduced as an example of the method available to the designer working with the educational client in the absence of a specific schedule of accommodation.

The basic principles of the calculation of the schedule of accommodation are set out below. This calculation is only possible if the curriculum, certain population data, special room requirements, the length of the teaching week, etc., are known.

Suppose the length of the teaching week is Y hours. This would be the number of hours any one room could be used if the utilisation factor would be 100%. In practice, however, only utilisation factors of 70% to 80% can be achieved in most cases, leaving this room in fact available for $0.7Y$ to $0.8Y$ hours. Suppose a particular room type would be required for X hours as revealed by a study of the curriculum.

The number of rooms of this particular type that would be required would thus be

$$\frac{X}{0.8Y} \quad \text{(always to be rounded up)}.$$

Example. Physics laboratory required for 92 hours per week. Length of teaching week 30 hours. Utilisation level assumed at 70%.

Number of laboratories required $\dfrac{92}{0.7 \cdot 30} = 4.3$ or 5.

DATA

HEIGHT GROUPING OF CHILDREN

The heights of children of age groups in each type or department of a school have considerable influence on the installation and size of equipment and furniture. In any age

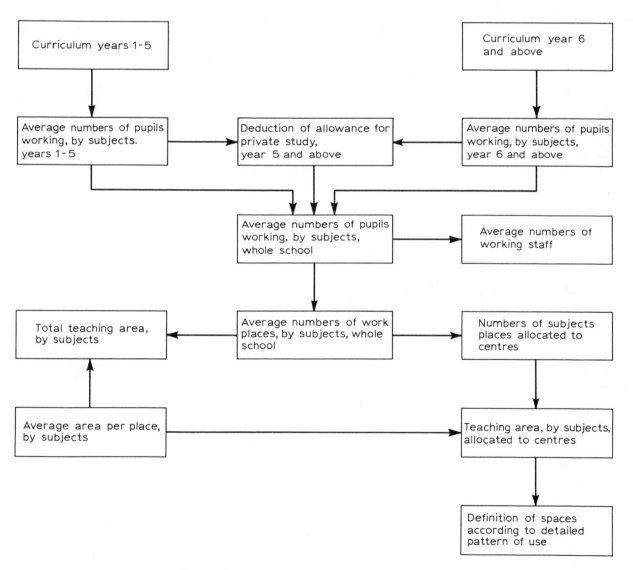

Fig. 2.3   Network showing derivation of teaching area allocation

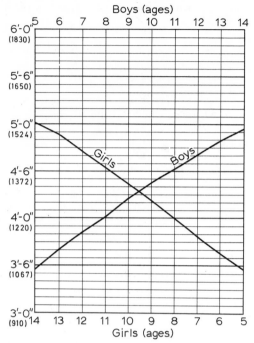

Fig. 2.4 Graph showing average heights of children at various ages in the UK (Approximate equivalents in mm are given in brackets)

group there are wide variations above and below the average height which must be taken into account in regard to seat and desk levels. The dimensions on which Fig. 2.4 is based are averaged from a number of sources, and heights in different parts of the country may be found to be slightly different.

These average heights must be used for fixing the heights of WC seats, cloakroom fittings, towel rails, lockers and all similar fittings and fixtures. Correct heights of all such fittings are of the utmost importance if full benefit is to accrue (Fig. 2.5). For seating and the working heights of desks and tables the correct height for each child is of the maximum importance to ensure good health and working comfort, and this matter will be discussed in greater detail in later sections on teaching spaces.

The heights of children are not given in the figure for ages over fourteen years, as for that age and onwards average normal adult height for fittings and fixtures begins to be satisfactory. It should be noted that although in the younger age groups there is little difference in the sizes of boys and girls, in the later years the girls grow more rapidly than the boys, ultimately, after school age, the boys' average height exceeds that of girls.

FURNITURE AND FITTINGS

The effective working capacity of the building, and its immediate adaptability to specific curriculum needs, depends to a considerable extent on the way it is furnished. A range of furniture types has been designed by the Development Group of the DES (see Bulletin No. 38).

The range is designed to allow scope for different teaching methods. Individual pieces are dimensionally related so that group sizes and arrangements of space can be changed

reasonably easily. Dimensions in the vertical plane are also related in order that wall treatment, such as dado, chalkboard and pin-up, and furniture can be co-ordinated in height, material and colour (see Fig. 2.6). The range conforms to the appropriate British Standards for materials and their use.

ACCOMMODATION—GENERAL

Table 2.6 gives a sample schedule of accommodation for a school of 1200 girls and boys, whilst Table 2.7 gives similar data for a secondary school of 810 pupils. Development of schedule of teaching accommodation for a typical 6th form unit is given in Table 2.8.

Table 2.6 SCHEDULE OF TEACHING ACCOMMODATION PROVIDED FOR A SCHOOL OF 1200 GIRLS AND BOYS

Lower School	Area in m²
3 Group rooms	158·02
Discussion room	29·26
General work area	319·30
Lectures, film and TV Studio	111·48
Social area	66·88
Science area	90·30
Tutorial	12·54
	787·78
Centre for English and Languages	
Languages presentation	64·38
Practice room (Language)	46·82
Practice room (Language)	25·08
Languages work area	37·63
Conversation and drama	20·90
3 Conversation rooms	37·63
Seminar room	20·90
Group room	40·97
2 Tutorial rooms	37·63
English work area, library and study space	91·97
Individual language practice	15·05
Social areas	133·04
Tutorial	25·08
	597·08
Centre for Humanities	
Group room	52·68
Group room	40·97
Discussion room	29·26
General workspace	221·94
Study area	49·84
Lecture room	56·57
Tutorial room	12·54
Library area	18·58
Social area	89·56
Tutorial	13·94
Typing group room	46·82
Seminar room	27·31
Seminar room	29·26
	689·27

Table 2.6 CONTINUED

Centre for Physical Science, Mathematics and Technology,		*Centre for Science, Home Economics, Art and Craft and Crafts*	
Physical Sciences		*Science*	
Tutorial room	14·86	Seminar room	25·08
Lecture/Demonstration	40·97	Lecture/Demonstration	40·97
Laboratory space	242·47	Laboratory area	248·70
		Garden room	58·53
		Food lab.	12·54
		Tutorial	6·04
			391·86
Mathematics			
Seminar room	23·78		
Group room	53·51	*Home Economics*	
Group room	35·67	Cooking 1	83·33
Mathematics lab/studio	98·10	Cooking 2	83·61
Technology area	140·47	Group room	28·24
Common: Library and Study	35·30	Home area	40·41
Social area	46·45	Needlecraft	71·63
Tutorial	14·12	Tutorial	6·60
	745·70	Laundry	11·71
			325·53
Drama, Arts and Music Centre			
Drama studio	207·36		
Group room	33·44	*Arts and Crafts*	
Practical area, needlecraft, art/craft/english	181·53	Pottery	41·25
Reference and study	50·54	Arts and Crafts	30·92
Orchestra room	82·76	Crafts	56·21
Music room	60·20	Art	58·53
Music group room	20·90	Tutorial	4·83
6 Practice rooms	44·79		191·74
Listening booths and study	26·76		
	708·28	*Workshop Crafts*	
		Metal shop	99·59
		Wood shop	74·04
		Construction projects	86·03
		Design area	17·84
Study Commons		Home workshop	7·43
Tutorial	25·08	Tutorial	5·57
Tutorial	12·54	*Common*	
Study area and common room	229·65	Group room	66·89
	267·27	Social area	46·45
		Library and study	37·16
			441·00
Centre for Physcial Education			
Gymnasium	229·47		
Sports Hall	541·81	*Central Buildings*	
Gallery	56·58	Library, library study and workroom	283·26
Hall	238·57	Teaching area (including integrated storage	
	1066·43	and circulation elements) *Total area*	6504·25

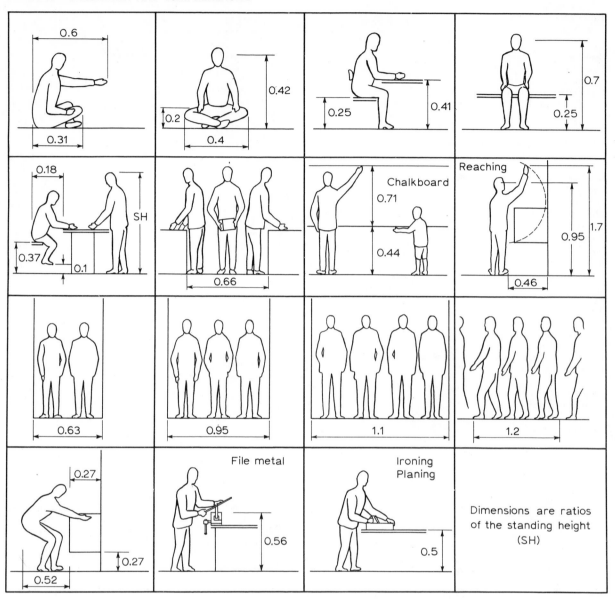

Fig. 2.5 Dimensions required for activities

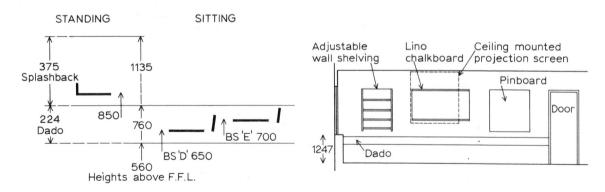

Fig. 2.6 Vertical relationships of furniture, wall treatments, sill and door heights

Table 2.7 SCHEDULE OF TEACHING ACCOMMODATION PROVIDED FOR A SECONDARY SCHOOL FOR 810 PUPILS
(Areas suggested include internal walls and space dividers)

General		*Area in m²*	*Business Studies*		
13 General Classrooms (30 pupils)	598		1 Commerce Room (30)	50	
4 Group Rooms (15)	90		1 Business Machines Area (16)	36	
Lecture Area (90)	108		1 Typing Room (30)	50	136
1 Special Tuition Room (8)	20				
1 Mathematics Room (30)	46	862	*Music and Drama*		
			1 Music/Drama Area (30)	85	
Library/Resources			1 Listening Room	11	
Library	190		1 Store	11	
Library Stock/Work Room	11		2 Music Cells	12	119
Audio-Visual Store	13	214			
			*Pastoral/Guidance/Social**		
Language			4 Year-masters' Rooms	36	
1 Language Laboratory (30)	65		2 Chaplains' Rooms	18	
1 Recording Studio	17	82	2 Guidance Counsellors' Rooms	18	
			1 Guidance Display/Waiting Area	9	
Social Studies			1 Guidance Seminar Room	18	
1 History/Civics Room (30)	60		4 Social Areas	144	
1 Geography/Environmental Studies Room (30)	60		1 Students'/Community Room	40 (min.)	283
Project/Group Areas	40	160			
			Dining/Assembly		
Science			1 Dining/Assembly Area	180	
3 Science Laboratories (30)	258		1 Kitchenette	30	
1 Preparation/Resource Area	55		1 Store	7	217
1 Optical Laboratory	9				
1 Demonstration Room (60)	50	372	*Administration/Staff*		
			1 Entrance Hall	24	
Practical Arts			1 General Office	24	
1 Junior Woodwork Room (24)	85		1 Principal's Room	16	
1 Woodwork Store	20		1 Vice-Principal's Room	12	
1 Junior Metalwork Room (24)	94		1 Teachers' Common Room + Lockers	95	
1 Junior Metalwork Store	11		1 Teachers' Work Area	17	188
1 Senior Metalwork Room (24)	130				
1 Senior Metalwork Store	11		*Toilets*		
1 Building Construction Room (24)	128 (ex. Paint'g)		Girls' Toilets	72	
	20 (Painting)		Boys' Toilets	72	
1 Painting Store	7		Staff Toilets	18	
1 Carpentry/Joinery Store	20		Others	14	176
1 Wet Trades Store	14				
2 Mechanical Drawing Rooms (24)	120		*Circulation/Cloaks/Lockers*		850
1 Mechanical Drawing Store	7	667			
			Other Ancillary Areas		
Arts and Crafts			Stores	18	
1 Open-plan area (60)	216		Boiler	60	
1 Store	11	227	Switch room	3	81
Home Economics					
1 Domestic Science Room (20)	104				
1 Dress-design and Materials Room (20)	62	166		*Total Area*	**4800**

*A welfare unit suited to the needs of this particular example.

Table 2.8 DEVELOPMENT OF SCHEDULE OF TEACHING ACCOMMODATION FOR A TYPICAL 6TH FORM UNIT

SCHEDULE	Area in m^2
Lounge	211·0
Common Room/Snack Bar	252·6
	463·6
Study Areas	154·0
	50·0
	51·5
	18·2
	117·3
	391·0
Seminar Rooms	99·0
	96·0
	100·0
	100·0
	75·0
	470·0
Lecture Theatre	280·5
Lecture Room	152·4
English/Drama Room	160·3
	593·2
Tutorial	58·0
	38·0
	32·0
	45·7
	44·0
	34·0
	46·0
	24·6
	38·0
	360·3
Open Suites	189·0
	160·0
	349·0
Exhibition Area	43·8
Rest Room	26·0
	69·8
Total Teaching Area	391·0
	470·0
	593·0
	360·3
	349·0
	2163·5

PLAYING FIELDS

Reference should be made to the paragraph on playing fields in the previous section on primary schools and also to the volume on *Planning: Buildings for Administration, Entertainment and Recreation,* where the sizes for various games are given, but it should be noted that some spaces of indefinite size are needed for practice pitches, long jumps, etc., which can be placed on odd spaces of suitable sizes in playing fields. Additional spaces and pitches are needed to rest the ground and maintain it in a playable condition. Sites which are reasonably level should be sought to avoid excessive cost in preparation.

The information on the planning requirements of various games given in the volume *Planning: Buildings for Administration, Entertainment and Recreation* is for general purposes; for school purposes these may frequently be reduced with advantage.

Building Bulletin No. 28 deals with playing fields and hard play areas.

Table 2.9 shows minimum areas required and possible schedules of pitches for mixed secondary schools of various sizes.

Fig. 2.7 shows an example of a layout for a school of 1350 pupils.

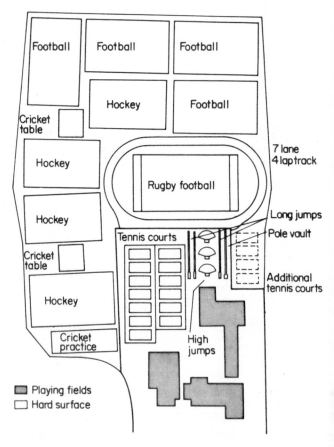

Fig. 2.7   Nine-form entry mixed secondary school: 10.5 ha

Table 2.9 AREA OF SITES, PAVED AREAS AND PLAYING FIELDS

MIXED SECONDARY SCHOOLS

Pupils under 16 years	150 1 F.E.	300 2 F.E.	450 3 F.E.	600 4 F.E.	750 5 F.E.	900 6 F.E.	1050 7 F.E.	1200 8 F.E.	1350 9 F.E.	1500 10 F.E.
AREAS										
Minimum areas in the Regulations										
(a) Regulation 15: hard surface area included in site area below in square metres	1·86	1·86	3·18	3·18	3·66	4·13	4·60	5·06	5·53	6·00
Site area in ha	0·63	0·83	1·25	1·56	1·87	2·18	2·50	2·81	3·12	3·44
(b) Regulation 16: grass playing fields area in ha*	1·87	2·91	4·16	4·16	5·41	5·41	6·66	6·66	7·92	7·92
Min. total area in ha	2·50	3·75	5·41	5·73	7·30	7·60	9·17	9·47	11·00	11·85
POSSIBLE SCHEDULE										
Winter games pitches										
Boys' pitches Small/medium	—	—	1	1	1	1	2	2	2	2
Large	1	1	1	1	2	2	2	2	3	3
Total	1	1	2	2	3	3	4	4	5	5
Girls' pitches Small/medium	—	—	1	1	1	1	2	2	2	2
Large	1	1	1	1	2	2	2	2	3	3
Total	1	1	2	2	3	3	4	4	5	5
Cricket										
Reserved space	1	1	1	1	1	1	1	1	2	2
Permanent practice wickets	3	4	6	6	6	6	6	6	8	8
Tennis courts Sited on the hard surface area at (a) above	4	4	7	7	8	9	10	11	12	13
Athletics track	—	1	1	1	1	1	1	1	1	1

*The Regulations provide that at least one-half the Regulation playing field area shall be in grass. With certain provisos, the remainder may be provided with a hard porous surface, such surface counting for three times its actual area.

FACILITIES FOR CHANGING

This problem is greatly simplified if the playing fields adjoin the school, when advantage may be taken of the normal cloakrooms and lavatories or gymnasium changing rooms; but it is desirable to extend the normal accommodation somewhat and to add shower baths, foot baths, and, if possible, a small plunge bath.

The same changing rooms might be used for games and a swimming bath, if both are situated near enough together. If, however, playing fields are provided centrally for a number of schools, or if they are far from the school itself, changing rooms or sports pavilions must be provided in connection with the playing fields. (See also under 'Gymnasium' later in this section).

SPORTS PAVILIONS

These vary considerably in size and character according to the type of school and whether near or far from the school buildings. They used to be, in fact, no more than changing rooms, together with the necessary lavatory and WC accommodation, and with apparatus stores. For secondary schools more elaborate buildings are frequently required, including refreshment facilities for one or two visiting teams and a similar number of house teams.

Opinions vary in regard to the number of changing rooms which should be provided. A frequent provision is a large room for junior pupils, one or more smaller rooms for senior pupils, and a room for visiting teams. Each room should have at least shower baths and lavatory basins with hot and cold water. Reference should be made to the section on 'Sports Pavilions' in the volume on *Planning: Buildings for Administration, Entertainment and Recreation,* but bearing in mind always that the needs of schools are more simple than of pavilions for other purposes.

The changing rooms can be very simply fitted up; wooden seats round the walls and island seat-fittings, if the rooms are sufficiently large, clothes hooks above and shoe racks under the seats are the chief needs. In changing rooms for outdoor sports, dirty areas connected with outside, and clean areas connected with the showers, are often separated by low benching. Lockers are generally unnecessary. Ample ventilation and light are very important, as also are floor materials; the latter should be such that they are easy to clean and do not suffer damage from studded boots, mud or wet feet.

The refreshment facilities, when required, usually consist of a large room to seat the necessary number of persons at one time, based on an allowance of 0·8 m² per person, together with a small combined kitchen and service room. Little actual cooking is required, as meals are generally ready-cooked or necessitate only the boiling of water for tea.

Adequate space for china and glass storage is important, with ample draining-board space near the sink. The chief need, otherwise, is table space on which meals may be prepared.

GAMES STORE

Adequate and properly fitted up storage is needed for games equipment either at the school or at the playing fields. The amount and type of accommodation needed will vary greatly from school to school, according to the amount of interest given to organised games.

Suitable storage may be provided to meet the needs of different games. Cricket bats require a shelf with raised edge about 150 mm wide, with a similar shelf fixed at 680 mm above it and perforated with holes at 100 mm centres which should be 80 mm diameter for bats and 50 mm diameter for stumps. Cricket, hockey and similar balls can either be kept in cupboards or on racks; it is advantageous if the balls are raised off the shelves to permit of adequate air circulation by resting them on three-pointed supports. Footballs and netballs can be stored on shelves about 300 mm wide with a high front edge; holes 50 mm diameter and 250 mm centres should be made in these shelves.

Sticks for rounders may be held in wall clips spaced at 150 mm centres. Hockey sticks require 80 mm diameter holes spaced 100 mm apart in a rack placed above a sloping base, a shelf 350 mm will accommodate three rows of sticks. Tennis rackets require a shelf about 320 mm wide with 50 mm diameter holes placed at 75 mm centres.

All these shelves and fittings must be strongly made and very securely fixed to the walls. Cupboards are also needed for the storage of cricket pads, gloves, score books and various similar smaller articles.

SWIMMING BATHS

Except in the larger secondary schools (over 1000 pupils) and in a few voluntary schools, swimming baths for the exclusive use of a school are not provided. It is usual to arrange for attendance of classes at public baths or to have a bath to serve a group of schools in an area.

When swimming baths are provided, it is desirable that they should be of the covered type, as the building may be used for certain other physical activities in the winter months if the bath is covered by a temporary floor. Swimming baths, open-air and covered types, are fully discussed in the Planning volume dealing with Recreation and also in Bulletin No. 26.

ACCOMMODATION—TEACHING SPACES

The Premises Regulations 1972 eliminate the two principal constraints on teaching space dimensions:
    (a) natural illumination level.
    (b) natural ventilation rate.
The requirements under these headings are as follows.

(a) LIGHTING

Section 52 (paragraph 2) requires that 'in teaching accommodation the lowest level of maintained illumination and the minimum daylight factor shall be 110 lux and 2% respectively.' However, this section also provides that if sufficient lighting can be provided by a combination of permanent supplementary artificial lighting and daylight *at less than a 2% daylight factor*, then the daylight factor can be at this lower percentage. This proposal is subject to the approval of the DES for any project. The measurement of illumination shall be on the work plane of normal use.

A further requirement limits the visibility of artificial light sources to the eye of an occupant in a normal position; and recommends that artificial lighting shall be arranged to illuminate ceiling and upper parts of walls to prevent excessive contrast. The effect of this measure is to eliminate the need for large areas of window glazing carried up to the ceiling in order to obtain penetration of light necessary to give 2% daylight factor at the rear of a room, with the problems of glare and solar heat gain associated with this solution. Clearly much smaller areas of window glazing are now possible with PSALI used to give an even spread of illumination by the installation of fittings in the rear of the room (see Fig. 2.8).

Equally, it now becomes possible to provide much deeper buildings with teaching spaces arranged in a more open and continuous fashion uninhibited by the critical dimension from a window wall of around 6 m which previously obtained. Ceilings heights of 3 m, or thereabouts, can now be maintained throughout large areas of multi-use teaching spaces thus permitting economies in elemental cost and flexibility in the positioning of internal partitions.

The critical factor in such deep buildings as now are possible will be the visual connections of the occupant with the outside environment for purposes of relief and stimulation and the availability of such views from the deepest portion of the building. It further seems desirable to introduce courts with planting or sculpture or paved for external activities into such buildings.

(b) VENTILATION OF TEACHING SPACES

The provision of natural ventilation to teaching spaces is no longer required by the Premises Regulations but minimum requirements of ventilation are laid down as set out in Table 2.10. The provision of such fresh air ventilation can be made by natural or artificial means or a combination of both.

If the average area per pupil work station for the purpose of reading, writing or private study is taken to be 1·87 m² in a space with a clear ceiling height of 3 m, then the air changes per hour required are $1·87 \times 3 = 5·6$ m² which, by Table 2.10, requires five air changes per hour.

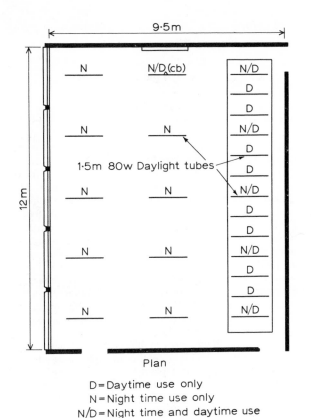

D = Daytime use only
N = Night time use only
N/D = Night time and daytime use

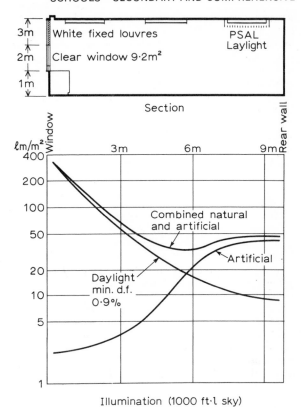

Fig. 2.8   Permanent supplementary artificial lighting

A higher level of ventilation coupled with the extract of noxious fumes will, of course, be required in spaces such as chemistry laboratories, workshops and kitchens.

The heating of teaching space is clearly related to ventilation rates and the Premises Regulations provides for the temperature in schools and the proportion of fresh air to be heated as given in Table 2.11. It will be observed that if, as in the example worked above, a teaching space required five air changes per hour on the basis of cubic space per person, then when the outside temperature is 0°C a temperature of 17°C must be maintained by heating two air changes per hour, that is 2/5 of the total air flow through the space. The temperature is to be maintained at a height of no more than 1 m from the floor.

Table 2.10 RECOMMENDED VENTILATION FOR TEACHING SPACE

Cubic space per person for whom the room is designed m³	Appropriate number of air changes per hour
Not more than 5	6
5–5·7	5
5·8–7	4
7·1–8·5	3
More than 8·5	1½

Table 2.11 RECOMMENDED HEATING LEVELS FOR TEACHING SPACES

Type of room or space	Number of air changes per hour to be heated by the heating system	Temperatures C
Convalescent sitting rooms	3	18·5
Medical inspection rooms	3	18·5
Changing rooms, bathrooms and shower rooms	3	18·5
Teaching rooms	2	17
Nursery playrooms	2	17
Common rooms	2	17
Staff rooms	2	17
Sanatoriums and sickrooms	3	14·5
Halls	1½	14
Dining rooms	2	14
Gymnasiums	2	14
Cloakrooms	2	13
Corridors	1½	13
Dormitories	2	11

ACOUSTICS IN TEACHING SPACES

An acoustic finish to the ceiling in teaching spaces is desirable in order to minimise reverberation time. It is becoming common to provide carpeting over much of the floor within a school and particularly in corridors or circulation spaces in order to eliminate the clatter from foot traffic. Rubber flooring can also be used but tends to be more expensive. Where it is necessary to isolate noisy activities it will be necessary not only to provide partitions of sufficient sound resistance but also to ensure that sound is not transmitted through the space above false ceilings or through open windows. In practice it is more effective to isolate the noise source locally than to attempt to screen other users from air-borne noise at a distance. Workshops require special attention in most cases.

SERVICE SPACES

Services Distribution

Services can be considered in two categories:
  (a) Environmental control services.
  (b) Activity services.

Environmental control services will be delivered uniformly around a school for lighting, heating and ventilation. Distribution should be through elements of the building which are permanent and not disturbed by alterations demanded in the normal course of teaching activities.

The development of false ceiling systems in which artificial lighting fittings are integrated, together with ventilation or air-conditioning equipment, has been a significant solution to the problem of the distribution of the environmental control systems throughout an inherently flexible interior. Fig. 2.9 shows the development of such a system in the SCSD programme of school building in USA.

Activity services will be limited to domestic level electricity power points and some water supply to sinks, in all but the specialised laboratory or workshop spaces. Mains should be distributed in spaces where they will not be disturbed, although access will be required to service runs. Local distribution for laboratories should be in benches as far as possible and on the surface where necessary. Services should not be run in partitions or buried in screeds, and the same applies to drainage runs.

GENERAL PRINCIPLES

The total area of internal teaching accommodation is determined by the minimum area per pupil given in the Premises Regulations. Within this total area, however, there has been a changed approach to the adoption of rigid areas for rooms for various purposes. Designers are now encouraged to treat suggested areas as minima and to increase them, keeping only within the maximum prescribed costs. The required allocation of space varies considerably according to the size and type of school; thus designers should follow carefully the various suggestions set out in the Building Bulletins of the DES.

One of the governing factors in the planning of schools is the number of storeys on which the accommodation is disposed. There is a tendency to use single-storey buildings for nursery, special and primary schools whenever land areas permit, which is, broadly, in all except very congested urban areas. Secondary schools, however, are often planned as single and multi-storey buildings, the latter tending to be the more usual. Single storey buildings tend to become very spread out if the school is large, thus involving long circulations and more difficult supervision. Other factors to be considered in the decision on the number of storeys are the site contours, type of construction, method of lighting to be used for rooms and local preferences.

Plans may vary greatly in shape, but the trend towards deep buildings with fewer rigid internal divisions must be noted, following the increasing acceptance that experiment and innovation are a constant factor in education. Buildings are increasingly expected to provide a variety of accommodation to permit flexible group sizes, timetabling options and facilities for individual work.

It is important to anticipate that extensions may be needed

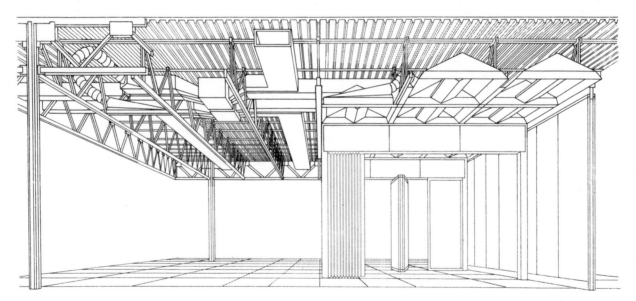

Fig. 2.9   Section showing lighting and conditioning systems in ceiling, over deep unpartitioned space. SCSD School Building Programme, USA

at some later date, and consequently very compact plans, especially if built round a courtyard and closed on all sides, are difficult to extend. Varying uses of school buildings during and after school hours also affect general planning greatly.

Analysis of general circulation in all school plans is dependent in the first instance, on a realisation of the relative importance of various parts, and their inter-relationship.

SOCIAL AND ORGANISATIONAL ASPECTS

Comprehensive organisation will usually lead to the creation of larger schools. This alone would make a replanning of

SECTIONS

TYPICAL SECTIONS: TRADITIONAL AND NON-TRADITIONAL TYPES

The provisions outlined above will not necessarily mean that the traditional type of school layout will disappear following the relaxation of requirements for natural illumination and ventilation. Indeed, a need to consider carefully cost-in-use for any proposed school will mean that the degree of artificial illumination provided and the cost, both capital and recurrent, of artificial heating and ventilation systems must be most carefully considered in order to ensure optimum use of energy.

Figs. 2.12(A) to 2.12(D) show a number of traditional arrangements whereby natural ventilation and illumination are distributed throughout teaching rooms. Figs. 2.13 and 2.14 show examples of buildings which make use of PSALI

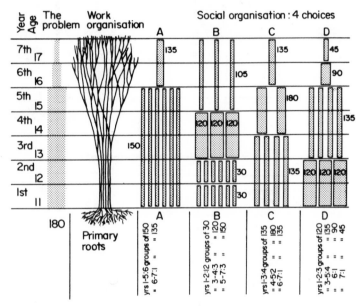

Fig. 2.10   Social groups: some choices
A school (11 to 18 years) with an annual entry of 180 and 135 students over 16 years. This diagram suggests four possible approaches to the sub-division of the enrolment into smaller communities with which individuals can feel a sense of identity. The pattern of this grouping may be quite different from the pattern of the working groups. (H.M.S.O.)

traditional organisation, with regard to teaching and social aspects, desirable since numbers of specialist teachers increase and a wider choice of subjects is given. Such changes tend to reduce the contact between teacher and pupil and tend to break down the compactness of groups.

The pupil may be a member of different groups and may be in contact with many teachers. This increases the need for carefully organised divisions of the whole (large) school into smaller communities. The form of such divisions, however, is subject of discussion. What is the best group size? Should they be organised horizontally or vertically? What would be the activities of such a group? What should be the relationships between social groups and work groups? These are the sort of decisions to be taken. It is clear that such decisions would have major implications for the design of buildings.

Fig. 2.10 gives some choices for social organisation, and Fig. 2.11 gives an example of a solution.

and artificially induced ventilation systems.

Figs. 2.12(A) to 2.12(D) show sections through classrooms and corridors. (A), and (B) and (D) show single storey types and (C) shows a multi-storey type. It is generally desirable that direct ventilation be available to classrooms over the corridor as shown in all figures except (C). Borrowed lights between classrooms and corridors are widely used and assist the lighting of wide types of classroom; an objection to the use of such lights is that the main light on desks nearest to the corridor is likely to be from the right-hand side and other rows may receive light of equal strength from two directions. Another objection to large borrowed lights is that the wall-space may be wanted for the accommodation of lockers, display boards or bookshelves.

Where rooms are planned on both sides of corridors, as in Fig. 2.12(B), the corridor may be top-lighted and, in consequence, may not be well ventilated; opening clerestory lights

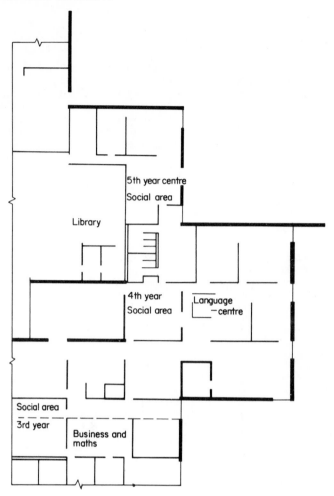

Fig. 2.11   A possible arrangement for social organisation within a comprehensive

for the classrooms above corridors of this type are, therefore, most essential. Classrooms with partial top or roof lighting are not generally favoured as they usually cause cold down-draughts which are difficult to overcome. Also, the cost of maintenance of roof lights, especially cleaning, is high. Vertical lights as shown in (D) are more easily maintained. When borrowed light across corridors is used sill heights must be kept low to avoid shadows across desktops nearest to them and also because the angle of light is necessarily low from the upper part of corridor windows.

GENERAL SPACES

Adaptability of classroom size may be important. Modern educational methods lay less and less emphasis on 'chalk and talk'.

Formal arrangements such as shown in Fig. 2.15(a) will not occur very often. More emphasis is laid on discussion, project work, team teaching, individual study etc. requiring more flexible and informal arrangements as shown in Figs. 2.15(b) and 2.16.

Equipment.   Cupboard(s).
    Desks, chairs: pupil, teacher.
    Chalkboard.
    Projection screen, table, TV.

INDIVIDUAL STUDY

Individual work places may range from a single table-top to a small private study room (Fig. 2.17).

Cubicles, carrels, etc. should have adequate lighting, book-shelves and filing storage and if tape recorders etc. are used, a power point. The advantage of the models shown is that they are movable.

STAFFROOM REQUIREMENTS

These should comprise a common room for teaching staff and a separate room for the head teacher.

ACCOMMODATION FOR MEALS

This is covered in the Planning volume dealing with recreation. The minimum space is:
    0.5 m² per person if two sittings.
    1 m² per person if one sitting.

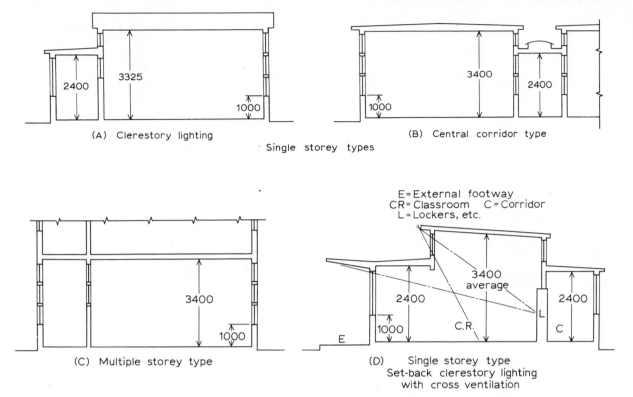

Fig. 2.12   (A) to (C) Classrooms and corridors : lighting and ventilation ; (D) Classroom and corridor sections

Fig. 2.13   (1) Example of buildings using PSALI and artificially-induced ventilation systems

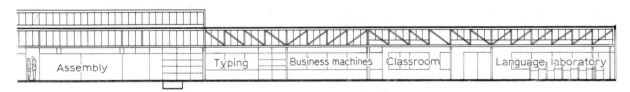

Fig. 2.14   (2) Example of buildings using PSALI and artificially-induced ventilation systems

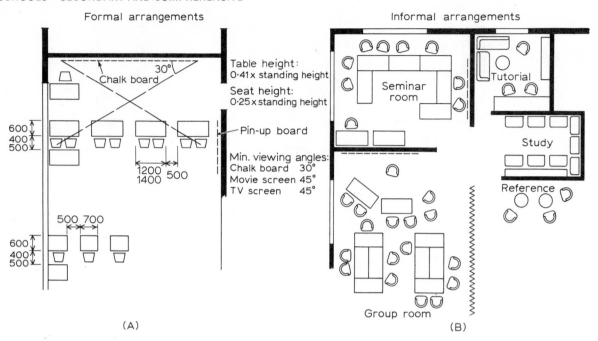

Formal arrangements

Informal arrangements

Table height:
0·41 x standing height

Seat height:
0·25 x standing height

Pin-up board

Min. viewing angles:
Chalk board   30°
Movie screen 45°
TV screen   45°

Seminar room

Tutorial

Study

Reference

Group room

(A)

(B)

Fig. 2.15   General teaching and learning spaces

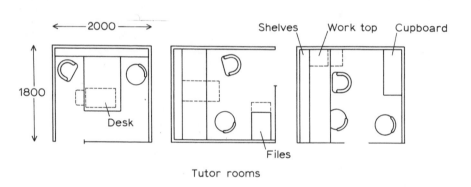

Shelves   Work top   Cupboard

Desk

Files

Tutor rooms

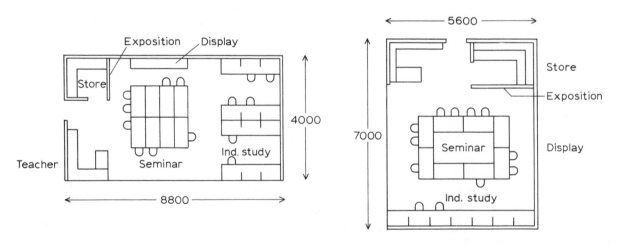

Exposition   Display

Store

Teacher   Seminar   Ind. study

Store

Exposition

Display

Seminar

Ind. study

Fig. 2.16   Teaching rooms for seminar and individual study

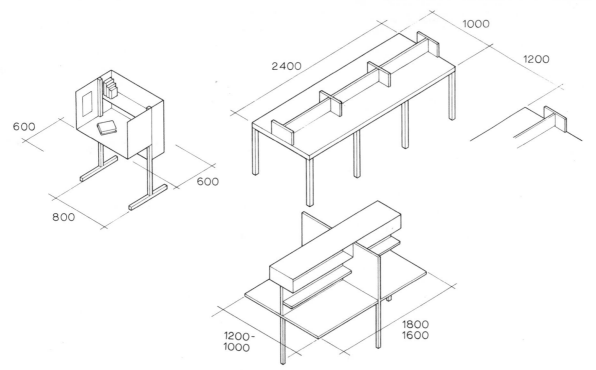

Fig. 2.17 Small private study room

SPECIALISED SPACES

WOODWORK

The layout is shown in Fig. 2.18 and includes:
  Equipment and workbenches.
  Space for planning and reference, equipped with tables, chairs, shelving, display shelves.
  Gluing area.
  Finishing area: polishing, painting, finishing
    a space free of dust with simple benches.
  Teacher's space.
  Storage space: for materials (i.e. length of timber up to 4800 mm; width of timber 150–300 mm; plywood).
    for work in progress
    for tools, first aid, fire-fighting equipment
  Changing and working area.

METALWORK (see Fig. 2.19)

The layout includes:
  Equipment and workbenches.
  Sheet metal bench (one), somewhat lower and room for manoeuvring of sheets of about 1200 × 600, with hand-level shearing machine.
  Planning and reference area (see woodwork).
  Forgework, brazing, soldering, casting and grinding.
    Forgework:
      forge water trough (600 × 300 × 300).
      fuel bin.
      two anvils.
      swage block (450 × 450).
      leg vice.
      wall fixing for anvil and forge tools.
      pegs for aprons.

    Brazing:
      brazing bench and accessories.
      an acid bath.
      a sink.
      a scouring and draining surface.
    Moulding:
      benches.
      casting tray.
      sand bins.
      guillotine.
  Storage.

WORKSHOP PLANNING ASPECTS

Both for woodwork and metalwork areas the following two points should be borne in mind:
  (a) Logical flow of materials.
  (b) Minimum movement of people.

OTHER WORKSHOPS

Other workshops which come under the heading of specialised spaces include:
  Electricity/Electronics.
  Power mechanics.
  Combined wood/metal.
  Advanced metal.
  'Uncommitted' workshop.
  Homecrafts.
  Building construction, masonry.
  Rural crafts.
  Spinning, weaving.
  Rattan/Bamboo }
  Leather   } arts related.

WOODWORK SHOP
Equipment showing clear working space required

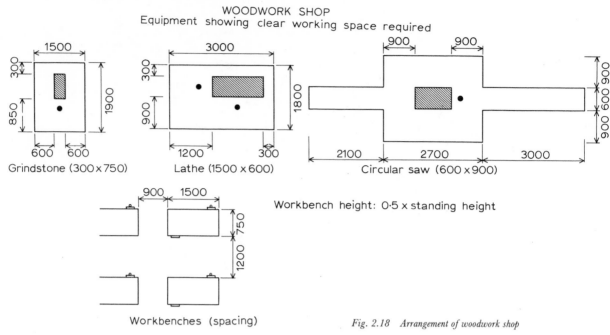

Grindstone (300 × 750)

Lathe (1500 × 600)

Circular saw (600 × 900)

Workbench height: 0·5 × standing height

Workbenches (spacing)

Fig. 2.18   Arrangement of woodwork shop

METAL WORKSHOP
Equipment showing clear working space required

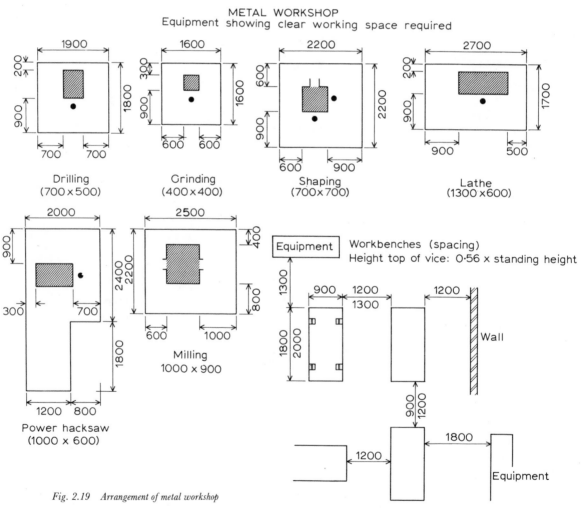

Drilling
(700 × 500)

Grinding
(400 × 400)

Shaping
(700 × 700)

Lathe
(1300 × 600)

Power hacksaw
(1000 × 600)

Milling
1000 × 900

Equipment

Workbenches (spacing)
Height top of vice: 0·56 × standing height

Wall

Equipment

Fig. 2.19   Arrangement of metal workshop

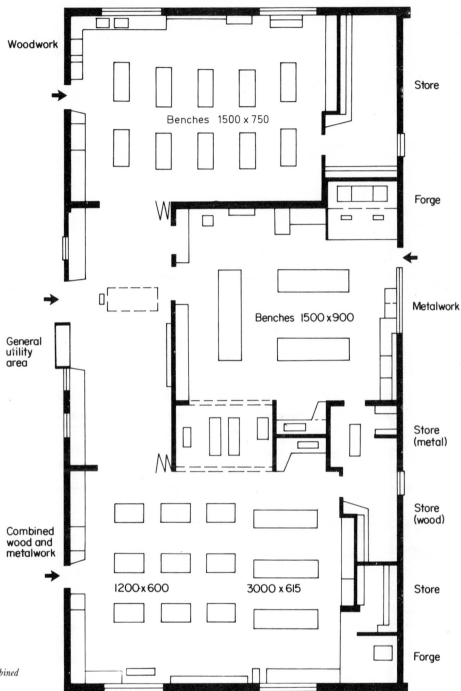

Woodwork

Store

Benches 1500 x 750

Forge

General utility area

Benches 1500 x 900

Metalwork

Store (metal)

Store (wood)

Combined wood and metalwork

1200 x 600   3000 x 615

Store

Forge

Fig. 2.20   Typical layout of a combined workshop (H.M.S.O.)

LAYOUT OF A WORKSHOP DEPARTMENT

Typical Examples

(a) In Fig. 2.20 three workshops (one equipped for metal-work, one for woodwork and for both wood and metalwork) share a general utility area.

This is used sometimes for large scale assembly work which cannot easily be done in the workshops, sometimes for evening work on engines etc, sometimes for study. It has double doors opening on to a yard. Two of the workshops also share a small 'interchange' area, containing lathes, hacksaw and grinder, which can therefore be made available to both workshops (by rolling up the two sets of shutters as shown) or to either one or the other workshop (by rolling up only one set of shutters).

A third point of interest is the inclusion of a small bay for individual work in two of the workshops, each equipped with benching, vice, lathe, a small panel of chalkboard and a socket outlet.

2—21

(b) The layout in Fig. 2.21 is in a technical high school for approx. 500 pupils. In addition, there is a combined wood and machine shop used by younger pupils. The lighting is from interior lights and perimeter clerestory windows. There are also screens between some of the spaces, above either bench or door head. While illumination levels are good, some windows at view level at selected points would have been welcomed.

Woodshops. Note the bay for the storage of work in progress and the placing of the teacher's demonstration bench. Sixth formers can use the lathes behind the guard rails while a class is in progress. The generous store provides for vertical stacking of unsawn timber and horizontal stacking of prepared pieces; for tool sharpening; for the use of special machines; and for some of the work of senior pupils.

Metalshops. This has been equipped in three distinct zones: the bench area (with locker for tools); the machines area (separated by a guard rail); the heat treatment area (with soldering bench and hearths but no forge).

Engineering Shop. The layout is similar to that of the metal-shop in principle, but there are more machines, and an area for the exclusive use of sixth formers.

'*Heat*'. A screeded floor with brick hearth. The sink has a sediment tank.

'*Testing*'. Used largely by sixth formers. Equipped with fixed worktops with drawers under, movable chalkboards, display surfaces.

'*Engines*'. Heavy equipment can be handled both inside and outside, for there is a block and tackle and a roller shutter.

'*Finishes*'. Fair-faced brick walls. Ventilation important.

Stores and office. Desk and bench for technician servicing the department. Racks for rods and sheets. Lockable cupboards for valuable equipment.

Staff H.Q. Here department staff keep their files, reference material and personal belongings. Equipped with basin, pegs, filing cabinets, drawing chest, shelving, desk and worktop, clock and 'phone.

Drawing rooms. Main room equipped for thirty pupils. Drawers under worktop for pupils' folders. Platform to enable pupils to see drawings and display material clearly. The room for advanced work is separated by a glazed screen, and equipped with drawing machines and facilities for printing.

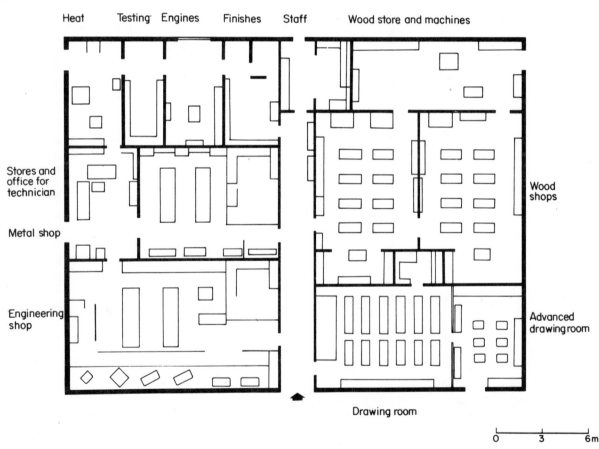

Heat   Testing Engines   Finishes   Staff   Wood store and machines

Stores and office for technician

Metal shop

Engineering shop

Wood shops

Advanced drawing room

Drawing room

0   3   6m

Fig. 2.21   Combined workshop area designed for technical high school

SPECIAL TEACHING ROOMS

These can be divided into groups comprising:

Languages

To look, listen and imitate.
To practise the skills of speech.
To develop these skills to acquire a deeper knowledge of the language in a widening context and with varying personal objectives.

Main areas

Presentation and follow-up work.
Individual practice (language lab.)
Store, maintenance, recording, books, reference.

TYPICAL EXAMPLES

Provision for Modern Languages: A 60-Group Unit (Fig. 2.22)

Average working area: approx. (2·0 m²) per pupil.

This layout allows for the broad division of the work on the lines previously discussed, with—at any time—roughly one-fifth of the sixty pupils practising individually with electronic equipment and the other four-fifths divided into groups which can vary according to how the teachers wish to organise the work. For example, a group of twelve, eighteen, twenty-four, or a maximum of about thirty-six pupils can watch slides, film strips, a film or television programme;

smaller or larger groups can work in the bays or on the raised areas for follow-up work; conversation, acting, reading, etc.

In space 1 there is provision for daylight projection, with adjacent recess fitted with shelves over a worktop and cupboard for the staff; a length of wall benching with display surfaces over and a couple of plug-in practice positions if wanted; and tables and chairs can be arranged in various ways.

In room 2 there are two slightly raised carpeted areas with tables and chairs at the curtained windows, while the central area is furnished with twelve individual work places, some with 'listen-respond-record' equipment, all under the guidance of the teacher at the console.

There is a small room for storage and repairs with a recording bay adjacent.

Provision for Modern Languages: A 120-Group Unit (Fig. 2.23)

Average working area: approx. (1·85 m²) per pupil.

In this example there are two spaces (1 and 2 on plan) each equipped for daylight projection, in which two groups of about twenty-four can watch film strips, etc. Individual practice can also be taken in groups of twenty-four. So can some of the follow-up work, though sometimes there might be smaller groups of about twelve, or larger ones of thirty-six —depending in part on the number of adults and also on the number of pupils working on their own at any particular time.

Spaces 1 and 2 are therefore each shown furnished with twenty-four chairs, which on occasion can be pushed back (as in space 2) to clear the floor for acting. If the sliding-folding doors are opened, the actors can split up into several groups. In both spaces there are shelves, cupboards, provision

Fig. 2.22 Provision for modern languages. A 60-group unit (H.M.S.O)

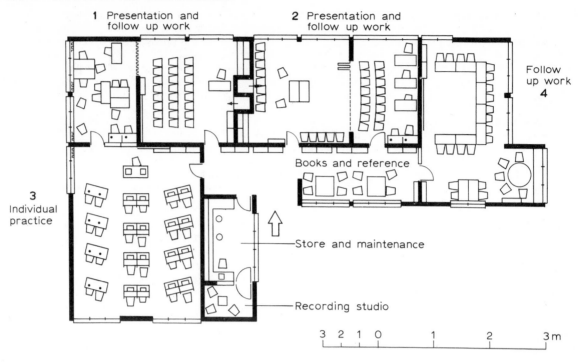

1 Presentation and follow up work

2 Presentation and follow up work

Follow up work **4**

Books and reference

3 Individual practice

Store and maintenance

Recording studio

3 2 1 0   1   2   3 m

Fig. 2.23   Provision for modern languages. A 120-group unit (H.M.S.O)

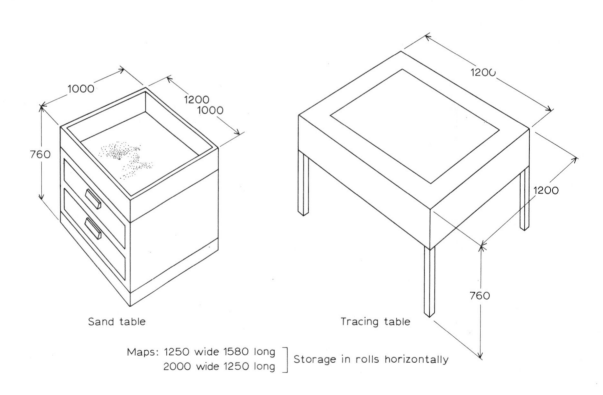

1000

1200
1000

760

Sand table

1200

1200

760

Tracing table

Maps: 1250 wide 1580 long
2000 wide 1250 long] Storage in rolls horizontally

Fig. 2.24   Equipment for a geography room

for display and power points into which trolleyed equipment can be plugged.

Space 3 is furnished with twenty-four individual practice places, eight of them with audio-active, sixteen with 'listen-respond-record' equipment, all linked to the teacher's console. An overhead projector or other visual aid can be trolleyed in if needed. In this instance, everyone faces the console. Opinions vary on the need for this, but many teachers feel it important to be able to watch the faces of the younger beginners, at least.

There is a central reading, reference and exhibition area, with one or two tables for reference, and again a small store/workshop and recording room.

SPECIAL TEACHING AND LEARNING ROOMS

Such spaces are, in principle, identical to normal teaching spaces, but have some additional furniture specific to the subject mainly taught in the room, such as geography, mathematics and social studies.

Geography (Fig. 2.24)

Large chalkboard, for map drawing.
Provision for hanging and storing of charts and maps.
Equipment display and storage: globes 400 mm. dia. barometers, compasses.
Display and storage of specimen of minerals, pictures, photographs (shelves, pin-up boards, cupboards).
Practical work area:
    a sand table for modelling projects.
    a tracing table.
    project tables.
Provisions for audio-visual aids:
    projection screen, projection table, overhead projection table, socket outlets, darkening possibilities.
Outside: meteorology station.

Mathematics

Chalkboard: large, well-finished, partly lined for drawing of graphs etc.
Pegboard for hanging of equipment.
Chart rail.
Provision for the production, display and storage of mathematical objects (e.g. small workbench, display and storage shelves, cupboard):
    geometrical solids.
    geometrical models.
    spaceframes.
    mathematical toys etc.
Provision for audio-visual aids: overhead projectors are often used.

ARTS AND CRAFTS

Areas

Display areas.
Reference and study.
Storage of materials, tools and projects.

Teacher bases.
Practical work areas (inside and sometimes outside) for:
    1. Pictorial work, such as drawing, painting, block-printing, bookcrafts etc.
    2. Three-dimensional work, such as carvings, sculpture, clay modelling, pottering etc.
    3. Work on textiles: fabric printing, weaving, spinning, costume making and design etc.

1. Pictorial Work

A mix of types of working surfaces might be the most flexible answer. Tables of about 2000 mm long and 900 mm wide would provide working space for 4 students. Paper storage in drawers (800 × 1400 approx.) would store most paper sizes. Most equipment and materials can be stored on shelves. Bulky items of equipment can be stored under workbenches. Two general-purpose sinks are generally needed. Block printing requires a firm working surface.

Bookcrafts require special equipment, depending on what is meant by bookcrafts, e.g. a press, sewing frame, cutter, zinc-covered bench for gluing, heating equipment etc.

2. Three Dimensional Work

An indication of the type of equipment that might be used (see Fig. 2.25):
    Tabling (some trestle tables and some heavier type).
    Benching with vices (for woodwork).
    Benching with vices (for metalwork).
    Felt and cork-jawed vices.
    Wedging bench for clay (0·4 m² area).
    Grindstone (600 × 600 mm), sharpening stones.
    Modelling stands, boards.
    Cross-cut saw.
    Gas ring and glue pot.
    Electric soldering iron.
    Small blowlamp.
    Large sinks or sinks with clay trap.
    Wood and metalwork tools.
More specialised equipment is needed for pottery, as follows:
    Storage of materials: clay bins.
    Preparation of clay: pugmill; wedging bench (600 to 670 high) sturdy construction; sink; plaster bats; buckets, sieves etc.
    Making and modelling: heavy tables, benches (750–600 mm length per person, 1000 mm width for 2 persons, 750–600 mm width for 1 person); wheels, banding wheels; moulds; plaster container; tools; damp cupboard.
    Decorating in clay state: benching, sink, shelves.
    Drying: shelving, well ventilated.
    Firing: kiln.
    Decorating, glazing: benching, shelving.
    Glaze firing: kiln.
    Storage and display: shelving etc.

3. Work on Textiles (see Fig. 2.26)

Fabric printing: equipment depending on the techniques to be learned:

1100

900 1000
1200 1300

Potter's wheel

1700

600 750

Small electric kiln

Modelling table

Fig. 2.25   Equipment for 3-dimensional work

Designing, experimenting: strong tables (could be trestle type). 1800 × 750 for 2 persons. Storage shelves, drawers, cupboards for tools, inks, paints etc.

Washing, drying, ironing: large sink, 1050 × 600 × 600 mm deep for washing, draining boards on both sides. Drying racks, lines, etc. (min. 1800 mm long). Ironing on large trestle table.

Setting out the fabric ready for printing. Table: minimum 2100 × 1050 mm.

Dye mixing, preparation of screens (zinc or formica top covered bench 1200 long). Shelves, cupboards for pails, pans etc. Storage and display area.

Spinning and Weaving:

Spinning: spinning wheels (needing 900 × 450 mm floor space), carders, spindles, skein holders, a yarn trolley (600 × 950), shelving.

Weaving: looms (table types, 350 × 450 mm, 450 × 450 mm, 900 × 800 mm). Treadle looms (850 × 850 mm; 1250 × 1050 mm).

Miscellaneous warping frames; a warping mill (1000 × 600 × 1800 high).

Shelving, cupboards etc.

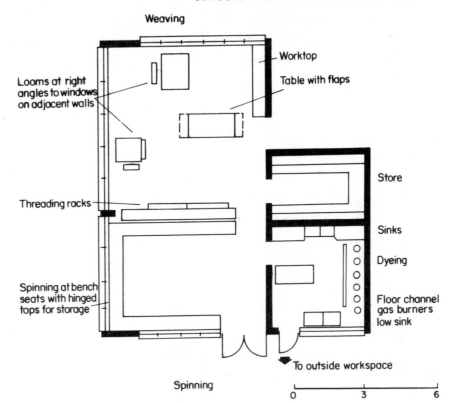

Fig. 2.26 Sequence of operations: spinning, dyeing, weaving, finishing. This diagram illustrates the four main elements of a weaving workshop.

Space and equipment for spinning.

Space and equipment for dyeing (and finishing)

Space and equipment for weaving.

Space and equipment for storage of materials and work
(H.M.S.O)

Weaving

Looms at right angles to windows on adjacent walls

Worktop

Table with flaps

Store

Sinks

Dyeing

Floor channel gas burners low sink

Threading racks

Spinning at bench seats with hinged tops for storage

To outside workspace

Spinning

0   3   6

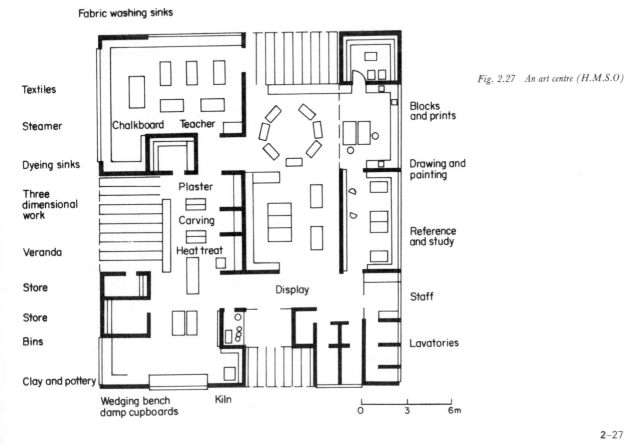

Fig. 2.27 An art centre (H.M.S.O)

Fabric washing sinks

Textiles

Steamer

Dyeing sinks

Three dimensional work

Veranda

Store

Store

Bins

Clay and pottery

Chalkboard   Teacher

Plaster

Carving

Heat treat

Display

Wedging bench damp cupboards   Kiln

Blocks and prints

Drawing and painting

Reference and study

Staff

Lavatories

0   3   6m

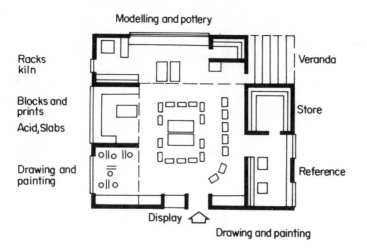

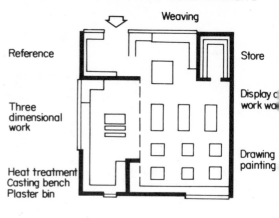

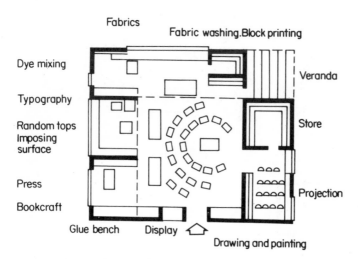

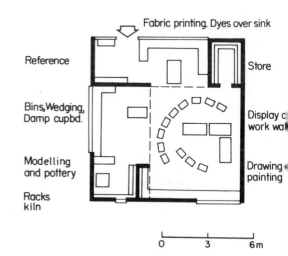

Fig. 2.28 A general studio (H.M.S.O)

HOME SCIENCE; HOME ECONOMICS; HOUSE CRAFTS
(SEE FIG. 2.29)

Subjects that may be taught:
    Foods and nutrition.
    Textiles, dressmaking.
    Family living.

DRAMA AND MUSIC ROOMS

Music (see Figs. 2.31 to 2.37)

1. Accommodation for class teaching—the music room.
2. Accommodation for instrumental practice and tuition.
3. Accommodation for orchestras, bands, choirs and other ensembles.
4. Storage.

Drama

1. Rooms for small scale drama work—easily movable furniture, such as platform units, chairs etc. Folding screens, curtains to cut down light, a neutral background (wall or curtain), socket outlets above skirting level area for record player and records, spotlights etc.
2. Drama studio—possibly useful for a variety of other activities e.g. lectures, discussions, etc. (see Fig. 2.38).
3. Space primarily on performance (see also section on 'Theatres' in the Planning volume on Entertainment and Recreation). Multi-purpose uses of theatres e.g. as halls, etc. Open stage. Proscenium stages (traditional).

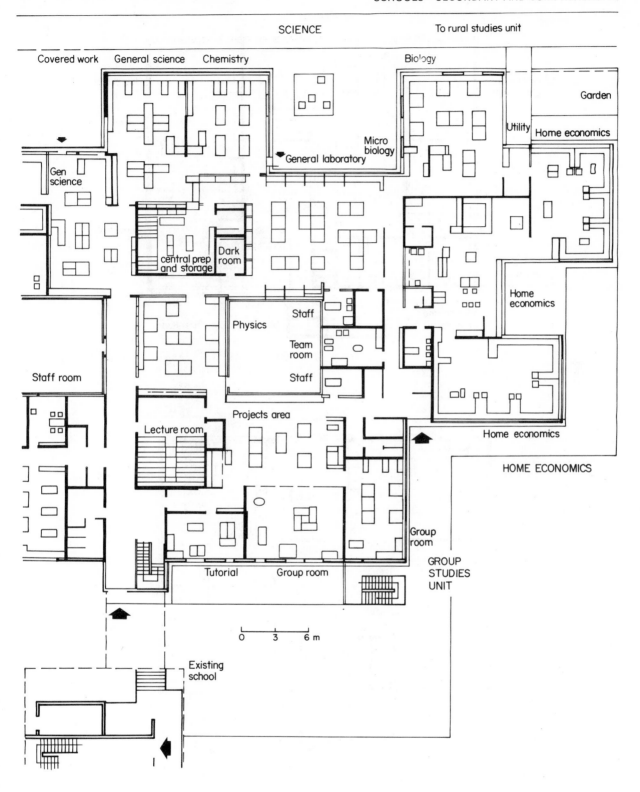

Fig. 2.29   Science, home economics and housecraft area (H.M.S.O)

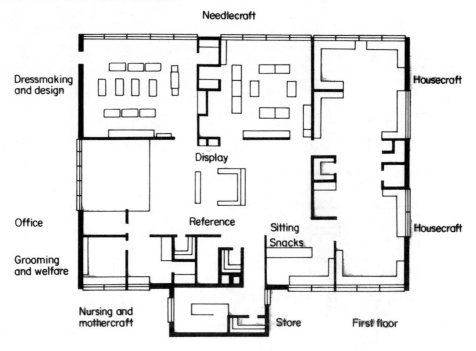

Needlecraft

Dressmaking
and design

Housecraft

Display

Office

Reference

Sitting

Snacks

Housecraft

Grooming
and welfare

Nursing and
mothercraft

Store

First floor

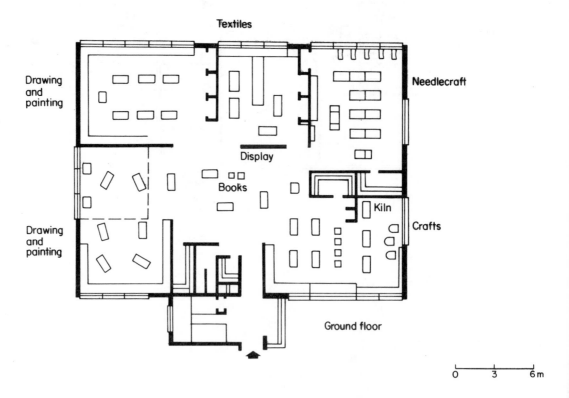

Textiles

Drawing
and
painting

Needlecraft

Display

Books

Kiln

Crafts

Drawing
and
painting

Ground floor

0   3   6 m

Fig. 2.30 A 'social living' project. Equivalent in area to what might have been about eight practical rooms, this centre was conceived as a series of intercommunicating spaces in which many different activities could achieve a certain unity of purpose, with flexibility in time-tabling and groupings (H.M.S.O)

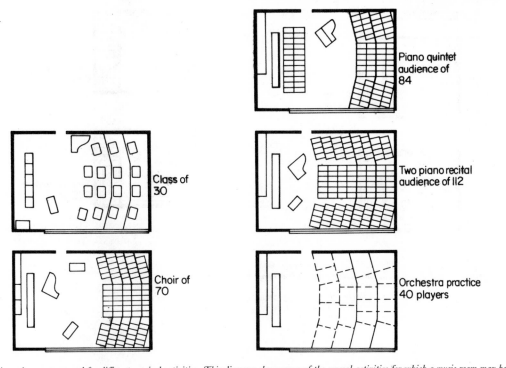

Piano quintet audience of 84

Class of 30

Two piano recital audience of 112

Choir of 70

Orchestra practice 40 players

Fig. 2.31 A music room arranged for different musical activities. This diagram shows some of the several activities for which a music room may have to cater. It can be used for an orchestra of about forty players or a brass band, as well as for class teaching, choir practice and recitals.

Hollow platforms 1500m to 1800m wide and about 20m high are confined to the back of the room in order to give maximum scope for rearrangements of space and furniture. They are splayed to give good sight lines to the conductor or the chalkboard.

The store behind the teacher's wall can take tables, chairs, music stands, etc, when these are not required. (The upright piano can if necessary also be stored in here.)

The cupboard fitting (at either end of which are curtains for easy access) provides a large chalk and display surface on one side, and, on the other, cupboards and shelves for record playing equipment, records, tape-deck, music and so on. A radio outlet is available both through a fixed loud speaker and through a jack for direct tape recording. An additional plug at the back of the room is provided for projection or other purposes. (H.M.S.O)

Fitted cupboards for records, sheet music, record player, tape deck and amplifier

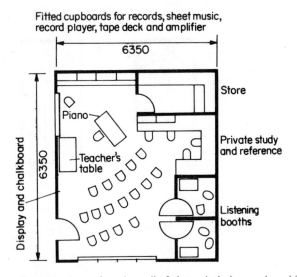

6350

Store

Piano

Private study and reference

Teacher's table

6350

Display and chalkboard

Listening booths

Fig. 2.32 A room for senior pupils. In large schools there may be need for a room designed for the use of senior pupils.

Equipment includes fifteen to twenty chairs, an upright piano, record player, tape recorder, fittings for music and record storage, chalkboard, wall surfaces for pictures and other display. There are also work tops for individual study and two small listening booths equipped with record players, and a store.

In some schools senior study groups might instead use a small room also used for instrumental teaching (H.M.S.O)

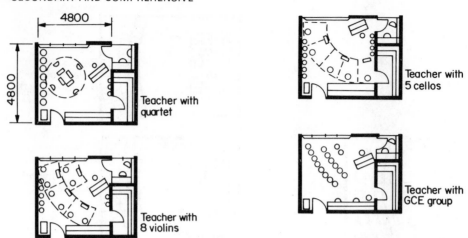

Teacher with quartet

Teacher with 5 cellos

Teacher with 8 violins

Teacher with GCE group

Fig. 2.33   A small teaching room.
This small teaching room is designed to accommodate the largest instrumental teaching groups that may occur (for example, about eight violins, or five 'cellos, together with an upright piano). Alternatively it can be used for small ensembles, or as a study room for senior pupils. (H.M.S.O)

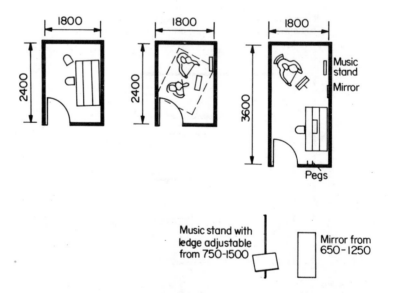

Music stand
Mirror

Pegs

Music stand with ledge adjustable from 750-1500

Mirror from 650-1250

Fig. 2.34   Practice rooms. This diagram shows the minimum internal dimensions of two kinds of rooms for music practice and individual tuition.
The smaller (2400 × 1800) will take an upright piano; alternatively it can be used for solo or dual practice of other instruments (1800 is needed for the full spread of 'cellos, double basses, bass trombones and some percussion).
The larger room is suitable for an upright piano and one or two other instruments. Useful wall fixtures are a mirror, an adjustable music stand, pegs and a small notice board. (H.M.S.O)

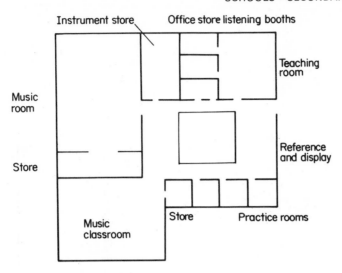

Fig. 2.35   A music centre which might be run by three full-time teachers. This is planned as a separate block, but alternatively the accommodation might be near a larger space for musical and dramatic performances. (H.M.S.O)

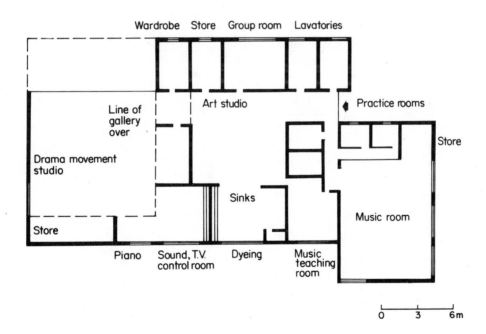

Fig. 2.36   A centre for music, drama, arts and crafts. This diagram shows an example of the grouping together of a drama-movement studio, an art and crafts studio and a music department, providing opportunities for combined work not often encouraged by more conventional planning.
The accommodation for music is slightly isolated for reasons of sound insulation. There is a main music room (with high ceiling) for day-to-day teaching, practice and performance; a smaller room for instrumental teaching and group work; two practice rooms, and a store for instruments.
In the drama studio, there are two curtained recesses for storage, with galley over, accessible by cat-ladder. Lighting can be mounted on ceiling battens and on rails over the gallery balustrading. A recess accommodates the piano, behind which is a small control room equipped for tape and record playing and a small television chain.
The art studio, where small scale properties and costumes can be designed and made, also has a high ceiling for good illumination and to allow for large areas of display wall surfaces. Off this there is a lower ceilinged bay which can be used for dyeing materials. There is also a general store, a wardrobe and a small group room for individual study, audio-visual work and staff consultations. (H.M.S.O)

2–33

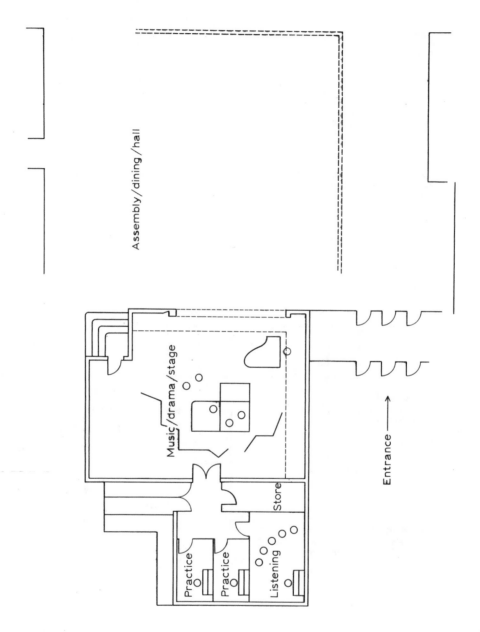

Fig. 2.37 Music and drama rooms for comprehensive schools—Ireland IBRD project (Delaney, McVeigh and Pike)

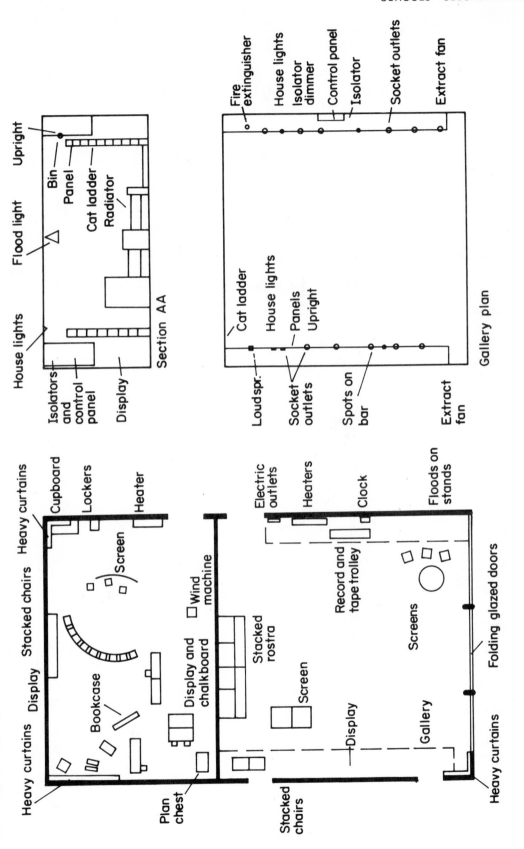

Section AA

Upright
Flood light
House lights
Bin
Panel
Cat ladder
Radiator
Isolators and control panel
Display

Gallery plan

Fire extinguisher
House lights
Isolator dimmer
Control panel
Isolator
Socket outlets
Extract fan
Cat ladder
House lights
Panels
Upright
Loud spr.
Socket outlets
Spots on bar
Extract fan

Cupboard
Lockers
Screen
Heater
Heavy curtains
Stacked chairs
Heavy curtains
Display
Heavy curtains
Bookcase
Display and chalkboard
Wind machine
Plan chest
Stacked rostra
Screen

Electric outlets
Heaters
Clock
Floods on stands
Record and tape trolley
Display
Screens
Gallery
Stacked chairs
Heavy curtains
Folding glazed doors

Fig. 2.38 A drama studio. This diagram shows two rooms in a drama department of a teachers' training college, each used by groups of up to thirty students. The smaller room (roughly 75 m²) is for work on scripts, recitation, recording, recitation, speech-rating, reading, research and discussion. In such a room, work connected both with English and drama come together. The larger room (roughly 110 m²) is designed and equipped as a drama studio. (On occasions up to about sixty onlookers can be accommodated, additional chairs being brought in.) The floor is of hardwood strip. The walls are plastered and painted. The high window can be covered by a heavy pelmeted curtain which blacks out the light. The wall opposite the large window is painted white for projection and background lighting. On the wall between the two single-leaf doors is a long display panel. The ceiling is of acoustic tiles. The two galleries (650 wide) are accessible by cat-ladders. These provide space for the lighting controls, for actors and for observers. Light fittings can be fixed at any point along the continuous bar over each balustrade. There is a generous provision of socket outlets both at gallery and at low level on the walls. In addition to the tables and chairs, etc., equipment in the two rooms includes:

(i) 3 fabric-covered folding screens on wheels (2400 long × 1800 high)
(ii) a complement of rostra (see below) and 12 stools (H.M.S.O)

2–35

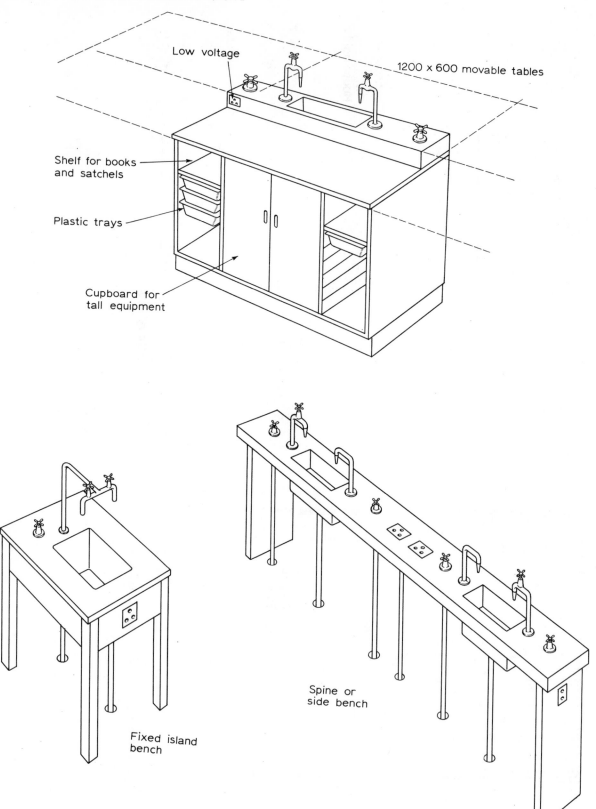

Low voltage

1200 x 600 movable tables

Shelf for books
and satchels

Plastic trays

Cupboard for
tall equipment

Fixed island
bench

Spine or
side bench

Fig. 2.39   Serviced stations for biology or physics

LABORATORIES

Biology

Biology laboratories should have easy access to the outside.

External facilities: gardens, greenhouse, animal houses, cages, outside teaching space.

Preparation and storage area: This should contain cupboards for models, transparent cases; refrigerator; deep freeze; potting tables; bins for food and refuse; workbench.

Equipment

High degree of blackout for micro-projection.
Good ventilation to extract smells of dissection.
One sunny bench with blinds for sun control.
A couple of medium sized and one large sink (at side benches).
Lockable storage for microscopes.
Storage of reference books, charts, maps, collections.
Chartrails, pin-up boards etc.
Storage for pupils belongings.
Side benches for dirty and wet work and for longterm experiments.
An area for aquaria, vivaria, potted plants etc.

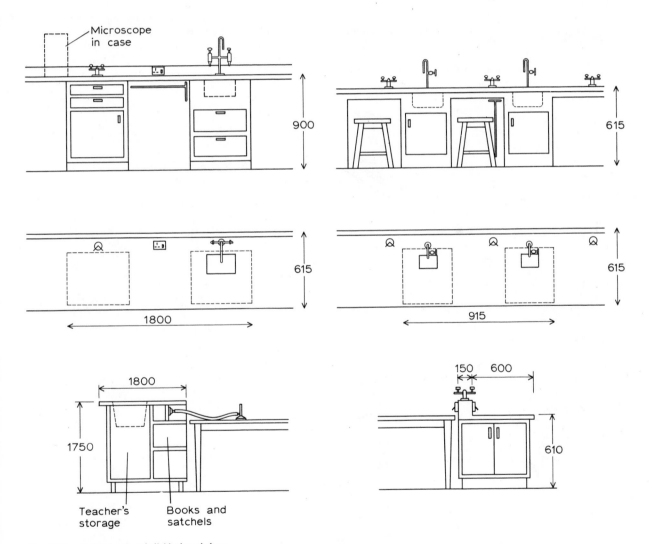

Fig. 2.40   Biology benches: individual workplaces.
The left-hand drawing shows a full range of facilities, with the routine equipment stored at the bench; in consequence a student occupies a larger space than is necessary for his practical work.
The right-hand drawing is a more economical design; the volume of storage is much smaller, and a certain amount of equipment has to be stored elsewhere.
The bottom drawing illustrates the relationship of movable tables to fixed island benches with services.

A PROPRIETARY METHOD FOR SERVICING WORK SPACES
IN LABORATORIES

*Overhead Service Laboratory: 'Metriscope' (Sintacel Ltd).
See Fig. 2.41*

The range of servicing items is so designed that any part of
the floor area of the laboratory can be serviced by moving
the particular service within the arc of its flexible connections
to the boom outlets or other connections.

Electrical and Gas services are carried into the work space in
a bollard which has a maximum capacity of four single way
switched socket outlets and up to three other services, i.e.
twin gas, vacuum and compressed air. Gas services are
completely self contained within the bollard to prevent
accidental ignition by electrical arcing.

The bollard which is colour coded for services can be
bolted to locations provided in the practical tables. The
frames are stove-enamelled Grey BS 3037 and the lids
Orange BS 0.004.

Cold water taps are a twin bib tap fitting which can be
bolted to the practical table to drain directly into a drainage
trough, or assembled as part of the cold water sink. The taps
are coloured dark blue.

The general laboratory sink consists of a white vacuum

formed polyethylene or stainless steel sink and drainer,
mounted on an epoxy coated sheet steel base coloured dark
brown BS 3-038. The sink is invariably fitted with a cold water
tap and can be located or bolted on to the practical table. It
drains through the back of the base via a flexible hose into
the drainage trough.

The drainage trough is available in three lengths 1200, 1800,
2400 mm and is constructed of white polythene dipped sheet
steel. It drains via a polypropylene flexible waste and bottle
trap, with a visual base, directly into the floor drainage
point. Ideally it is mounted on to the frame of the practical
table with a detachable clamp supplied as an extra or it can
be mounted free standing on the floor.

The wash up sink is an item intended primarily for small
preparation rooms. It consists of a white vacuum formed poly-
ethelene or stainless steel double bowl sink mounted on an
epoxy coated sheet steel base, coloured dark brown, BS
3-038. The upstand with shelf is also in brown epoxy coated
sheet steel and contains the hot and cold mixer control for
the water supply and a switched fused spur with neon light
which switches on the 14 litre 1·2 kW storage heater mounted
behind the PVC coated closing panel in the front of the table
frame. The end panels of the unit and the base of the upstand
are constructed from 18 mm oil-tempered hardboard.

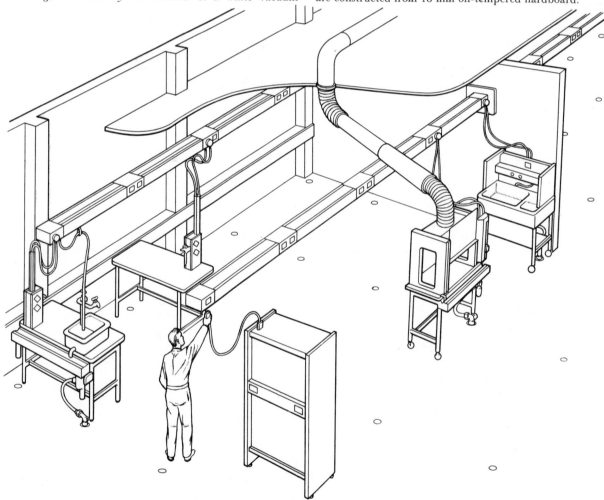

Fig. 2.41   Servicing workspaces (Sintacel Ltd.)

The mobile fume cupboard is constructed mainly of oil-tempered hardboard, but the internal surfaces can be changed to meet particular requirements. The sash, back, baffles and end windows are all 6 mm toughened glass. A modified service bollard is mounted on one corner of the cupboard. Drainage from the cupboard can be via a standard trough mounted on the table frame or via an internal drip cup. Up to 3 m of flexible extraction can be provided with each cupboard through the rate of extraction and general performance of the cupboard should be discussed with the manufacturers.

Double sided cupboards can be provided.

Electrified rails can be installed in the backs of 1800 mm high storage units where these are being used as room dividers.

Light and optics, sound and acoustics.
Fluid and hydraulics, electricity and
Magnetism, matter and atomic energy.

Laboratory
Side benches.
Island benches.
Tables of different sizes $(1200 \times 600, 1500 \times 750, 1000 \times 900, 1200 \times 1200)$.
Storage space.
Demonstration bench.
Workshop area.
Preparation and storage.
Darkroom.

PHYSICS (SEE FIG. 2.42)

Includes disciplines:
Mechanics.
Heat and thermodynamics.

CHEMISTRY LAB (SEE FIGS. 2.43 AND 2.44)

Activities:
Practical work, sometimes in groups.
Note taking, reference books consulting etc.

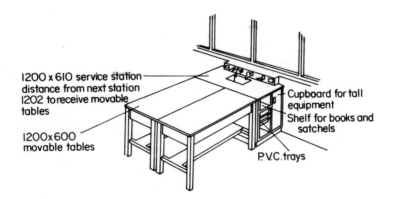

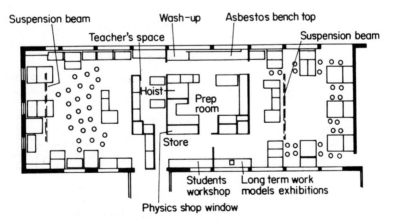

Fig. 2.42 Physics service station at an Oxford school. The activities likely to take place in laboratories are numerous, and shapes and types of fittings are designed with this in view.
The main unit is a service station shown in the diagram. It contains a cupboard for a few standard items of equipment, a shelf for students' books and satchels and a number of interchangeable plastic trays for kits of apparatus which are replaced when topics of study change.
The unit provides all basic services and its working surfaces can be extended by movable tables (1200×600 or 1200×1200). The elements can be combined in a variety of ways. (H.M.S.O)

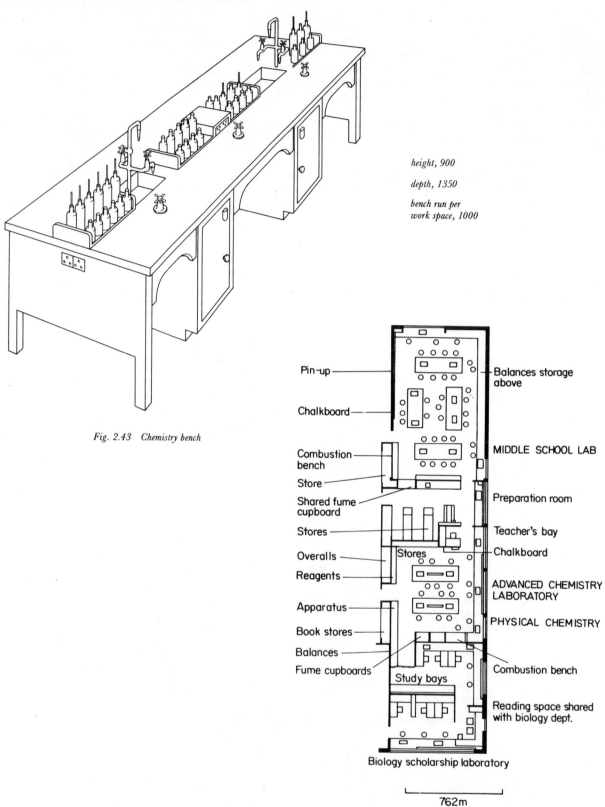

height, 900

depth, 1350

bench run per
work space, 1000

Fig. 2.43   Chemistry bench

Pin-up

Chalkboard

Combustion
bench

Store

Shared fume
cupboard

Stores

Overalls

Reagents

Apparatus

Book stores

Balances

Fume cupboards

Study bays

Biology scholarship laboratory

Balances storage
above

MIDDLE SCHOOL LAB

Preparation room

Teacher's bay

Chalkboard

ADVANCED CHEMISTRY
LABORATORY

PHYSICAL CHEMISTRY

Combustion bench

Reading space shared
with biology dept.

Stores

762m

Fig. 2.44   Layout of chemistry department at an Oxford school.
(H.M.S.O.)

Demonstration.

Lecturing (only at lower levels).

Chemistry benches require gas and water, and sometimes electricity. Working surfaces should be very stable for safe and comfortable working. Storage of reagents on benches might be on removable scaffolding.

Safety: showers, blankets, appropriate extinguishers.

Direct reading balance does not need balance room.

Fume cupboards. The need for these has been reduced by the introduction of different methods of analysis. Some provision is still needed, though especially at higher levels.

Preparation Room

Preparation bench (3000 × 900 mm) with sink and all services.

Fume cupboard.

Balance, small oven, a still.

Combustion bench, glassworking bench.

Vice for wood and metalwork.

Trolley space, trolley.

Cupboards for equipment, material, reagents etc.

Cupboards for first aid, fire equipment.

Changing area.

Table, locker, filing cabinet.

Store room for reagents, expendable material (glass tubes etc. 1300 mm long), general equipment. Storage of dangerous chemicals requires special attention: in special store outside main building, locked.

SIXTH FORM CENTRES (SEE FIGS. 2.45 TO 2.47)

At the upper end of the age range in the larger secondary schools it is becoming usual to make provision for the different requirements of sixteen to eighteen year old pupils. Sixth form centres bridge the gap between second level education and higher education. Emphasis is on individual study, seminar and tutorial teaching methods. In the larger schools of more than 1000 pupils the community served in this way can be 200 or more.

Evening use of such a centre will be normal, with generally expanded links to the community at large.

The examples shown in Figs. 2.45 to 2.47 illustrate additions to existing schools to provide sixth form centres, and give an idea of the accommodation required. Detailed programmes for such centres will be as agreed for any such project.

RESOURCE CENTRES

Developments in educational technology have meant that special accommodation for the range of new activities and equipment is often provided in 'resource centres'. These house both the media and materials used in audio-visual systems and the spaces necessary for their preparation, such as darkrooms, studios, small laboratories and workshops.

Material may be disseminated for use around the school, or may be used in or local to the centre, in projection rooms, lecture theatre or study carrels.

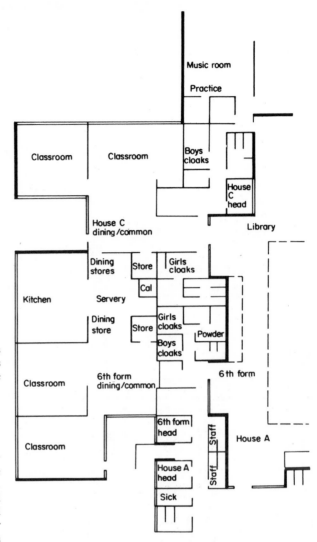

Fig. 2.45   Chaddesdon School. Sixth form centre Scale, 1:200 (Architects Co-Partnership Inc.)

Centres are often associated with a central library facility. In some circumstances local resource centres may be associated with those areas of a large school where the needs are different, such as in the first year or the sixth form, although duplication of expensive facilities should be avoided.

The example shown in Fig. 2.48 is associated with a senior Teaching Base for Humanities and is a resource centre for the storage and preparation of non-book materials and media. It will serve the whole school; trolleys of mixed media equipment and materials can be prepared here for distribution to any other base. The centre contains a store room, technician/assistant's office, small studio and recording room and a work room for use by staff and students on the preparation of materials.

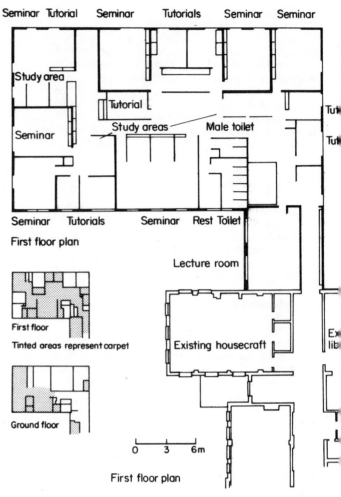

First floor plan

Tinted areas represent carpet

First floor plan

Fig. 2.46   Sixth form centre. (1) (DES Bulletin)
Scale, 1:200 (H.M.S.O)

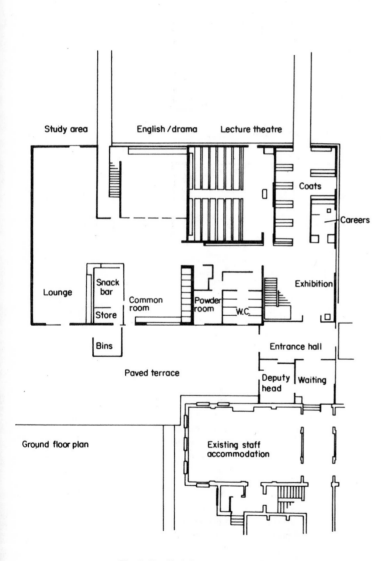

Ground floor plan

Fig. 2.47   Sixth form centre. (2) (DES Bulletin)
Scale, 1:200 (H.M.S.O)

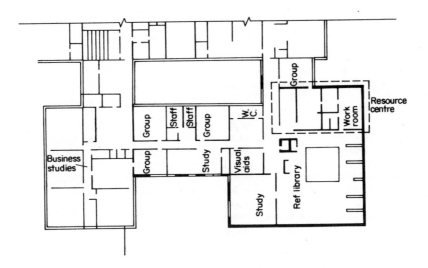

Fig. 2.48   Resource centre in a teaching base for humanities

ANCILLARY ACCOMMODATION

ENTRANCES

Entrances must not lead directly into an assembly hall or into any teaching room, nor should they be used as cloakrooms. In large schools more than one entrance may be needed, and several exits are essential. Service entrances for deliveries should be quite separate from those giving access to the school proper. Entrance doors should open outwards, and external steps must have ample landings between the doors and the top step.

Outside steps should be protected to prevent slipperiness in frosty weather. An outside artificial light point is essential. Doors should be at least 1350 mm wide, in two leaves, and are better if the upper part is glazed, unless there is a lobby with internal glazed doors and the outer doors are kept open during normal school hours.

A mat-sinking of a large size is desirable. Facilities for anchoring the doors open are needed. School halls are frequently let for meetings, etc., after school hours, and therefore corridor approaches and exits must conform to established regulations for places of public entertainment.

The main school entrance should give access to the head teacher's room or rooms, in the case of mixed schools, and, unless the assembly hall is placed away from the head teacher's room, this entrance can well serve as the main public entrance to the hall. It is generally desirable that the head teacher's room should be near the hall and the main entrance is, conveniently, of dual purpose.

The main entrance to the school should not be cramped in area if it is used in conjunction with the hall for either school functions or for public lettings of the school's assembly hall. Care should be taken that doors opening outwards do not obstruct footpaths or playgrounds; they should therefore be set in recesses or in projecting porches.

CLOAKROOMS

Cloakroom requirements vary with each type of school, although there are many factors which are constant. There are various positions in which cloakrooms may be placed in relation to the entrance and the classrooms. The more general method adopted is to plan large cloakrooms near the entrances of each department. There are, however, indications pointing to the adoption of alternative methods, namely, planning small cloakrooms to serve two classrooms only, between pairs of classrooms, or even single class cloakrooms attached to each classroom.

SANITARY ACCOMMODATION

Lavatories may be attached to cloakrooms and WC's; if grouped with the former they should be in such positions that the cloakroom can be closed and used separately if desired.

Hot and cold water supplies are essential. Basins should be 550 mm long and 450 mm from back to front, and fixed at the normal adult height of 850 mm. Floors should be of impervious materials, such as asphalt tiles, ceramic tiles or granolithic, laid to fall to floor channels or gullies for easy cleaning. Similar materials should be used for wall facing to a height of at least 1800 mm.

The number of washbasins provided should equal the number of sanitary fittings, in schools up to 1000 pupils. In larger schools the number is to be agreed.

Sanitary fittings should be provided at the rate of two for every 30 pupils. In a school attended by boys not less than one third of the fittings for their use should be WC's, the remainder urinals.

Urinals should be of the stall type and if slab types are used divisions should be provided; each stall or division should be served by automatic flushing apparatus. Stalls should be planned on a basis of 520 mm run per person and should be 1050 mm high. Adequate entrances and exits to the urinal apartment are essential to avoid congestion. Urinals should be in an enclosure separated from the WC's, although this may prove to be difficult to plan in some instances. Floors should be finished with materials such as hard asphalt or tiles and should be laid to fall to the urinal channel for easy washing down.

Pads have been widely used instead of seats but it is considered better training and more hygienic if seats are provided as should be found in the homes of the children; plastic seats with flat undersides are hygienic and more easily cleaned. Each WC must have its own flushing apparatus but this is best met by the provision of trough-type flushing-cisterns which avoid the refilling time lag involved by the use of separate flushing-cisterns.

WC partitions must be 750 mm wide in the clear, 150 mm clear of the floors and should be 1950 mm high above the floor; doors should be 150 mm clear of the floor and 150 mm short of the framing at the top. Partitions in tubular metal framing with metal-faced partitions are light and easy to keep clean. If partitions are not carried up to within a short distance of the ceiling, the space between the framing and the roof or ceiling should be unclimbable. Doors for all older children require fastenings and are best hung on 'falling' butts so that they remain open when not in use.

Consideration should be given to protection of plumbing in frosty weather and it is an advantage to form a heated passage or duct behind the fittings in which all plumbing and drainage is placed. This has the added advantage that all plumbing except the 'pull' is out of reach of the children and is easily accessible.

STAFF LAVATORIES

The head teacher, and possibly the head of each department, if they are of opposite sexes, may need a private cloakroom, lavatory and WC near his or her room but not communicating directly with it.

The remainder of the teaching staff should have separate accommodation for each sex; it should comprise a cloakroom, perferably with lockers, a lavatory and WC's; these rooms should not communicate directly with staff common rooms but should be planned near them. WC's should have full height partitions.

The number of fittings is not specified but the following is a guide:

Staff	Basins	Closets
3–6	2	1
6–9	2	2
10–20	3	2
20–35	4	3

VISITOR'S LAVATORIES

Lavatory provision should be made for visitors of both sexes in all schools. When the building is likely to be used for purposes other than the normal school routine it is essential that cloakrooms and sanitary accommodation for both sexes should be available in adequate proportions, and in positions convenient for the expected use.

PUPILS' STORAGE

When students' lockers are provided in corridors, the latter must be increased by the dimensions of the lockers and allow standing spaces for those using the lockers; this is likely to involve an increase of at least 600 mm. Rooms from which doors open outwards into corridors must be planned to avoid the doors obstructing the corridors. In other countries, cloakrooms are often formed in corridors and this matter has been discussed in the previous paragraph on cloakrooms.

With extension of the use of tables and chairs, in lieu of desks, the locker problem is intensified; if table drawers and desk lockers are not provided book storage has to be found elsewhere. There are objections to lockers being placed in classrooms or to the use of desk lockers, in that the pupils must always return to their own rooms after each lesson period to put away or change books; nor can a book be fetched from a classroom without disturbance. All these difficulties may be avoided by the provision of lockers in circulation spaces or by planning separate locker rooms or recesses, or if lockers are placed in cloakrooms; the latter arrangement is generally the least preferred.

Lockers for normal book storage purposes need not be more than 300 mm overall from back to front, but either width or height should allow for an attache case or satchel to be placed in the locker, and this needs about 390 mm or more. The overall height of locker fitments should not be too great for children to reach, or when a full glazed partition is used between the corridor and classroom.

The size of book lockers varies considerably according to the grade of school; small lockers 300 mm × 300 mm × 300 mm are adequate for junior classes, increasing to 300 mm × 450 mm × 300 mm and fitted with an intermediate shelf for secondary schools, where students need more and larger size books, and may have, in addition, instruments or tools. The number of tiers of lockers is dependent on the length of walls available, but lockers must be kept within easy reach, bearing in mind the average heights of the children to use them in each type of school. The lowest row of lockers should be at least 200 mm and better 450 mm above the floor, and the space so left should be clear of all obstructions to permit easy cleaning.

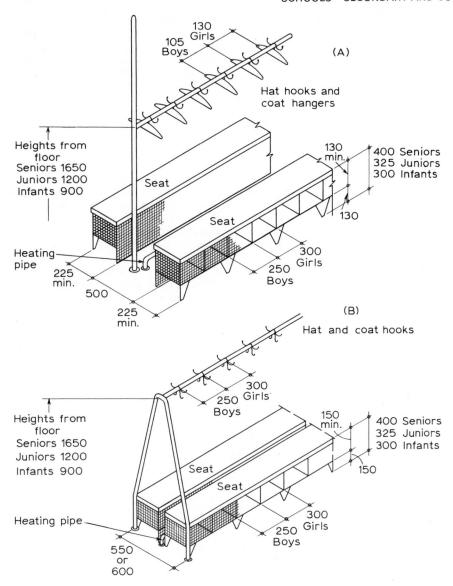

Fig. 2.49   Two typical fittings for school cloakrooms. Sizes suitable for children of various ages are given.

DRYING ROOMS

Drying rooms in which wet clothing may be dried are essential in all schools (see Figs. 2.49 and 2.50). The amount of space needed is likely to vary considerably according to the locality of the school, but it is unlikely that provision ever needs to be made for more than about 40% of the children.

Drying rooms present some problems, as the time available for drying clothes may be limited to about three hours; as, however, children from long distances are probably those who remain for lunch, a longer period is usually available. Excessive temperature should be avoided as it is detrimental to clothing. Any efficient system will need a considerable amount of heat and almost certainly mechanical ventilation. Since the drying room may be needed in summer time when school heating, other than that for domestic hot water, is not in use, it is better to rely on methods giving intermittent facilities.

Various systems of handling wet clothing have been tried in schools and factories; many depend, basically, on moveable 'horses' or similar devices, from which the clothing is suspended. Fig. 2.50 illustrates a typical layout, using movable 'horses' in one or two tiers, according to the ages of the children. A simpler arrangement is to provide fixed rails on which fixed coat hangers are spaced about 150 mm apart, under which are placed heating coils or rails; these coat rails may be about 1500 mm apart giving 1000 mm for gangways and 500 mm for the clothes racks; and gangways should be about 1500 mm wide. It is also desirable to have a number of projecting pegs fixed on the walls on which boots may be suspended upside down.

The drying room should adjoin or be entered from the

general cloakroom, to avoid unnecessary movement of clothing about the building.

CIRCULATION SPACES

The distribution of circulation space in relationship to usable space will vary in different schemes, mainly because of the trend towards the multiple use of space, open planning and integration of circulation into usable space.

Many specialised uses will still require exclusive space, segregated from circulation. Formal circulation spaces are subject to dimensional rules and often to statutory regulations.

Widths of corridors should be decided with regard to the number of rooms to be served, but should never be less than 1800 mm. Good lighting of circulation spaces both natural and artificial is essential. It is sometimes desirable to increase corridor widths as entrances are approached, or where persons from many different parts of the building may need to congregate, as, for example, near the assembly areas. Very long corridors should be broken up at intervals, to reduce draughts and noise, with doors swinging both ways. Cul-de-sac corridors should be avoided whenever possible.

Circulation spaces are often used as exhibition spaces for such articles as models or handicraft work requiring more space than would be occupied by such articles as drawings or pictures hung on the walls. If corridors are to be put to these uses a proportionate width increase is necessary to allow a 1800 mm to 2400 mm clear circulation space; or, alternatively, exhibition bays may be provided.

STAIRCASES

At least two staircases are essential in every multi-storey building; it is desirable that such alternative staircases be at opposite ends of the building, but they should not be more than 60 m apart, a requirement which may mean that additional staircases have to be provided. Staircases must have adequate light and ventilation, which can be provided by having at least one external wall.

Construction must be fire-resisting and of non-slip surface materials; staircases are best constructed of concrete with hardwood treads, or of artificial stone with inserted non-slip

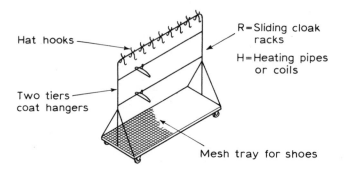

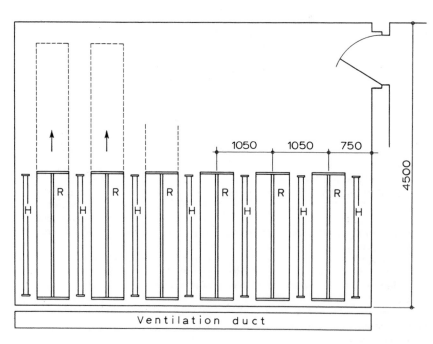

Fig. 2.50 Typical drying room—dimensions and fittings

strips near the nosings. The minimum width should be 1200 mm and the maximum flight should be 14 steps, unbroken by landings.

(See also Planning volume for *Habitation, Commerce and Industry*, Section 2 'Office Buildings and Banks')

SERVICE SPACES

Caretakers' Cupboards

A slop sink and hot and cold water taps at a height convenient for filling pails are required for the use of cleaners, together with suitable storage cupboards for brooms, pails and general supplies. The sinks are frequently placed in the lavatories, but are better if placed in a small cleaner's cupboard with proper ventilation; a window is desirable and for convenience in arranging plumbing services cleaners' facilities should be planned adjacent to sanitary blocks.

Large schools should have a number of cleaners' cupboards suitably placed in relation to the various parts of the school, and should have a main store for bulk storage of materials and cleaners' general supplies.

Adequate ashpits, dustbins and garbage bins must be provided in positions accessible to vehicles but at the same time screened from view and inaccessible to the children.

Plant Rooms

Plant rooms must be carefully ventilated and access must be cut off so that pupils cannot enter. It is preferable that access be arranged externally to overcome any risk of penetration of fumes into the school buildings. Fuel storage must be adequate in size for the supplies to be delivered in large quantities, and for this purpose convenience to roadways for easy delivery is of the utmost importance.

Fuel storage should be properly arranged in relation to boilers to reduce handling of fuel to a minimum. Care should also be taken to ensure that the boiler room is of a sufficient area and height to avoid difficulties in plant layout.

Meters

Proper provisions must be made for gas and electric meters, distribution boards, fuse boxes and similar apparatus in positions convenient to the entrance of supplies and for easy distribution; they should be so placed as to be accessible only to the caretaker or his staff.

MEDICAL FACILITIES

Medical Suite for a Large Mixed School (Fig. 2.51)

This accommodation includes a medical room, changing cubicles and lavatories, two rest rooms and a waiting area.

Too clinical a character is avoided in the medical room by the planning of the store and sink recess, somewhat screened from the rest of the room, and by the furnishing. There are cupboards and drawers for record files and equipment, one or two comfortable chairs, a rug and curtains. The hatch through to the rest room gives added length for eye testing and might be useful for supervision. The number of rest beds could be decreased if double bunks were provided.

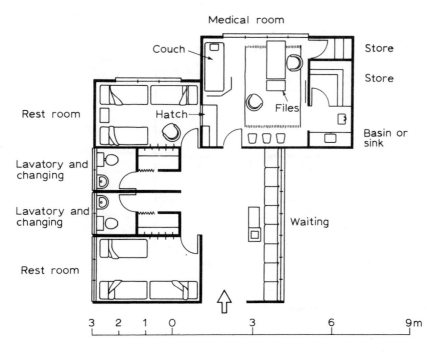

Fig. 2.51   Medical suite for a large mixed school (H.M.S.O)

Medical Suite for a Mixed School (Fig. 2.52)

This medical suite has similar features to those outlined above but the rest rooms are smaller. Four people, instead of two, could rest at the same time if double bunks were provided.

By opening the door or the hatch additional length for eye testing is available.

SPECIAL SCHOOLS

The Premises Regulations are primarily concerned with schools for the Educationally Sub-Normal (ESN). Other special schools will be the subject of specific briefs and programmes.

SITES

Minimum areas of sites shall be as follows:

Number of pupils
Not more than 25	0·2 ha
26–50	0·25 ha
51–80	0·3 ha

and for every additional unit of 40 pupils, the minimum areas shall be increased by 0·05 ha.

These areas are increased in a school for senior pupils as follows:

Number of senior pupils
Not more than 50	0·05 ha
51–120	0·1 ha
121–160	0·15 ha
More than 160	0·2 ha

PAVED AREAS

The amount of paved area is included in the minimum site area given above.

The following provision should be made for paved area:

	Number of pupils	
(i) *Schools for infants and juniors*	Not more than 105	612 m²
	More than 105	910 m²
	Number of senior pupils	
(ii) *All-age schools and schools for seniors*	Not more than 50	910 m²
	51–120	1122 m²
	More than 120	1850 m²

Where a school contains more than 120 senior pupils, this provision can be made by a combination of hard paved area and hard porous area suitable for team games.

PLAYING FIELDS

Every school for ESN pupils shall have a playing field extra to the site given above. The minimum area to be as follows:

Number of pupils
Not more than 120	0·5 ha or such smaller areas as may for special reasons be approved in the case of any school.
121–200	1·0 ha.

Playing fields should adjoin the school site unless otherwise approved.

TEACHING ACCOMMODATION

The minimum internal teaching area is to be:

Number of pupils
Up to 100	520 m²
120	576 m²
140	632 m²
160	688 m²
180	744 m²
200	800 m²

A hall is required and for each class a room of 28 m² for the first ten pupils plus 2·2 m² for each additional pupil.

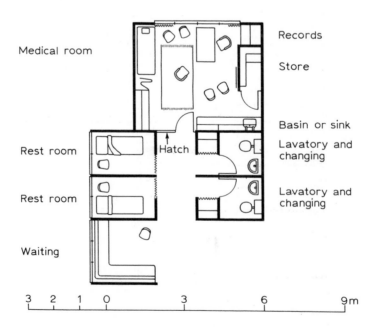

Fig. 2.52   Medical suite for smaller school (H.M.S.O)

SANITARY AND WASHING

The minimum number of sanitary fittings shall be one for every ten pupils. Urinals are to be provided for boys over eight years of age, not less than one third of the fittings for boys are to be WC's. At least one washbasin is to be provided for every ten pupils.

OTHER ACCOMMODATION

This will be in all respects similar to that for normal secondary schools.

BOARDING SCHOOLS

The Premises Regulations set out the requirements for boarding accommodation.

Up to the passing of the 1944 Education Act very little, if any, boarding accommodation was provided in State assisted schools, except in the case of remand homes and homes for orphans and similar special classes of children. Boarding schools are usually provided either by charitable organisations or as schools run privately as preparatory and public schools.

The Regulations do not give a lead as to whether boarding accommodation should be grouped with teaching accommodation, or whether the boarding accommodation should be separate. Practice has, in the past, varied very considerably; some schools have had part of the boarding accommodation attached to teaching buildings and in some cases the whole has been very closely related, whereas in other plans this accommodation has been arranged in separate 'houses' either on the same site or on sites completely separated from that providing teaching buildings and playgrounds.

SITES

No requirements are made for site areas.

RESIDENTIAL ACCOMMODATION

Standards for School Premises Regulations.

DORMITORY

The minimum conditions are:
  ≥ 5 m²/bed for first two beds.
  ≥ 4·2 m²/bed for additional beds.
  At least 900 mm between beds.
  Cubicles should be ≥ 5 m² and have a window.
  Bedrooms should be ≥ 6 m².
  1 slipper bath or shower per 10 residents.
  1 washbasin per 3 residents (first 60).
  1 washbasin per 4 residents (next 40).
  1 washbasin per 5 residents (additional).
  1 closet per 5 residents.
Dormitories are to be sex segregated above the age of eight.

DAY ROOM SPACE

Internal day room space is to be provided at 2·3 m² per pupil, although this may be reduced where school accommodation is adjacent to boarding space and dual use is possible; or where boarding accommodation is other than in dormitories and common rooms, i.e. study bedrooms, or where there are only weekly boarders. (See Fig. 2.53).

SICK ROOMS

A sick room must be provided and where boarders exceed 40 an isolation room. Beds are to be provided at a rate of one bed for every 20 boarders.

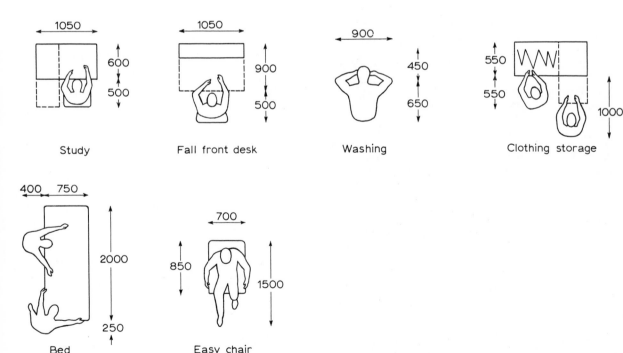

Fig. 2.53 Day room and study bedroom space requirements

Areas of sick rooms shall not be less than 7·4 m² per bed and the minimum distance between beds shall be 1800 mm.

GENERAL

In general it can be taken that requirements, unless otherwise stated above, will be similar to those governing secondary schools for all non-boarding activities.

STATUTORY REQUIREMENTS, LEGISLATION, AUTHORITIES

There are numerous Statutory Acts, and Statutory Instruments and Regulations made under these Acts, which make provisions with regard to the planning, construction and usage of educational buildings.

The most important of these Acts is the Education Act 1944. Section 10 empowers the making of regulations prescribing the standards to which the premises of schools maintained by local education authorities are to conform.

Section 63(1) amends Section 71 of the Public Health Act 1936 to exempt from the provisions of the building regulations any educational establishment erected or to be erected in accordance with plans approved by the Secretary of State for Education and Science.

With regard to the regulations made under the Act, Statutory Instruments Nos. 1959–890, 1968–433, 1971–1553 and 1972–1255 set out standards of educational amenity and of health and safety for school premises. They include requirements on site and teaching areas, structural stability, fire precautions, lighting, heating, ventilation, washing and sanitary accommodation.

Regulations made under Section 100 of the Act, and Section 3 of the Local Government Act 1958 contain requirements on the use of premises and specify that the approval of the Secretary of State must be obtained before premises can be provided or altered.

The following regulations are also applicable:

Direct Grant Schools Regulations (SI 1959–1832).

Handicapped Pupils and Special Schools Regulations (SI 1959–365).

Handicapped Pupils (Boarding) Regulations (SI 1959–362).

Schools Regulations (SI 1959–364).

Training of Teachers Regulations (SI 1967–792).

Further Education Regulations (SI 1969–403).

In addition, the Department of Education and Science publishes advisory literature from time to time, of which its Building Bulletins and Safety Series are just two examples.

Index of subjects, in alphabetical order, with the relevant Act(s).

ACCESS

To buildings by disabled persons	Chronically Sick and Disabled Persons Act 1970.
For vehicles	Restriction of Ribbon Development Act 1935, S.17.
For removal of refuse	Public Health Act 1936, S.55.
To premises from highway	Highways Act 1971, Ss. 29, 40.

ASSEMBLY BUILDINGS

Ingress and egress	Public Health Act 1936, S.59.
Fire certificates	Fire Precautions Act 1971, S.1.

BUILDING(S)

At corners of highways	Highways Act 1959, S.81.
Forecourts	Public Health Act 1961, S.46.
In conservation areas	Town and Country Planning Amendment Act 1972, S.8.
Line	Highways Act 1959, Ss. 72, 73.
Projections from	Highways Act 1959, S.131.
Sanitation generally	Public Health Act 1936, Part 11.
Within inner London	London Building (Construction) Bye-laws 1972.

CAR PARKS

Multi-storey or underground	Petroleum (Consolidation Act) 1928.

CHILDREN

Homes, community	Children & Young Persons Act 1969.
Homes, voluntary	Childrens Act 1948, S.29.
Nurseries	Nurseries & Child Minders Regulation Act, 1948.
Nurseries	Health Service & Public Health Act 1968, S.60.

CHIMNEY(S)

Height of	Clean Air Acts 1956, S.10 and 1968, S.6.
Flue pipes	Building Regulations, Part L.

CLOAKROOM

Requirements	Offices, Shops & Railway Premises Act 1963, S.12.

COOKING APPLIANCES

Installation of	Building Regulations 1972, Part M.

DRAINAGE AND SEWERAGE

Generally	Public Health Acts 1936 and 1961.
Regulations	Building Regulations 1972, Part N.

ELECTRICITY

Supply	Electricity Acts 1947 and 1957.
Works by undertakers	Electric Lighting Act 1882.

FIRE

Generally	Fire Precautions Act 1971.
Means of escape	Public Health Act 1936, S.60.
Means of escape in London	London Building Act (Amendment) 1939, S.34.
Structural precautions	Building Regulations, Part E.

FOOD

Catering, storage, etc.	Food & Drugs Act 1955, S.13.

BOILERS

Details	Clean Air Acts 1956 and 1968.

GAS

Generally	Gas Act 1972.

HANDICAPPED PERSONS

Facilities in buildings	Chronically Sick & Disabled Persons Act 1970.

LIGHTING

In offices	Offices, Shops & Railway Premises Act 1963, Ss. 8, 42–43.
Emergency	See under FIRE.

OFFICES

Drinking water, floors, passages and stairs, heating, overcrowding, sanitary conveniences, washing facilities and ventilation	Offices, Shops & Railway Premises Act 1963.

PETROL

Garages and storage	Petroleum (Consolidation) Act 1928.

SMOKE CONTROL

Areas	Clean Air Acts.

REFUSE DISPOSAL

Generally	Building Regulations, Part J.
Access for	Public Health Act, S.55.

STAIRCASES

Offices	Offices, Shops & Railway Premises Act 1963, Ss. 16, 42–43.
Within inner London	London Building Act (Amendment) 1939, S.34.
To a 'high' building within inner London	London Building Act (Amendment) 1939, S.20.

TOWN & COUNTRY PLANNING

Generally	Town & Country Planning Acts 1971 and 1972.
Buildings in conservation areas	Town & Country Planning Act 1971, S.28.
Listed buildings	Town & Country Planning Act 1971, Ss. 54–58.
Tree preservation orders	Town & Country Planning Act 1971, S.60.

VENTILATION

Generally	Building Regulations, Part K.
Offices	Offices, Shops & Railway Premises Act 1963, S.7.

EXAMPLES

Benfleet Sixth Form College, Thundersley, South Benfleet.
Architects Journal (25 July 1973).
Madeley Educational and Recreational Centre.
Architects Journal (28 June 1972).
Maiden Erleigh Secondary School.
DES Bulletin No. 48.
Abraham Moss Centre.
DES Bulletin No. 49.
Comprehensive School, Horsforth, Lee Lane East, Horsforth, Near Leeds, Yorkshire.
Architects Journal (29 May 1974).
Sedgefield School, Durham.
Design Note 6.
Castle Vale Comprehensive School, Birmingham.
Building (7 February 1969).
Comprehensive School, Bingham Notts.
Architects Journal (18 June 1969).
Secondary School, Pudsey Crawshaw.
Building (14 March 1969).
A new approach to school for the over sixteens.
Description of design of colleges at Andover and Havant, Hampshire.
Architects Journal (23 January 1974).
Aujourd'hui l'Ecole
L'Architecture d'Aujourd'hui, March/April 1973 No. 166.
An issue describing problems and solutions in educational building design. 25 examples from Europe and the USA.
Swedish Comprehensive Schools (e.g. Vannhög, Malmo).
Architects Journal (29 November 1972).
Schooling in the Street, Risskov Grammar School, Jutland, Denmark.
Architects Journal (1 December 1971).
Six Schools, e.g. Countesthorpe College, John Hunt of Everest Comprehensive School.
Architects Journal (1 September 1971).
Skelmersdale Comprehensive School.
Architects Journal (5 August 1970).
Winning Competition. IBRD Second Level Schools Programme, Republic of Ireland.
Delany, McVeigh & Pike with Architects' Co-Partnership Incorporated, 1974.

BIBLIOGRAPHY

Department of Education and Science Building Bulletins:
No.
35. Problems in School Design: Middle Schools—Implications of Transfer at 12 or 13 years (1966).
25. Secondary School Design: Sixth Form and Staff (1965).
26. Secondary School Design: Physical Education (1965).
30. Secondary School Design: Drama and Music (1966).
31. Secondary School Design: Workshop Crafts (1969).
34. Secondary School Design: Designing for Arts and Crafts (1967).
39. Designing for Science: Oxford School Development Project (1967).
40. New Problems in School Design: Comprehensive Schools from Existing Buildings (1968).
41. Sixth Form Centre, Rosebery County School for Girls (1968).

43. Secondary School Design: Modern Languages (1968).
29. Harris College, Preston (1966).
28. Playing Fields and Hard Surface Areas (1973).
33. Lighting in Schools (1967) (out of print).
38. School Furniture Dimensions: Standing and Reaching (1967).
44. Furniture and Equipment Dimensions: Further and Higher Education, 18 to 25 Age Group (1970).
48. Maiden Erleigh Secondary School (1973).
32. New Problems in School Design: Additions to the Fifth Form (1966).

Building Bulletins— Technical Subjects
No.
4. Cost Study (1957).
7. Fire and Design of Schools (1961).
9. Colour in School Buildings (1962).

Publications from Scotland
Scottish Education Department, Educational Building Note 9.

Home Economics Departments: Secondary Schools. Edinburgh HMSO 1970.

Publications from other countries
School Building Design Asia (1972). Asian Regional Institute for School Building Research (ARISBR), sponsored by UNESCO.

Construction Scolaires. Recueil de Normes. Ministere des Enseignements Primaire et Secondaire Republique Algerienne Democratique et Populaire.

School Building Resources and Their Effective Use: Some Available Techniques and Their Policy Implications. OECD 1966.

Schools Without Walls. Educational Facilities Laboratories, New York.

Educational Change and Architectural Consequences. Educational Facilities Laboratories, New York.

SCSD: The Project and the Schools. Educational Facilities Laboratories, New York.

SOURCES OF INFORMATION

Department of Education and Science, London.
Educational Facilities Laboratories Inc., 477, Madison Avenue, New York, NY 10022, USA.
UNESCO Headquarters, Place de Fontenoy, Paris, France. and UNESCO Regional Offices for Education.
Building Research Station, UK.
School Planning and Building Research, Ontario Department of Education, Canada.
Central Building Research Institute, Roorkee, India.
National Building Research Institute, Republic of South Africa, NBRI, P.O. Box 395, Pretoria.
Information Centre for School Building, Bouwcentrum, Weena 700, P.O. Box 299, Rotterdam, Holland.

Jordan, John, *Dip. Arch. (Birm.) RIBA is a director of Architects' Co-Partnership Incorporated where he takes a particular interest in educational building and brief preparation. He did some original development work on CLASP, has been in charge of ACP offices in Nigeria and Bristol and has practical experience of projects in several countries. Held a research lectureship at the Birmingham School for two years and has subsequently published numerous articles on educational work and system building and is a regular consultant to UNESCO.*

Mooij, Dirk, *M.Sc. (Delft) has been employed with Architects' Co-Partnership, and his main field of work is educational facilities planning. He was a Unesco expert for three years, in the Educational Facilities Section, and in this capacity worked in a number of educational building projects, both in the U.K. and elsewhere, in addition to consultancy services to IBRD and UNESCO.*

3 POLYTECHNICS, TECHNICAL COLLEGES, COLLEGES OF FURTHER EDUCATION AND UNIVERSITIES

JOHN JORDAN, Dip. Arch (Birm.), R.I.B.A., and DIRK MOOIJ, M.Sc (Dlft)
Architects Co-Partnership Inc.

INTRODUCTION

This section comprises all buildings concerned with further education, that is education from the age of approximately 18 years onwards, following secondary level education. In most countries this level is distinguished from the earlier education levels by the following factors:

1. Further education is generally non-compulsory, therefore very much smaller numbers of students are involved.
2. The numbers of young people going into further education direct from secondary education are in the case of most countries subject to a selection process of some type or other. In many countries the attainment of a particular standard at the final secondary level education examination, the equivalent of the U.K. 'A' levels or the French baccalaureat, will automatically give the opportunity for a place in a further education institution. In other countries, such as the U.K., selection is carried out by the institution concerned having regard to the secondary level performance of the pupil concerned and no automatic right to further education is conferred on a student by reason of attainment at that level.
3. Further education is characterised by a much greater investment both capital and recurrent per head of student population than any other level of education.
4. Further education demands an increased definition of study content, but at the same time may offer in the later stages of a course a considerable number of options for study. The course component can therefore achieve considerable complexity.

Research work is an important part of further education. This does not normally involve the undergraduate category of student who will generally be doing a course of three years duration in the U.K., and of similar duration in most other countries. After the completion of a first degree, selected students may have the opportunity to continue study and attain further degrees, in which case they will become involved in research work probably first as research assistants whilst doing their Ph.D. or other second degree. The stress laid on research will vary from country to country, but the basic assumption is that research is necessary in a university as a means of keeping teaching staff interested in the frontiers of their disciplines. It is assumed that research will be done in universities but not necessarily carried out to the same extent in other institutions of further education and probably not at all at technical college level. (See Section 6, 'Research Laboratories').

The degree of autonomy enjoyed by a further educational institution will vary and may be the object of controversy. Universities in U.K. retain a considerable autonomy compared with institutions in other countries. However, the agency providing funds to the universities or other institutions will in practice be found to link such funding with systems for controlling the expenditure of resources and it will be the duty of architects to work within such systems.

Further education in the U.K. is controlled by two different systems, although funds are ultimately drawn from central government in both cases. Under the binary system, university funding is directed from central government via the University Grants Committee (UGC) directly to the individual institutions. All other institutions such as polytechnics, technical colleges, colleges of further education, are funded by the local education authority in whose area they are situated, these funds being drawn from central government but administered by the authority, under the system of regulations drawn up and supervised by the Department of Education and Science (DES). The universities of Oxford and Cambridge enjoy considerable funds of their own and are often therefore in a position of carrying out capital programmes outside the direct control of UGC or DES.

Both UGC and DES publish 'Notes on Procedure' which set out the methods of seeking approval to capital and recurrent expenditure including minor works. Both sets of procedures require the submission of proposals to a relevant degree of detail at various stages of a project; usually at the stages of Project Definition, Sketch Design and Tender Report.

The UGC requires Universities to prepare Outline Growth Plans to which projects should relate. Both UGC and DES support their procedures with published 'Norms' which give guidelines for the amount of space permitted for particular functions. Both agencies also operate cost limits which are revised periodically in the light of building cost inflation and which are used to set an expenditure limit for each project.

Similar systems of control over space and expenditure are exercised in most countries in the developed and developing world.

Universities traditionally do not serve their immediate neighbourhood alone but draw students from a national or international context. It is therefore normal for universities to provide residential accommodation for a proportion at least of their students. Most institutions of further education provide in addition a range of supporting facilities for students, such as cafeterias, social accommodation and facilities, sports facilities, etc. (See Planning volume on *Buildings for Habitation, Commerce and Industry* for details of student accommodation and facilities.)

In contrast to the universities, which will in many cases be extremely old establishments, the polytechnics and colleges of technology have historically been more oriented towards the needs for graduates and technicians for industry, business and commercial systems of their immediate locality. In addition to full time courses, these colleges have the facilities for part time, sandwich and day release courses for students. As would be expected, this category of further education institutions normally provides less residence than the universities.

This building type will be concerned in the main with the provision of teaching space and the necessary support facilities. In the case of universities and polytechnics these will tend to be large complexes of buildings comprising a number of different building sub-types. The most common form of building activity in this area is that of extensions and additions to existing institutions or departments within those institutions. The foundation of complete new institutions is relatively infrequent. As the stock of buildings increases so the development of institutions will encompass the re-cycling of the existing building stock to an increasing extent.

THE FUTURE

Forecasts of the future in higher education are notoriously inaccurate. The one trend which can be identified with any certainty is that the delivery of continuing education to a greater number of the population will be an ambition of an increasing number of countries. There will therefore be an increasing demand for flexible, open-ended and innovatory further educational systems. Architects and planners will be required to bring an understanding of this situation to capital programmes in this building type.

SITING

The siting of buildings for higher education can be considered at three levels:
1. The level of macro-location.
2. The level of micro-location.
3. The level of the specific location.

Macro-location siting decisions will normally lie outside the interest of the architect although planners and architects may be involved in feasibility studies related to such decision. Siting at this level is determined by national government and takes into account such matters as demography, regional priorities, cost benefit studies and relationships to other institutions in the educational, industrial or commercial world.

Micro-location; siting decisions taken at this level follow the decisions taken at the higher level and will lead to the location of a site for a total institution or for a major addition to an existing institution.

The factors to be taken into consideration can be grouped in two sections:

1. Academic and social factors such as relationships with the local industry and community; relationships with existing institutions in the area; the local infrastructure and communications systems; the possibilities for residential provision in the area in addition to residences provided by the institution; recreational and social facilities in the area; the catchment area itself, considered for availability of staff and students; and finally the whole field of the impact of a new or enlarged institution on the locality including availability and capacity of utilities and manpower.

2. This section would include technical factors such as the area, topography, shape and extension possibilities of potential sites; the possibilities for the acquisition of potential sites having regard to the time scale of the proposed developments and the costs of such sites; existing regional or town development plans will have to be taken into account and finally the details of the site qualities of water table, foundations, drainage, gradients, etc. With all these factors impinging upon a decision it will be seen that a number of agencies are inevitably going to be involved in arriving at the choice of a specific site. Architects, planners and designers will be called upon to advise the agencies and to quantify the advantages and disadvantages under the above factors.

It may be noted that the trend towards a greater community and social involvement in further education systems will lead to an increasing interest in the subject of siting at a micro-location level in order that developments may easily integrate into the local fabric of communities.

There are in practice two categories of university site, campus type or integrated type. The campus type of development indicates that all the university facilities are gathered together in one place on a contiguous site including residential, social and all supporting facilities for the normal teaching activities. The integrated type of university development can mean the buildings being intermingled with a small town or the fabric of a major city and the supporting facilities are often distributed about the urban area; in this case the individual development site is often on the scale of a city block.

QUANTIFYING THE SITE DEVELOPMENT

The UGC and the DES offer guidelines for the development of sites for further education buildings. It will be the case in most countries that regulations or guidelines are laid down by the competent authorities in this area. Table 3.1 shows the numbers of students which can be accommodated per hectare for given plot ratios. The plot ratio is a ratio determining the density of building and represents the ratio between the total amount of floor space on a given site and the area of that site.

RESIDENTIAL AREAS

The density of development of residential areas is generally measured by the number of students accommodated per hectare. A plot ratio of 0·72 : 1 has been found to be an optimum density for medium rise construction of up to 4 storeys and in this case it produces a density of 420 students per hectare.

ACADEMIC AREAS

Assuming non-academic and library areas at 5·6 m² per student the following numbers can be accommodated at varying plot ratios:

Table 3.1 ACADEMIC AREAS

Plot Ratio	Students per hectare	
	Arts Based	Science and technology
0·5 : 1·0	340	190
1·0 : 1·0	685	385
1·5 : 1·0	1025	575
2·0 : 1·0	1370	770
2·5 : 1·0	1710	960

PLAYING FIELDS

The *net* area of grass pitches required is likely to be:

Table 3.2 PLAYING FIELDS

	Per 1000 Students FTE
	ha
Up to 3000 students	2·80
Over 3000 students	1·45

The *gross* are will vary with topography. All weather pitches are equivalent to some four times the same area of grass and their use will reduce total requirements pro rata. 0·7 ha is adequate for soccer and rugby pitches although one or two first team pitches may well be about 1 ha.

In the case of a campus type of university it will be found normal for playing fields to be provided adjacent to the other university facilities. In the case of integrated type of universities these facilities will probably be located further afield. The recommended net area of grass pitches required is set out in Table 3.2. These areas are recommended by the UGC. (See Planning volume on *Buildings for Administration, Entertainment and Recreation* for details of sports facilities).

Site density will be determined in the integrated type of development by factors such as plot ratios set down by local planning authorities.

Other facilities which will have to be provided within the curtilage of a campus type of development will include car parking, service roads and access systems and central plant, together with an allowance for landscaping and amenities.

A major consideration will be flexibility and the ability to extend the buildings, often in a manner which cannot be predetermined. This consideration will not only affect land for building but will also require a policy for distribution of

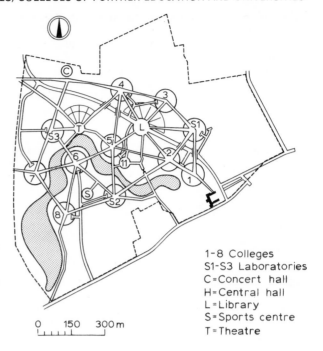

1–8 Colleges
S1–S3 Laboratories
C = Concert hall
H = Central hall
L = Library
S = Sports centre
T = Theatre

*Fig. 3.1   Molecular type of University Plan—York University
(Robert Matthew Johnson-Marshall)*

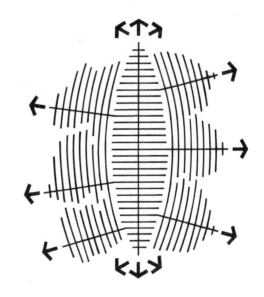

Fig. 3.2   Linear type of University plan—Bath University
The linear pattern of growth allows the central 'core' of general teaching space and social and commercial facilities to expand at either end as the population of the University increases. The specialised teaching and research buildings of the Schools of Study grow outwards from the core along lateral circulation and service points and new Schools are added to extensions of the core.

(Robert Matthew Johnson-Marshall)

main services and communications within the site. A number of solutions exist which take account of this and Figures 3.1 to 3.4 show most of the common types of development patterns for total institutions. For the siting of a specific building the most important considerations will be the relationship of that particular element of the total development to the surrounding buildings and to the overall development philosophy outlined in the above paragraph.

SPACE REQUIREMENTS

Space required for higher education buildings is ultimately controlled by the systems of maximum allowable areas operated by the University Grants Committee and the Department of Education and Science in U.K. or by their counterparts in other countries. The maximum allowances, or 'Norms', take account both of the minimum areas required to perform specific functions and of the utilisation levels which can be achieved for different categories of space.

Norms are expressed in terms of area per work station or area per Full Time Equivalent student (FTE). The FTE concept is required to even out the anomalies in student numbers due to part time or sandwich courses and service

Fig. 3.3   Linear zig-zag type of University plan—University of Essex. Development plan for a University of 6000 students

(Architects Co-Partnership Inc.)

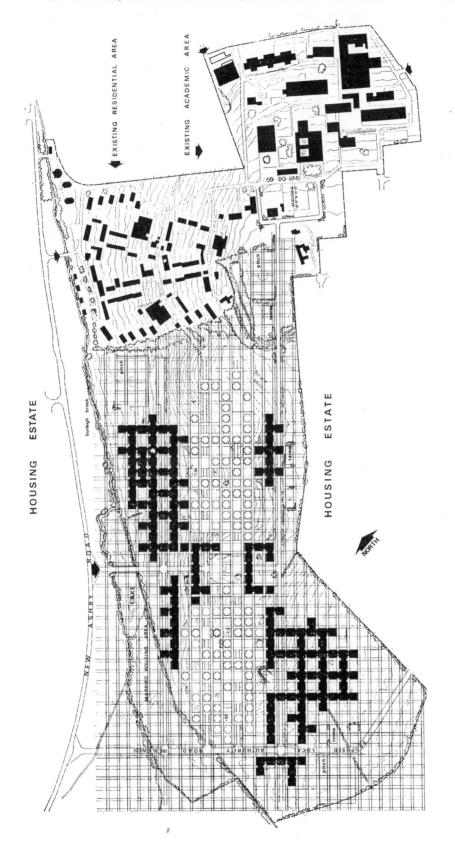

Fig. 3.4 Grid-iron type of University plan—University of Loughborough. Possible arrangement of the academic area within the master grid. (Arup Associates; architects, engineers and quantity surveyors)

teaching between departments. Rates per FTE vary with staff/student ratio.

Differences exist between the UGC and DES systems. The Universities' Norms, differentiate between students following courses, undergraduate (UG) or postgraduate (PG) and those involved in Research. The DES apply one rate to all students.

Under both systems, the total allowable space is a net usable area, to which must be added space for circulation, toilets, plant rooms etc., to arrive at a gross area for the building, which when multiplied by a cost limit per sq. metre of building produces the total expenditure limit for the project. The DES procedures apply a varying percentage addition to the net allowable areas to give 'Calculated Balance Areas', which when totalled gives a 'Calculated Gross Area' for the purpose of arriving at the Expenditure Limit. Within this cost limit the architect must provide the usable areas allowed but has some tolerance within the gross area. The Calculated Gross Area is an artificial figure

which is multiplied by a cost rate per m², revised from time to time by the Department.

Under UGC procedures an expenditure limit is set by the committee after consideration of the project.

DES Norms are summarised in Table 3.3. It will be seen that teaching accommodation earns an area allowance per work space; total work space numbers will have to be agreed. Communal space is allowed by area per FTE total for the Institution.

UGC Norms are summarised in Table 3.4 and are arranged by Departments; the space is allowed per FTE total for that department.

Once usable areas are determined, these are allocated over the functions to be accommodated, ultimately producing a room by room schedule. (See examples in Planning volume *Buildings for Habitation, Commerce and Industry*). Also in this volume the specific functions are studied and examples given illustrating the way net usable space is distributed over work spaces and activities.

Table 3.3 SCALES OF ACCOMMODATION AND CALCULATED BALANCE AREAS USED FOR CALCULATING EXPENDITURE LIMITS

Summary	Area per working space (% age for storage), m²	Calculated balance area (% age addition)
Teaching accommodation (Percentage addition for storage in brackets)		
Non-specialised		
Teaching rooms with informal seating and tutorial rooms	1·85	
Teaching rooms with tables or desks	2·3	
Teaching rooms with demonstration facilities	2·5	
Lecture theatres and lecture rooms with close seating	1·0	40
Drawing offices		
(a) using A1 and smaller boards	3·7 (10%)	
(b) using AO and larger boards	4·6 (10%)	
Specialised Area standards for different disciplines vary too greatly to be summarised		
	Area per FTE student	
Library (supplemented by up to 0·5 m²/FTE from non-specialised teaching areas)	0·8	25 (applicable to the basic allowance of 0·8 m²/FTE)
Administration (0·44 m² for the first 3000 FTE students, thereafter)	0·36	50
Academic staff workrooms	0·69	
Communal	1·65	30
Catering	0·47	25
Non-academic staff workrooms		
Departments of science and technology	0·5	40
Other departments	0·3	
Staff research		
Humanities	0·29	40
Science, technology, art and design	0·58	

Table 3.4(a) DEPARTMENTAL AREAS—ARTS, SOCIAL STUDIES, MATHEMATICS AND ARCHITECTURE

	UG and PG course, m²	PG research, m²
Basic arts		
Academic offices and tutorial teaching (assuming 1:8 staff/ student ratio)	1·75	1·75
Other office space and storage	0·50	0·50
Other group teaching	0·65	–
Study places	–	3·20
Total	2·90	5·45

For specialist subjects (i.e. languages, mathematics, etc.) the area per FTE student will be increased.

Table 3.4(b) TOTAL DEPARTMENTAL AREAS—SCIENCE

The total area in a departmental building will vary with the mix of subjects accommodated because of different staff/student ratios and different specialist subject requirements for laboratory space and ancillary accommodation. Where a full range of group teaching facilities (other than lecture theatres) is provided for a science department the usable area per FTE student might be as shown

	UG and PG course, m²	PG research, m²
Staff office and research:		
assuming 1:7 staff/ student ratio (including ancillary related to staff research)	4·35	4·35
Secretaries, administrative staff and technicians	0·45	0·45
Seminar/class/syndicate rooms	0·35	–
Special subject addition for laboratories and ancillaries —variable with disciplines		
(a) Biology	5·0	15·20
(b) Physics	4·9	13·80
(c) Chemistry	5·0	14·25

Table 3.4(c) TOTAL DEPARTMENTAL AREAS—TECHNOLOGY

(i) *Electrical Engineering*
Standard base unit of 276 m² plus the following areas per FTE student.

	UG and PG course, m²	PG research, m²
Staff offices and research assuming 1:7 staff/ student ratio (including ancillary related to staff research)	3·70	3·70
Secretaries, administrative staff and technicians	0·45	0·45
Drawing offices/ seminar/classrooms	0·70	–
Special subject additions for laboratories, workshops, preparation and storage	2·70	12·00

(ii) *Mechanical and Civil Engineering*
Standard base unit of 728 m² plus the following areas per FTE student.

	UG and PG course, m²	PG research, m²
Staff offices and research assuming 1:7 staff/student ratio (including ancillary related to staff research)	4·05	4·05
Secretaries, administrative staff and technicians	0·45	0·45
Drawing offices/ seminar/classrooms	2·40	–
Special subject additions for laboratories, workshops, preparation and storage	3·95	14·30

(iii) *Other technologies and overall allowance for development planning*
The usable area per FTE student in a typical departmental building for technology might be:

	UG and PG course, m²	PG research, m²
Staff offices and research (variable with staff/ student ratio but assuming here 1:7)	3·95	3·95
Secretaries, administrative staff and technicians	0·45	0·45
Drawing offices/ seminar/classrooms	1·70	–
Special subject additions for laboratories, workshops, preparation and storage (variable with discipline)	say 7·80	say 18·30

Table 3.4(d) TOTAL DEPARTMENTAL AREAS—MEDICINE

Where a full range of teaching facilities are provided, the usable area per FTE student might be:

	Pre-clinical medicine		Clinical medicine	
	UG and PG course, m²	PG research, m²	UG and PG course, m²	PG research, m²
Staff office and research space (assuming 1:8 and 1:5 staff/student ratios) including ancillaries related to staff research	3·80	3·80	6·15	6·15
Secretaries, departmental administration and technicians	0·45	0·45	1·00	1·00
Seminar/class/syndicate areas	0·35	–	0·35	–
Teaching laboratories				
(a) Multi-disciplinary	7·50	–	–	–
(b) Anatomy	1·88	–	–	–
assuming 2½ year pre-clinical course				
Additional research space including ancillaries	–	16·0	–	16·0
Total	13·98	20·25	7·50	23·15

ACCOMMODATION	REMARKS	ACCOMMODATION
Administration Principal's office Principal's secretary Vice-principal's office Registrar's office Secretary/ies Waiting room/Reception Main office Records office Committee/Boardroom Porter's office Bookshop Medical/Sickbay Rest-recovery room Stores/Stationery DEPARTMENT HEADS Engineering Building Science Architecture Art and Crafts Commerce/Business man Womens subjects Catering Related studies Dept.Heads' secs.rooms Depts. Staff rooms Depts. Workrooms	adjacent to each other for administrative efficiency — at Main Entrance — tends to be a noisy crowded area adjacent to each other — for all admin. clerks/secs. Elem. and advan. — related to the departments they serve part of physics complex —	**Elec. eng.** Electrical installations Electrical science Radio engineering Photometry and Darkroom Stores:Prep room. Tech.off Drawing offices Demonstration classrooms **Building** Carpentry and joinery Wood Machine shop Timber store Work store Brickwork Plastering Plumbing shop Stores: Maint.tech's Building science labs. Drawing offices Demonstration classrooms **Science** Chemistry - elem and advanced Prep. and store rooms Balance room Biology - elem and advanced Prep. and store rooms Physics - elem and advanced Prep. and store rooms Optics and Darkrooms General labs Demon./Lecture rooms
Communal Main Hall Dressing rooms (M and F) Stores Lecture Theatres Dining Hall Staff Dining Hall Kitchen Kitchen Stores: Preps. Library Librarian's office Reading room Bookstack Staff common room Students common room	— close to main entrance — backstage Main Hall - drama prod's — Main Hall chair store,props,etc. — available to all departments — central pos. to all departments is desirable etching, litho, printing — adjacent	**Arch.** Studios Stores Visual Aid/Lecture Darkroom: Reproduction Criticism/Exhibitions **Art and crafts** Sculpture Pottery Work and Material stores Kiln room Metal and Silversmiths Graphics Textiles - design and workshop Fashion Fitting room Display Photography studio Process and darkroom General studios
Gen. teach. Gymnasia (Nos.1 and 2) Changing/Showers Gymnasium stores General Gym. Stores Instructor/s Changing Tutorials Classrooms Lecture/Demonstration Drawing offices Studios	— heavy equipment next to Gym. — other light equipment — equipped with easy chairs,etc. life drawing, painting, etc.—	**Business** Typing Accountancy Geography Retail Trades/Commodities Display Stores and prep. rooms
Mech. engineering Machine tool shop Stores: Technicians' Off. Motor engineering Sheet metal/Welding Foundry Stores: Technicians' off. Engineering science lab. Store Materials testing Heat engines Metrology Metallurgy Stores: Technicians' off. Drawing offices Demonstration classrooms	veg, meat, etc.—	**Women** Household economics Needle and housecraft Cookery Stores and prep. rooms Classrooms Food technology **Catering** Bakery and confectionery Kitchens - elem. and advanced Larders and dry stores Prep. areas Demonstration classrooms **Ancill.** Coats: Lockers'-Maintenance Cleaners:WC's: Heating Chamber Corridors: Ent. Hall: Lifts: Lobbies

Fig. 3.5 A basic schedule of accommodation for a polytechnic institute. This is not intended as a complete list (Reprinted from 'The Design of Polytechnic Institute Buildings', by permission of Unesco,© Unesco 1972)

ACCOMMODATION

The norms described in the previous chapter are not sufficient in themselves to arrive at a room by room schedule of accommodation, but only give total areas per accommodation category, as the two examples hereafter show, for a Chemistry Department, and for a newly built University. (Tables 3.5 and 3.6).

The types of individual rooms that can be classified under such accommodation categories will depend on the project under consideration and on each Department concerned. Fig. 3.5 lists commonly found room types for a range of Departments. However, the list below gives an indication of such room types in a Chemistry Department and Table 3.5 shows the areas by category.

The determination of a room by room schedule of accommodation, would firstly require a detailed functional analysis of the institutional (sub-) unit, in order to arrive at a 'quantity' of activities, and a schedule of room types needed for such activities.

Such analysis would include study of policy and organisational considerations affecting space needs. For example; teaching group size policy, central timetabling, the relative importance of research, undergraduate teaching and postgraduate teaching, population, full-time and part-time students, expansion etc., and study of social activities.

First, an approximate schedule of accommodation is established, along the lines described. One then needs to derive the types of spaces with their capacity, and in order to arrive at an approximate area per room, area norms per unit capacity are normally applied.

A schedule of accommodation can only be finally established after room data sheets have been completed.

Two main categories of space must be identified:
(a) *Non-timetabled space.* This is generally a straightforward problem. If the institution provides one office per faculty member, then the number of offices will equal the number of staff. If one is programming for electron microscopes, the same logic applies. Common space such as libraries are also considered under this heading.
(b) *Timetabled space.* This space is shared and is affected by utilisation levels. If one is concerned with an existing faculty or programme, a schedule of rooms might be generated from the existing timetable. Alternatively the application of generally accepted utilisation factors can permit the calculation of the schedule of accommodation from a curriculum. Such schedules of accommodation must be checked by hypothetical timetables before finalisation.

TYPICAL LIST OF ROOM TYPES IN A CHEMISTRY DEPARTMENT

Lecture theatres.
Seminar rooms.
Offices.
Administration.
Library.
Graphic and reproduction rooms (darkrooms, Xerox etc).
Audio-visual aids centre.
Tutorial rooms.
Workshops (glassblowing, electrical, mechanical).
Chem. services.

Stores, including stores for dangerous materials.
Laboratories: Teaching and research; special rooms e.g. Hydrogination rooms, autoclave rooms, overnight experiment room, cold room, centrifuge room, computer room, chromatography rooms, X-ray rooms, crystallising rooms, micrograph, spectrographs, microscopes, micro-densitometers, spectro-meters, osmometers, balances, spectrophotometers, micro-analysis labs, deep freeze, high temperature rooms.
Common rooms.
Garages.

GENERAL ACCOMMODATION DATA

Under this heading can be included administration, offices, tutorial rooms, seminar rooms and rooms for individual study.

1. ADMINISTRATION (CENTRAL)

Although the requirements for administration areas will vary by project, certain rooms will always be needed, such as

Table 3.5 EXAMPLE OF A SCHEDULE OF ACCOMMODATION ALLOWANCES FOR A CHEMISTRY DEPARTMENT

224 UGs (Undergraduates)
140 PGs (Research Postgraduates)

	UGC allowances, m^2 FTE		Allowable usable area, m^2
	UG	*PG*	
1. Academic Staff Office	1·40	1·40	510
2. Academic Staff Research	1·20	1·20	437
3. Academic Staff Prep and Ancillary	0·60	0·60	218
Labs. Person Oriented:			
4. UG Teaching Labs	3·34	–	747
5. UG Prep & Ancillary			
6. UG Stores & Workshops	1·66	–	373
7. UG Research Labs	–	9·50	1331
8. UG Prep & Ancillary			
9. UG Stores & Workshops	–	4·75	665
10. Labs. Equipment Oriented:*	–	(4·05)	567
11. Secretaries, Admin, Technicians	0·45	0·45	164
12. Seminar/Class/ Syndicate Rooms	0·35	–	78
13. Lecture Theatres	0·50	–	112
14. Ancillary Teaching Lab.	–	–	–
15. Ancillary Prep & Ancillary	–	–	–
16. Chem. Research Group*	–	–	108
17. Unclassified	–	–	–
Total Usable Areas	9·50	17·90 (21·95)	5310

*Claimed as an 'abnormal'

Table 3.6 EXAMPLE OF A SCHEDULE OF ACCOMMODATION AT TOTAL INSTITUTIONAL LEVEL IN m²
This table is based on a schedule of accommodation for 3600 students at the proposed University of Bath.

'Organisational Units'	'Categories of Space'					Total area
	Administrative space	Communal space	General teaching space	Specialised teaching space	Residential space	
ACADEMIC AND ADMINISTRATIVE FACILITIES						
School of architecture and building technology	320	144	461	3055		3980
School of biological sciences	576	209	594	5047		6426
School of chemical engineering and materials	256	144	339	2971		3710
School of chemistry	588	209	612	5489		6898
School of education	186	88	334	299		907
School of electrical engineering	565	209	753	7182		8709
School of engineering	753	251	1127	7504		9635
School of humanities and social sciences	679	140	639	1044		2502
School of management studies	374	130	837	997		2338
School of mathematics	720	153	517	1349		2739
School of pharmacy	456	200	439	4052		5147
School of physics	518	153	453	3797		4921
Centre for nuclear studies	121	74	74	1393		1662
Central workshops				1023		1023
Animal house	46			790		836
Biological research station			schedule not yet agreed			—
Botanical garden			schedule not yet agreed			—
Central library			4916			4916
Central lecture rooms		167	1572			1739
Administration centre	1567	46				1613
Total: academic and administrative facilities	7725	2317	13667	45992		69701
COMMUNAL FACILITIES						
Restaurant-bases		4278				4278
Senior common room		739				739
Students' union and postgraduate centre		1172				1172
Non-academic staff centre		558				558
Conference centre	46	84	344			474
Main hall		1163				
Small hall		418				2325
Theatre/lecture theatre		744				
Indoor sports centre		2790				2790
Sports pavilion		1042				1042
Supplementary facilities		2223				2223
Total: communal facilities	46	15211	344			15601
RESIDENTIAL FACILITIES						
Students		2046			49104	51150
Academic staff (including vice-chancellor)					5827	5827
Non-academic staff		56			3766	3822
Visitors (university 'hotel')		56			614	669
Total: residential facilities		2158			59111	61269
Total, all facilities	7771	19686	14011	45992	59111	146571

offices for principal, secretary, registrar etc., and related secretarial staff, as well as appropriate cloakrooms and lavatories. Storage space for records, archives, stationery etc., meeting room, medical facilities, female staff rest room, general office with enquiry desk near entrance, sales counter, bookshops, etc.

Administration facilities should be of a flexible nature, so that if there are changes in organisation, or expansion, these can take place without major alterations. The UGC states:

'In a university of 3000 students a range of central ad-ministrative facilities including conference rooms, senate house, and committee rooms can normally be provided within 0·55 m² per student'.

Separate provisions are required for student' offices and administration, health services, etc.

2. OFFICES FOR TEACHING STAFF

UGC norms: (Notes on Procedures 1971)	*Net area*
Rooms for Professors and heads of major departments	18·5 m²

Table 3.6 (continued)

(only some of these
are funded by government)

	area m²
Medical centre	139·5
Chapel	465·0
Bookshop	186·0
Other shops	148·8
Barber	18·6
Post office	46·5
Branch banks	46·5
Launderettes	46·5
Pub	55·8
Sports and repairs	93·0
University Press	186·0
Filling station/garage	93·0
Public lavatory	46·5
Childrens' play centre	186·0
Maintenance building	232·5
Maintenance stores	232·5

Rooms for tutorial teaching staff, per working
place   13·5 m²
Office space for other teaching, clerical and
typing staff, per working place   7·0 m²
Staff offices may be located next to staff research facilities,
however, it should be borne in mind that such an arrangement would take up valuable laboratory area. Sometimes
additional offices for guest teachers will be required.

Office equipment

B.S. 3893 : 1965 gives recommendations for standard sizes of
desks, tables and seating, and reference should be made to
this. The AJ Metric Handbook is also another useful source
of reference in this connection.

3. TUTORIAL ROOMS, SEMINAR ROOMS, INDIVIDUAL
STUDY

Tutorials are normally given in staff offices, however, sometimes special tutorial rooms are provided (Fig. 3.6).
Seminar rooms (Fig. 3.7) are a common type of accommoda-

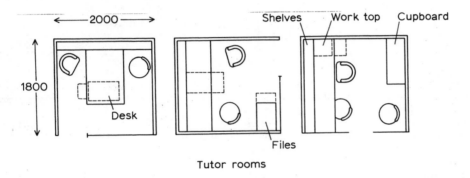

Fig. 3.6   Tutor rooms

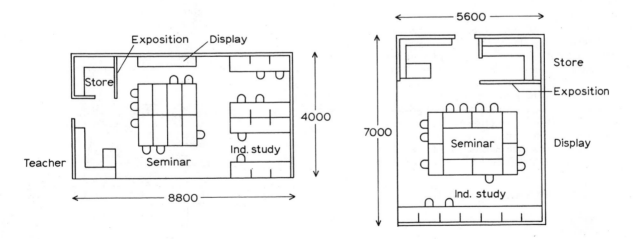

Fig. 3.7   Teaching rooms for seminar and individual study

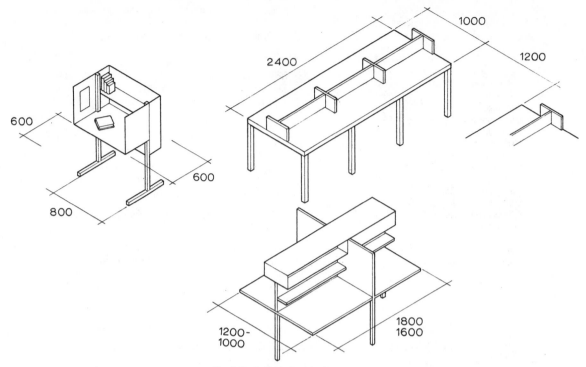

Fig. 3.8   Individual study places

tion. Group sizes making use of such rooms may vary, however normally are between 10 and 20 students. Both furniture and room should allow different arrangements for group work. One room capable of taking a group of 30 can be useful. Modern educational methods lay less emphasis on 'chalk and talk'. More emphasis is laid on discussion, group work, project work, requiring less formal arrangements of furniture. Increasing use is made of Audio Visual equipment, such as overhead projectors, TV, film and slide projectors (see Fig. 3.17).

Individual study spaces

In Higher Education, a great deal of individual study will occur. Often such individual study places are provided in the library, where they will also be used for consulting reference material, using library books. However individual study places may also be placed elsewhere. A great deal of individual study is normally done in the students residence. The suitability for study, and the distance of student accommodation will have an effect on the number of individual study places to be provided. Individual work places may range from a single table top to a small private study room, and may or may not be provided with teaching machines, microfiche readers, tape recorders etc. Cubicles and carrels should have adequate lighting, book-shelves and general storage. Movability of carrels is an advantage. (See Fig. 3.8).

LECTURE THEATRE (Fig. 3.9)

TRENDS

A lecture theatre is an expensive facility and the utilisation of lecture theatres is often very low, being used for a few

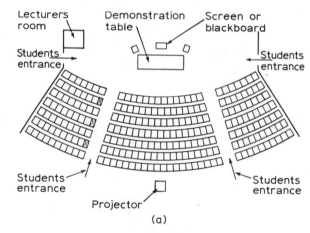

(a)

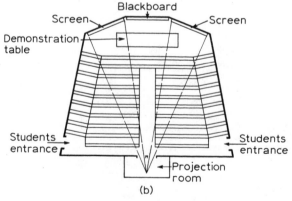

(b)

Fig. 3.9   Typical auditorium layouts

hours a day, and only by a few people at a time.

At present normal utilisation requirements are high. This certainly has implications for the lecture theatre:

1. It should be flexible, in that it should be able to perform different functions (e.g. lecture, cinema, demonstration, theatre etc).

2. It may be flexible in size, to be able to fit different audience group sizes. Divisible auditoriums are more and more accepted in the USA. (See Fig. 3.9).

3. It should be shared and centrally timetabled and not be the 'territory' of one Department.

SEATING DATA

The dimensions and relevant data for seating are shown in Table 3.14 and Figs. 3.11 to 3.13. Minimum dimensions are:

	Minimum recommendations (mm)
Width of seats with arms	500
Width of seats without arms	450
Back to back distance for	
Rows of seats with backs	750
Rows of seats without backs	600
Spaces between rows (See Table 3.14)	300
Width of gangway	1000
Normal max. distance from gangway of seats (See Table 3.7)	

Table 3.7 RECOMMENDED DISTANCE OF SEATS FROM GANGWAYS

Minimum seatway (measured between perpendiculars) (mm)	Maximum distance of seat from gangway (500 mm seats) (mm)	Maximum number of 500 mm wide seats per row	
		Gangway both sides	Gangway one side
300	3000	14	7
330	3500	16	8
360	4000	18	9
390	4500	20	10
420	5000	22	11

SIGHT LINES

The viewing quality of an auditorium depends on *raising the eye level* and setting up a viewing curve; uniform change of eye level is required at every seat in the auditorium; staggered seating permits view between heads of row in front:

Min change of eye level (°min), 60 mm

Medio change of eye level (°m), 125 mm

(Full information on viewing and sight lines will be found in the section on Theatres in the Planning volume *Buildings for Administration, Entertainment and Recreation*).

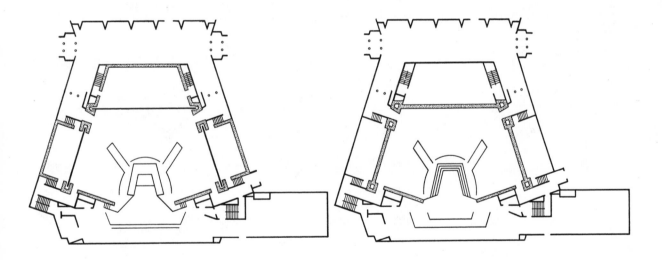

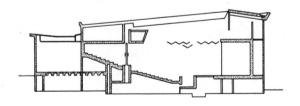

Fig. 3.10   Divisible auditoriums. Example shown is the Loretto Hilton Centre for the performing arts, Webster College, Missouri, USA

	Dimensions in mm		
	A Seat to eye short person sitting slumped	B Seat to head tall person sitting upright	C Difference
18-40 years Males Females	687 662	937 887	250 226
Optimum	675	750	75

Fig. 3.11   Application of existing body sizes to lecture theatres

	Dimensions in mm		
	Width	Length	Area per person
Space in existing lecture theatres	450-750	750-900	100%
Space required for large persons, posture changes, and easy access	750-900	900-1100	166%

Fig. 3.12   Comparison between width and floor area per person

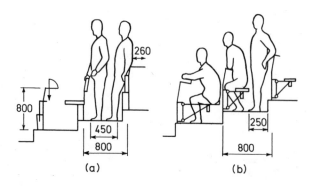

(a)   (b)

Fig. 3.13   (a) Layout with folding seats and folding desks; (b) Arrangement with fixed desks and swinging swivel seats. (Reproduced from Neufert Architects Data, published by Crosby Lockwood & Son Ltd.).

SEATING DESIGN

Main factors influencing seating arrangements are:

(a) *Seat design.* Which includes the dimensions, leg room, etc. of an individual seat and writing area. (See page **3**-13).

(b) *Audience arrangements.* The positions of seats relative to each other and to views of the lecturer, screen, demonstrations etc. (See previous Data and Figs. 3.18 to 3.25).

The following figures serve as a guide line for the seat design and determination of audience arrangements.

FUNCTIONS AND THEIR REQUIREMENTS

A lecture theatre may perform different functions. Such functions should be established in detail, to enable the determination of the design criteria.

Basic functions are: lecture function; cinema function; demonstration function.

(a) *Lecture function.* If there is only talking by the lecturer, then there is little problem. The audience should basically be able to hear and see the lecturer. The use of a chalkboard adds extra viewing requirements. Viewing angles should be checked, viewing distance is normally limited to about twelve rows of seating.

Trends in teaching are towards more participation. This means that the audience should be as close to the lecturer as possible, and should be turned towards itself (discussions). This can be achieved by a U-form arrangement with few rows of audience, resulting in area saving as well (See Fig. 3.14).

Instead of chalkboards, various audio visual devices, requiring visible screens, etc. Such devices are indicated in Figs. 3.15 and 3.17.

(b) *Cinema function*

Obviously the screen should be well visible. Criteria for good vision are shown in Fig. 3.15 and are:

Max. horizontal viewing angle	30°
Max. vertical viewing angle	35°
Critical angle of projector	12°
Max. viewing distance	6 × width of screen
Min. viewing distance	2 × width of screen

Acoustics should be right for sound films, while the need for blackout is obvious.

(c) *Demonstration function*

Good visibility of the demonstration is essential. The rake will be steep, and can be calculated, with the data in figures given.

Good visibility limits the number of seat rows to about 12. An example of a removable demonstration bench is given in Fig. 3.16. Demonstrations for large audiences, especially small sized demonstrations, often make use of closed circuit television.

The criteria for good visibility of TV screens are set out in Figs. 3.21, 3.22 and 3.23. The trend is towards movable TV screens.

GENERAL DESIGN

General design criteria are given below:

Basic shape. A square or fan shaped room is to be preferred, since the audience to lecturer distance variation is less.

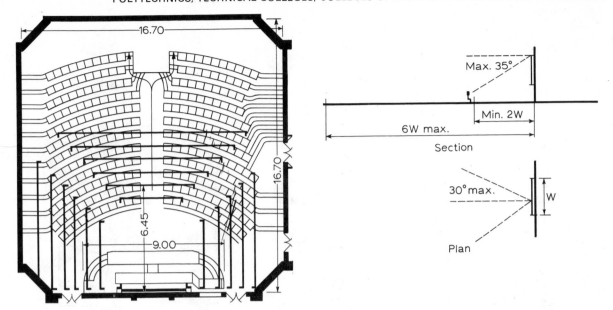

Fig. 3.14   Lecture theatre seating plan, redrawn to the same scale in the form of a lecture-theatre-in-the-round

Fig. 3.15   Critical dimensions for good visibility of cinema screen

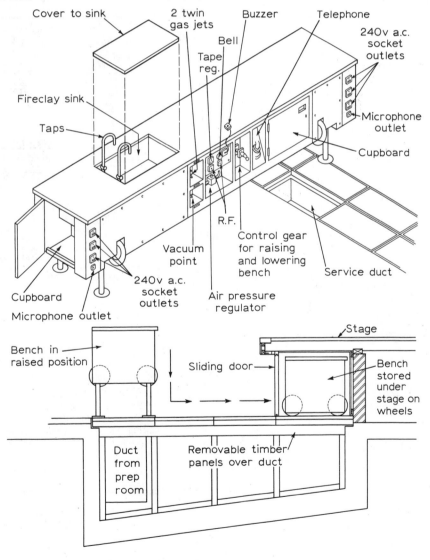

Fig. 3.16   Lecture theatre demonstration bench—Harris College, Preston

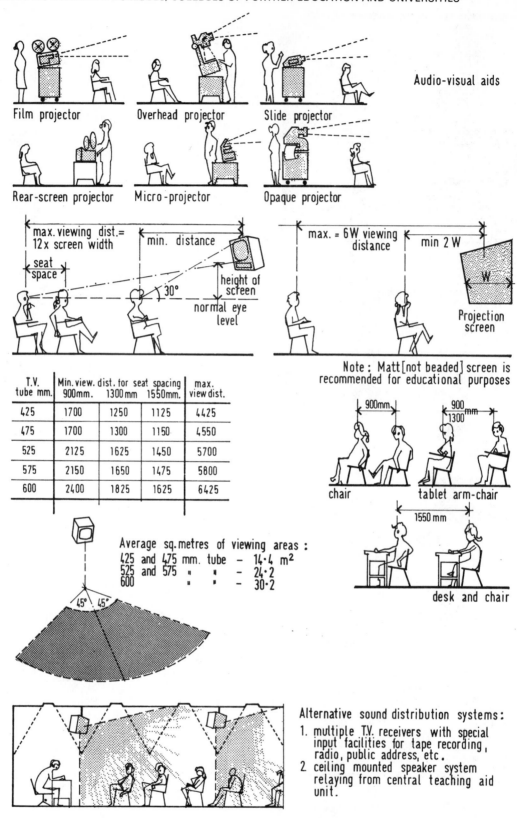

Fig. 3.17 Dimensional data relating to various types of audio-visual aids used in modern teaching. (Reprinted from 'The Design of Polytechnic Institute Buildings', by permission of Unesco.© Unesco 1972)

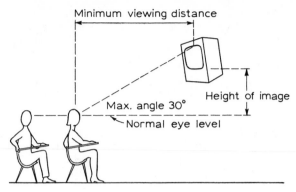

Fig. 3.18   Minimum viewing distance

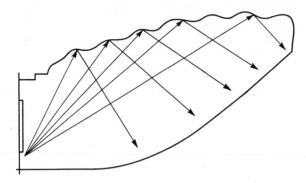

Fig. 3.20   Lecture theatre with good viewing conditions and favourable projection of sound

MINIMUM VIEWING DISTANCE

Size of T.V. tube	Seat row spacing		
	900	1300	1550
425 (17in.)	1650	1250	1125
465 (19in.)	1700	1300	1150
520 (21in.)	2125	1625	1459
570 (23in.)	2150	1650	1475
595 (24in.)	2400	1825	1625

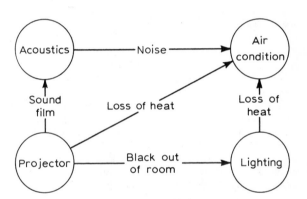

Fig. 3.21   Interaction between projection, lighting, air conditioning and acoustics

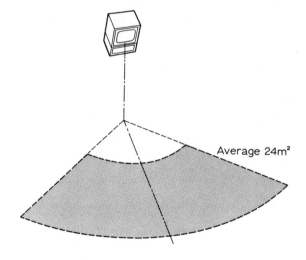

Fig. 3.19   Shape and square frontage of viewing area for a 21 in. receiver

HEIGHT OF TELEVISION IMAGE
(normal eye level to bottom of image)

Size of T.V. tube	Seat row spacing		
	900	1300	1550
425 (17in.)	650	425	350
475 (19in.)	675	450	375
520 (21in.)	850	562	462
570 (23in.)	875	575	475
595 (24in.)	962	620	520

Circular auditoria have pitfalls, one being the lack of a flat front wall surface for screens or chalkboards, another a possible sound focusing effect. A raked floor is advisable, but a dais is then an unnecessary danger and restricts flexibility, unless it is intended to promote dramatic separation and is generous in size. Steps should be wide, risers shallow, even, and illuminated in large halls. Curved windows are difficult to black out and portholes and slits seem always to allow shafts of light to strike the screen for forward areas at critical times. Windows and outside distractions are best avoided in serious areas. It must be possible to reach walls, floors, and ceiling to clean easily.

Size effects. If the front wall is too low then screens cannot be fitted to show pictures without the lecturer's head being shadowed in the picture, nor can full height chalkboards be used, with adequate capacity for mathematics and science lecturers. Too low a ceiling, especially at the back, can be oppressive.

Entrances and exits. Apart from being obvious they should be quiet, with provision for movement after commencement of the lecture and in darkness or semi-darkness. They should lead naturally into flat standing area to allow adaptation and filtering in.

Heating and Ventilation. Should be neither seen nor heard, particularly the latter. Exposed heating elements always cause trouble with dirt tracks. Ideally the whole installation should be automatic, monitored and controlled from outside, and only in special cases under the lecturer's control.

Acoustics. Provided the shape is right, and the ventilation plant quiet, good acoustics will depend mainly on the finishes around the lecturer and the avoidance of flutter echoes from roof and side walls, and direct echoes from the back wall. These problems are all soluble if acoustics are placed before fancy aesthetics (which they are sometimes not). The necessity for speech reinforcement for an audience under 500 indicates inferior design.

Chalkboards and Chartboards. Chalkboards which rattle or bump as they are written on are not amusing. Chartboards which are slung from pulleys should be eschewed in favour of sliding types with sashes, with magnetic fixings or with felt on softboard. Use oilite or oilable bearings which are accessible. If motorised, avoid too great a width for the mechanical bearings used, and see that adequate stiffness is provided to prevent whip. Use a cleaning fluid and applicator not the duster or old fashioned felt 'rubber'.

Screens and pointers. Screens should be fixed and stretched taut, since roller types are rarely flat and rarely still. They should be out of reach and optical pointers, not sticks and poles, should be provided. If the atmosphere is clean, special optical surfaces will generally give better results than the ubiquitous white matt plastic. It is common sense not to cater to the extreme ends of the first five rows, but rather for the great bulk of the audience. See that the picture is large enough for only moderately sighted viewers from the back row (and use thick chalk in large auditoria for the same reasons). It may be necessary to tilt a screen forward at the top to suit an overhead projector. Double width or two screens will generally be necessary for fine art, architecture, and similar 'comparative' disciplines.

Floors. Should not squeak or mark with rubber soles and should be dust free and easily maintained.

Windows and blackout. Curtains, although acoustically acceptable, are an unmitigated nuisance in hard worked locations and need careful control and maintenance of runners, hooks and cords when used as blackout. If used they should fit, and preferably be fastened at the sides. Windows should be sealed or they will let in dust, noise, and disturb blinds or curtains, and may be better fitted with obscured glass. All-in-all a windowless, curtainless environment is easier to handle. Skilled use of lighting can reduce or eliminate any suggestion of confinement. Blackout need not be perfect, dim-out can often be used provided it is completely controllable, and does not vary during the actual lecture.

General illumination. Should be adequate for reading and writing and totally non-directional. Clusters of spotty lights are a particularly irritating feature. Fluorescent tubes can be used if a rigid specification on chokes and dimming gear is adhered to. If positive pressure ventilation can be arranged so that only clean air passes over the fittings, much cleaning can be obviated.

Special illumination. Should be restricted to basic necessities and be well concealed but controllable. A whole battery of special chalkboard and dais lights, all separately switchable, with special spotlights are rarely required. If a theatre type installation is desired, have a proper bridge with operator at the rear as in better theatre practice.

Fixtures. A bench is not so necessary as sometimes imagined, so avoid it whenever possible and substitute a transportable lectern placed to one side of chalkboard or screen area. Fixtures in general should not call attention to themselves. Similarly it is better to build simple line-source speakers, and hide the wires to them rather than to design elaborate combined fascia units. Remember it is difficult for someone to sit on a chair behind a bench without the effect of appearing to be beheaded.

Seating. Above all this should not create noise by squeaking and banging—ideally it should be individual, be provided with put-down space, with ledges to prevent things rolling off and should be easy to get in and out of. Loose chairs and tables are difficult to silence in a crowded room. Toe room is essential for 55 minutes continuous lectures and surfaces should be medium tone and non-glossy. A soft seat is desirable and helps the acoustics in a partly filled theatre.

Projection bays or booths. If open to the audience they should be accessible during the lecture, and preferably protected by glass screens or acoustic shields. Duplicate controls should always be provided. Booths should be large enough and well ventilated and substantially built. Avoid wooden constructions on the floor which 'drum' and open ports which transmit the projector noise to the auditorium. Adequate communication is essential, and some provision for human intervention should all else fail. Avoid small square ports, use large generous windows but paint the back wall a dark colour and use a properly shaded light in the booth, a separate exit is useful.

Television. It is difficult to avoid having to use a number of separate display units, but keep these off the floor if at all possible and out of easy hand reach as they are a temptation to 'fiddlers'. A key switch may be necessary if broadcast reception is possible. Check the position for unwanted reflections from windows, or lights and see they are hooded if necessary.

Controls. Should be simple, standardised, well labelled and functional and progressive in layout so that first things come first. Remove all unnecessary operations to an auxiliary panel. Separate-out various functions. Chalkboard controls need to be at the chalkboard not elsewhere. Basic controls must be duplicated at box and some outside.

RESEARCH LABORATORIES

CLASSIFICATION

1. (a) *Bench scale laboratories.* Laboratories that are mainly fitted out with benches, although also accommodating equipment such as refrigerators, fume cupboards, etc.
   (b) *Pilot scale.* Somewhat more equipment is involved, although mainly small equipment. Change may be more frequent, and service arrangements and requirements are special.
   (c) *Factory scale.* Equipment-oriented. Mainly heavy equipment. Special service requirements.
2. (a) *Wet* (Chemistry, etc.).
   (b) Dry (e.g. Physics).
3. (a) Routine. Control of quality. Testing. Basically, activities in such a laboratory will be repetitive.
   (b) Research.
   (c) Teaching.
4. (a) Chemistry.
   (b) Physics.
   (c) Biology.
   (d) Others.

TEACHING AND RESEARCH

Teaching and research practices will have to be established.
In case of teaching: Teaching methods: demonstration, practical work, theory teaching, groupwork, group sizes. The tendency is towards smaller groups and more practical work.
Research categories: Group formations will usually be smaller, varying from 1 to about 12 workers.
For all categories the following information should be established:
Relationships between major groups.
Relationships within groups.
Types and frequency of communications (consultation, trolleys, etc).
Relationships with ancillary spaces.
Supervision systems.
Nature of activities.
Relationships with centralised facilities.

TRENDS (TEACHING AND RESEARCH LABORATORIES)

There is a trend towards 'multi-purpose' laboratories, in which students are given a permanent working place. This idea is more and more accepted already in the USA.

An architect's concern for the effective use of a laboratory throughout its full life span may sometimes conflict with the user's short term views. There is a danger that the building will be designed too closely around descriptions of immediate use, that are not related to a long term view of its operations.

In Primary, or early stage Briefing, trends and long term views should be clarified, while solutions should be sought to accommodate any of the situations likely to occur,

including that of the first set of users.

RESEARCH LABORATORIES—BENCHES

LENGTHS OF BENCHES FOR RESEARCH

1. *Long*
   Biochemistry
   Chemistry (some)   3300 to 4600 mm per scientist

2. *Medium*
   Chemistry
   Biophysics
   Physiology   3000 to 4000 mm per scientist
   Pathology and
     related subjects

3. *Short*
   Botany
   Animal subjects   2100 to 3700 mm per scientist
   Groups of up to three workers sharing facilities, will require noticeably less; around 1500 mm per worker.

Space between benches See Fig. 3.22

Increase may be needed because of:
Safety (quick backing away in case of hazard).
Traffic (access to other rooms, use by trolleys, etc.).
Equipment (place for equipment).
Flexibility (future arrangements).

Table 3.8 SIZE OF TEACHING LABORATORY WORKBENCHES

Subject	Bench area/student work station
Biology, biochemical labs.	1753 × 686
Biology, experimental labs.	1676 × 838
Chemistry	1753 × 686
General laboratories	1220 × 686
Physics	1676 × 838

Table 3.9 gives bench lengths required to give various degrees of satisfaction based on the time during which same bench was in use, for *Scientists* and *Assistants* in high, medium and low groups of disciplines. Figs. 3.23 and 3.24 show the anthropometric constraints governing the spacing between benches. The relationship between the anthropometric constraints governing bench spacing, recommended bench lengths and widths for teaching and research laboratories and alternative module sizes are also shown.

(Figs. 3.23 and 3.24 and Table 3.9 are reproduced by courtesy of the Nuffield Foundation from 'The Design of Research Laboratories' (O.U.P., 1961) published by the Division for Architectural Studies.)

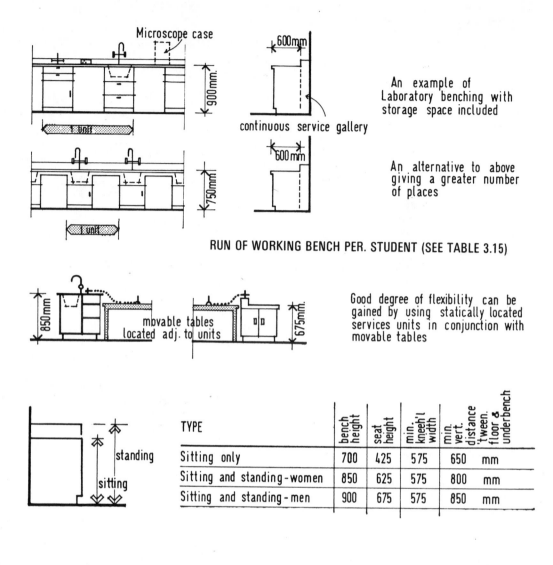

An example of Laboratory benching with storage space included

An alternative to above giving a greater number of places

RUN OF WORKING BENCH PER. STUDENT (SEE TABLE 3.15)

Good degree of flexibility can be gained by using statically located services units in conjunction with movable tables

TYPE	bench height	seat height	min. kneeh'l width	min. vert. distance 'tween. floor & underbench	
Sitting only	700	425	575	650	mm
Sitting and standing – women	850	625	575	800	mm
Sitting and standing – men	900	675	575	850	mm

Working spaces between benches :

a. One worker no thro' traffic — 1050 mm.
b. One worker plus passage way — 1200
c. Two workers no through traffic — 1350
d. Two workers plus passage way — 1800
e. Gangway only no working spaces — 1425

Fig. 3.22   Dimensional data relating to laboratories—working benches
(Reprinted from 'The Design of Polytechnic Institute Buildings', by permission of Unesco.© Unesco 1972)

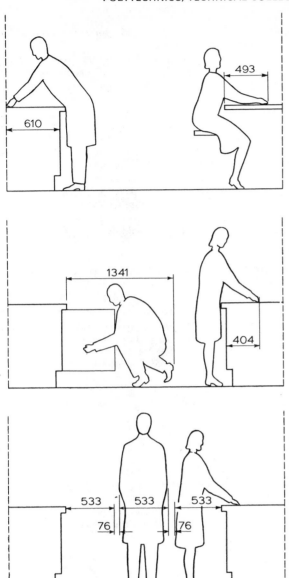

Fig. 3.23 The anthropometric constraints governing the spacing between benches

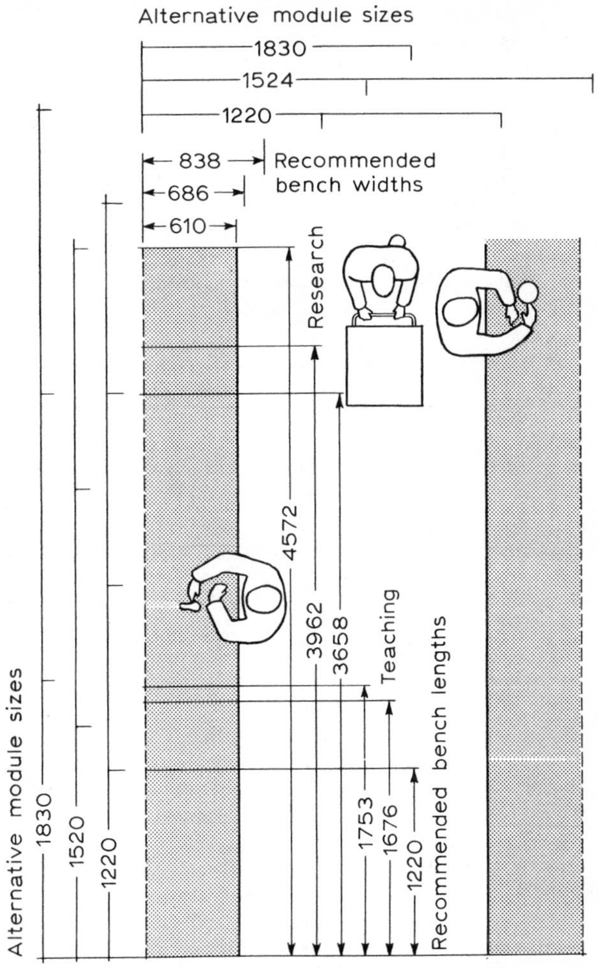

Fig. 3.24 The relationship between the anthropometric constraints governing bench spacing, recommended bench lengths and widths for teaching and research laboratories, and alternative modules size

Table 3.9 RECOMMENDED BENCH LENGTHS

	Scientists	Bench length in feet to give levels of satisfaction between 90 and 99%									
		90	91	92	93	94	95	96	97	98	99
Discipline class	High	13·4	13·7	14·0	14·3	14·7	15·0	15·3	16·0	17·2	18·5
	Medium	11·4	11·6	11·9	12·1	12·4	12·8	13·5	14·1	14·7	15·4
	Low	8·8	9·0	9·1	9·3	9·4	9·8	10·4	11·1	11·8	12·4
	Assistants										
		90	91	92	93	94	95	96	97	98	99
Discipline class	High	9·3	9·5	9·8	10·2	10·6	11·0	11·4	11·8	12·3	–
	Medium	9·5	9·9	10·3	10·8	11·3	11·7	12·2	12·8	13·9	15·1
	Low	10·1	10·4	10·8	11·1	11·5	11·9	12·2	13·1	16·0	18·5

RESEARCH LABORATORIES—SPECIAL FACILITIES

Special facilities are facilities in which equipment or techniques require a special environment, or create conditions not acceptable in general working areas, or calling for privacy of a kind not available in general working areas.

The most generally occurring special facilities are:

Cold stores. (Research, routine and teaching biology; research, routine chemistry; research physics). Degree of tolerance in temperature is important. Safety systems for people locked inside should be provided. Air-locked if frequently opened.

Cold laboratories. (Research, routine biology; research, routine chemistry; research physics). Degree of tolerance in temperature is important. Artificial ventilation is required.

Warm rooms, incubator rooms, hot rooms. (Research, routine biology, chemistry, physics). The degree of tolerance in temperature is important. Often combined with humidity control. Working in these rooms requires artificial ventilation.

Sterile rooms, dustfree rooms. (Reseach, routine biology, and any room with high grade electronic equipment, mostly in research laboratories for physics). Often required are air locks, air treatment, washing and changing facilities.

Dark rooms (all categories). Usually for photographic purposes. The trend is to centralise such facilities. Artificial ventilation required when in use.

Room with a special acoustic environment. Specialist involvement in designing such rooms is required. Important aspects: Sound absorbtion, reflection, reverberation, sound transmission through room enclosing elements.

Fume producing techniques (all biology and chemistry categories). Normally fumes are controlled in fume cupboards (Figs. 3.25 and 3.26). If quantities of unpleasant, toxic or otherwise dangerous fumes are high, so that they are not easily controlled in the open laboratories, this would require special rooms.

Chromotography rooms (all biology categories). Often produce unpleasant solvent fumes (heavier than air) and use large quantities of flammable solvents: special rooms required. Gas chromotography is usually carried out in the open laboratory. Paper chromotography will usually involve temperature control, as well as fume extraction: special room and fume cupboards.

Chemical distillation. (Research, routine chemistry; research, teaching biology). Extracting of fumes is important, while large scale processes require special rooms.

Steam production. (Chemistry, biology: all categories). Steam production is very common (washing, sterilising, etc.) and extraction is often necessary.

Heavy apparatus. This comprises equipment such as computers (which often require a special environment), ultra centrifuges, workshop equipment, testing rigs, compressors including vibration). These all require floors with high loading factors. Check pointloads as well.

Vibration producing equipment. Most equipment, and especially heavy equipment with moving parts, produces vibration. This must be prevented from affecting sensitive apparatus like balances, etc. Noise is often produced simultaneously.

Sensitive apparatus. Often requires guarding against vibration, and also may require a controlled (dustfree) environment. Balances and measuring apparatus often require special rooms. Electron microscopes require special rooms.

Animal rooms. Special environment.

Animal operating theatres. Special environment and procedures as in human surgery (hygiene).

Animal post-mortem rooms. Often infective materials to be used. Compulsory washing and changing. Air quality control.

For all *special facilities* the question should be asked whether *centralisation* is feasible in terms of organisation (control, supervision, distances etc.). Centralised special facilities will normally be more economical.

Radiation rooms including X-Ray rooms. Require correct screening, access security system, monitoring system and clear signposting.

Hazardous experiments. Can be segregated to special rooms.

Overnight experiments. Require separate safe facilities.

Explosive hazard. A special facility with a directional failure element usually a lightweight roof. Must be located in safe area, often on roof of highest building.

LABORATORIES AND RELATED SPACES

Relationships may necessitate location of such spaces in the laboratory area. The importance of such relationships should be studied, as location of such related spaces outside the costly laboratory areas may be more economical.

Libraries. Although policy trends are normally towards central libraries, departmental, or even laboratory libraries are likely to remain popular. Policies concerning libraries should be clarified.

Staff rooms, seminar rooms, reading, writing and thinking spaces. Consider relationships. Staff rooms may be used for teaching purposes. Staff common rooms may perform dual roles. Often some writing space is required in the general laboratory.

Cloakrooms, Storage. Consider central storage. Special storage: cold storage, explosive materials, radioactive materials. See 'Storage' below.

Plantrooms, Glass washing, Preparation rooms. Often used in connection with teaching laboratories.

STORAGE

Categories:

1. *Central storage* Organisation aspects are important: staffing, control, deliveries, handing out, etc. Special storage is often centralised: workshop stores, flammable solvents, explosives, poisons, animal food storage.

2. *Local storage* Storage in or next to laboratory required if frequently used (with the exception of highly dangerous materials).

3. *Storage at work place* Small quantities, very frequently used.

LABORATORIES—SERVICES

See also Section 2 'Secondary Schools' (Fig. 2.41). A high demand can exist for the following services:

Biology lab
   Gravity cold water
   Compressed air
   Inert gases
   Air extract
   A.C. mains electricity, single phase

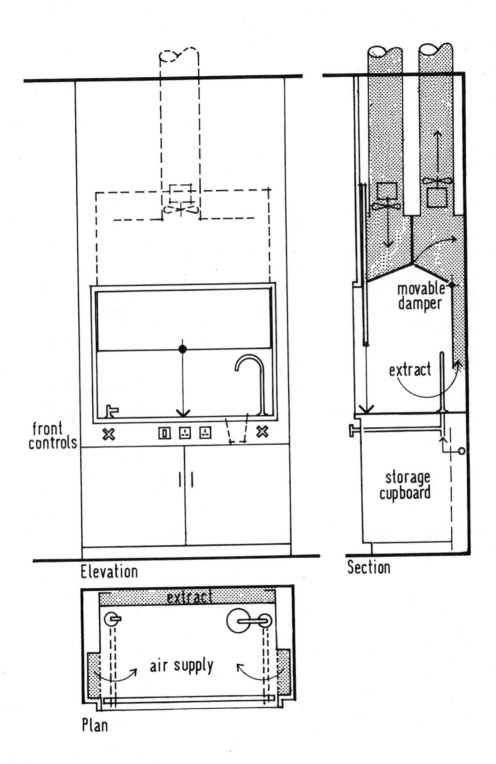

Elevation

Section

movable damper

extract

storage cupboard

front controls

Plan

extract

air supply

Fig. 3.25   The basic requirements of a laboratory fume cupboard. Each fume cupboard must be separately ventilated.
(Reprinted from 'The Design of Polytechnic Institute Buildings', by permission of Unesco. © Unesco 1972)

Chemistry lab

    Gravity cold water
    Town or natural gas
    Inert gases
    Air extract
    A.C. mains electricity, single phase

Physics lab

    A.C. mains electricity single- and 3-phase
    D.C. electricity
    Monitor circuit
    Screened circuit
    Control circuit

The establishment of future requirements and measures to accommodate these is absolutely vital.

There is a tendency for services to become less rigid, more easily adaptable, more flexible (see examples of flexible furniture arrangements). This even extends so far as providing bottled gas, in preference to piped supply, bottled air, etc.

Important aspects in service design are, maintenance, extension, adaptation, cost implications, minimalising disturbance, access. Generally, there is a tendency to *over-provide* services, and the absolute need for a piped service should have been proved before provision. For example, hot water is normally only needed at very few locations, and in this case local heaters may be much more economical.

A central vacuum service is another example of an often unnecessary central service as local vacuum pumps have proved. Similar considerations apply to electrical supply, where local stabilisers, rectifiers, transformers, etc., are often quite sufficient.

PUBLIC SERVICES AND WASTE DISPOSAL SYSTEMS

The following aspects should be checked: availability, accessibility, future needs, reliability of pressures. The Local Authority requirements for waste disposal should be established. A check should be made of all emergency systems, in case of failure. Private supply and disposal systems may be feasible.

DISPOSAL SERVICES

Laboratory waste systems may differ from waste systems in other buildings, only in so far as the substances to be carried away can be of a different kind. In most chemical and biological categories, laboratory wastes may carry corrosive agents, or may be of a high temperature. Sometimes it is necessary to trap valuable substances. Waste runs should be immediately visible and accessible in the room to which they belong.

The latest trend is towards pumped drainage as this system gives flexibility. In complex systems it is the routing of drainage that determines services layouts. Most of the supply services can be routed in almost any direction, but liquid waste disposal with a gravitational character will impose limits.

Solid waste is normally dealt with by local bins. However in animal experiment laboratories, incineration of carcasses and soiled bedding is obligatory.

Infected and radioactive waste are special problems.

ENVIRONMENTAL SERVICES

It should be stressed that the need for accurate control over large air volumes could be carefully checked. It has been found that expensive controlled environment rooms are sometimes not totally suitable for many chemical and biological disciplines, owing to their inflexibility. The trend again is towards local, individually controlled devices housed in the general laboratory area.

In the general laboratory area itself, there is a growing demand for some degree of environmental control stemming from the use of more sensitive, refined equipment. The use of a greater variety of dangerous substances, has increased the demand for artificial ventilation.

Hot water heating systems with attendant appliances have always proved inconvenient in laboratories where free wall space is of great functional importance. Compact heating devices are needed, for example radiant heaters.

It is obvious that many factors lead to complete combined heating and ventilation systems using air as the sole medium, and indeed the increasing use of heat-producing apparatus in laboratories may eventually lead to full air-conditioning. In rooms where fume extracting occurs, ventilation requires special attention.

Acoustical environment needs special attention in teaching laboratories, and also there where noisy activities or apparatus are to be accommodated. A number of rooms require a special environment, these are cold rooms, warm rooms, and anechoic chambers. (See subsection on 'Special Rooms').

SAFETY IN LABORATORIES

Fire and explosion danger. The correct fire fighting appliances must be provided. Alternative means of escape are required and care should be taken to avoid any obstructions.

Services to increase safety. These include under fume disposal, air balance, safety showers. In microbiology, surfaces should be non-porous, in order to avoid contamination and unwanted bacteria breeding.

For radioactivity, special safety precautions need to be taken. Two publications which deal with this aspect of safety are

Code of Practice for the protection of persons exposed to Ionizing Radiation in University Laboratories.

Radiological Protection in Universities. The Committee of Vice-Chancellors and Principals of the Universities of the U.K.

(Published by the Association of Commonwealth Universities, 36 Gordon Square, London, W.1)

LABORATORIES—EQUIPMENT AND FURNITURE

A full description of each item is required. This should include, make, supplier, new or existing, exact function, frequency and period of use, quantity, size, weight, required working space, services and connections, required environment, safety aspects, storage aspects, installation and fixing, special conditions such as vibration, etc.

Equipment, may be accommodated at benches (on framed rigs, bench refrigerators, bench fume cupboards, etc.) or elsewhere in the laboratory, or in another room.

Chemistry and Physics require large pieces of apparatus (often mounted on trolleys) such as vacuum pumps, electric or electronic banks, power packs, etc.

Supplementary equipment and installations include fire alarms, and other fire safety devices (smoke detectors, automatic doors, etc.); lifts; mechanical handling plant; telecommunications, including telephone and TV (especially in teaching areas).

FURNITURE

The determination of the furniture module is an important aspect of furniture design, as such a module is one of the most important factors that establish the building module. Such modules should be standardised, so as to accommodate all benches, under-bench and over-bench storage units, shelves, fume cupboards, desk spaces and blackboard units.

Trends in furniture design are towards mobility so as to accommodate various teaching situations, or to fit in with large equipment, that cannot be placed on the furniture.

Service outlets will be preferably located in service spines, or service bollards, or from flexible service runs of the ceiling, in such a situation (Fig. 3.26).

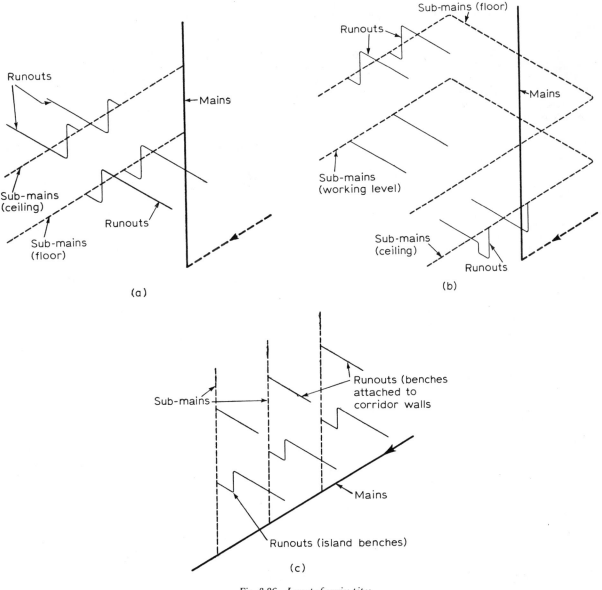

Fig. 3.26 Layout of service pipes
(a) Horizontal submains from vertical mains
(b) Perimeter submains from vertical mains
(c) Vertical mains from horizontal mains

Important aspects of furniture design are:
Dimensions to create comfortable and safe working conditions.
Dimensions and designs should be able to accommodate the required functions.
Selection of suitable materials, especially important in chemical laboratories.

LABORATORY PLANNING

Three basic arrangements of bench layout are:

Island benches
Perimeter benches
Flexible arrangements

Perimeter benches have the advantages of easy servicing. Flexible arrangements have advantages that are obvious, for instance, a number of types of experiments can be accommodated (varying sizes, varying services). Also, in the teaching situation, different group sizes can be accommodated.

Services should be planned such that they are easily adaptable to short term changes, and convertible for long term changes. Thus they should be easily accessible, and be able to cover economically any part of the laboratory (Fig. 3.26).

It is usual to accommodate services in specially reserved zones. The ceiling is the most common of such areas, with the disadvantage that drainage unless pumped still has to be accommodated either in bench units, or in the floor.

Accommodating services in the floor or under-floor means disturbance of the rooms below if changes take place. Accommodating services in the benches tends to reduce flexibility of such bench units. For really flexible arrangements, drainage needs to be pumped back up to the ceiling zone drain runs.

ACCESS AND CIRCULATION

Vehicular access is normally required for the following: loading bays, workshops, kitchens, boiler house, fuel tank inlets, plant rooms, incinerator, solvent stores, cylinder stores, isotope delay tanks, refuse collection disposal points, animal house, etc.

Circulation is best analysed by flow diagrams. An important aspect of circulation is occasional interference (e.g. service access).

Schramm sets out the following general rules:

Where doors open into corridors, the corridor width should be from 2·25 to 2·50 m, otherwise 2 m will be sufficient. As a first principle, alternative means of escape will be required in case of fire from any position immediately outside any room above ground floor.

Movement occur, of people and of goods. Such goods may include materials, trolleys, (large) equipment furniture.

Circulation, including doors should be able to take such movement.

Access is often to be controlled, in interests of security.

EXAMPLES

Typical examples of laboratory and workshop planning are given in the following diagrams:

Typical laboratory layouts for Polytechnic Institutes (Fig. 3.27).

A typical laboratory layout at Hatfield Polytechnic (Fig. 3.28).

U.C.L. Chemistry building. A typical teaching laboratory (Fig. 3.29).

Equipment oriented teaching laboratories (Figs. 3.30 and 3.31).

Workshops in Polytechnic Institutes (Figs. 3.32 to 3.35).

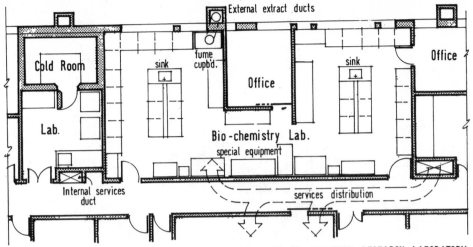

A. AN EXAMPLE OF AN ADVANCED RESEARCH LABORATORY

SCALE 1:200

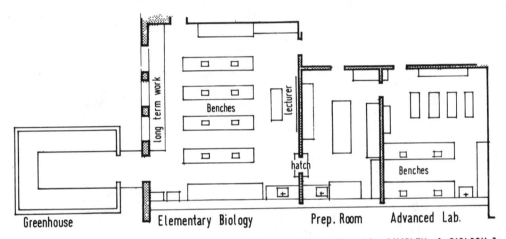

B. AN EXAMPLE OF A TEACHING LAB. COMPLEX [BIOLOGY]

SCALE 1:200

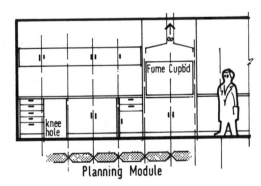

C. PLANNING MODULE:

It is advisable that all laboratory furniture be planned on a standard module. Removable under-bench storage units may then be interchanged to give great flexibility and adaptability to laboratory layouts

SCALE 1:100

Fig. 3.27   Typical laboratory layouts (a) a group of advanced research laboratories suitable for post-graduate work. (b) a smaller teaching laboratory complex (biology); the relationship of advanced and elementary study areas should be noted; (c) diagram showing typical laboratory planning module.
(Reprinted from 'The Design of Polytechnic Institute Buildings' by permission of Unesco.© Unesco 1972)

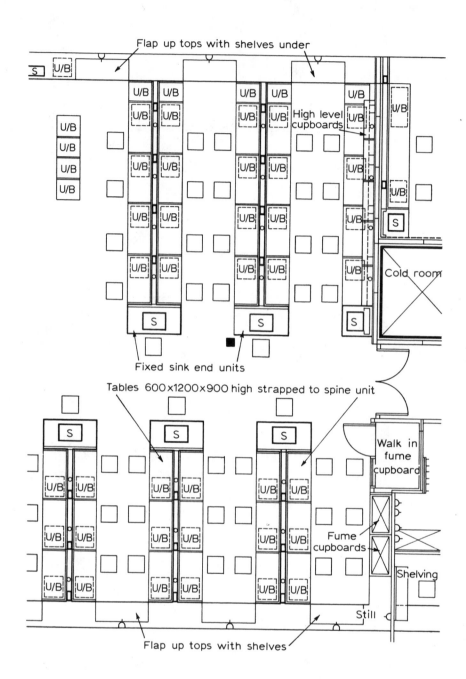

Fig. 3.28   Typical laboratory—Hatfield Polytechnic (Architects Co-Partnership Inc.)

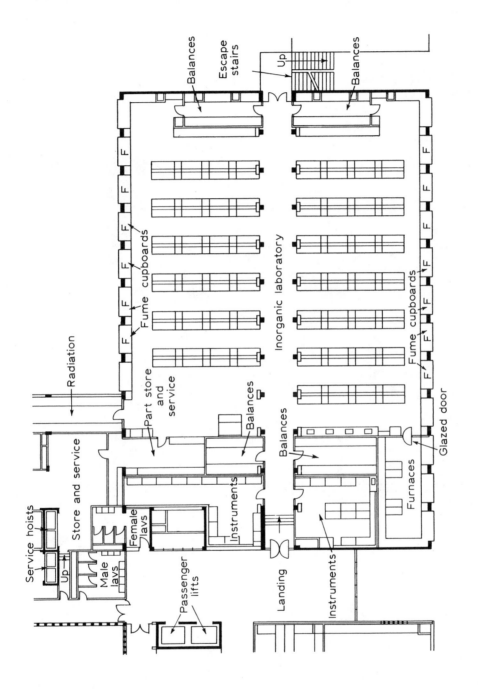

Fig. 3.29 A large chemistry teaching laboratory—UCL (Architects Co-Partnership Inc.)

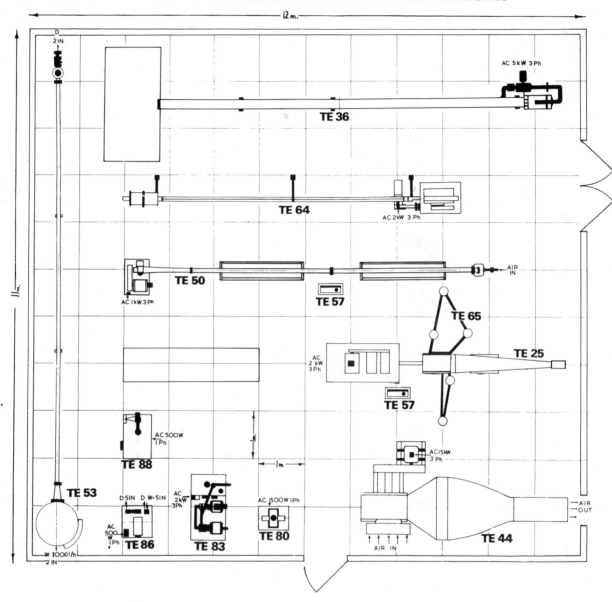

Fig. 3.30   Advanced hydraulics/fluid mechanics laboratory (Plint & Partners Ltd.)

TE 25. 100 × 25 supersonic wind tunnel.
TE 36. Universal modular flow channels.
TE 44. 460 × 460 subsonic wind tunnel.
TE 50. Pipe flow and nozzle apparatus and fan test set.
TE 53. Surge tower or oscillating liquid apparatus.
TE 57. Multitube manometer.
TE 64. Laminar turbulent pipe flow apparatus.
TE 80. Smoke tunnel.
TE 83. Two-stage centrifugal pump test set.
TE 86. Water hammer apparatus.
TE 88. Air jet and ground apparatus.

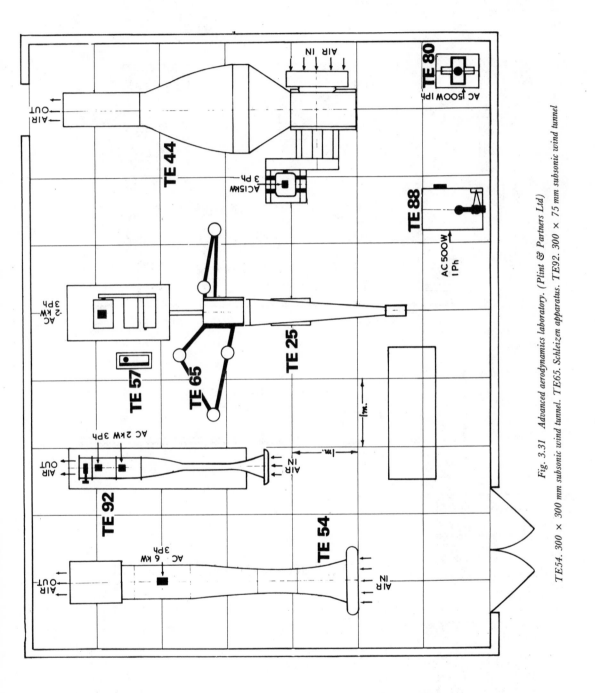

Fig. 3.31   Advanced aerodynamics laboratory. (Plint & Partners Ltd)

TE54. 300 × 300 mm subsonic wind tunnel. TE65. Schleizen apparatus. TE92. 300 × 75 mm subsonic wind tunnel

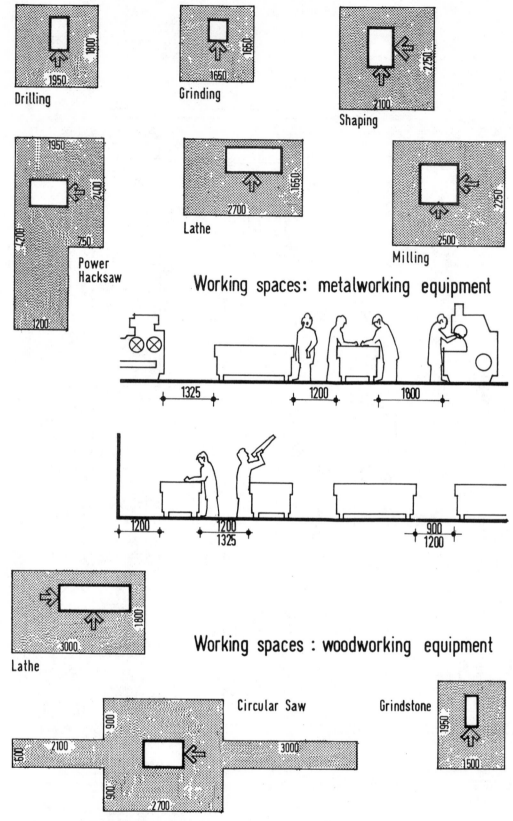

Drilling

Grinding

Shaping

Power Hacksaw

Lathe

Milling

Working spaces: metalworking equipment

Working spaces: woodworking equipment

Lathe

Circular Saw

Grindstone

Fig. 3.32 Dimensional data (in mm) relating to workshops and space required around machines.
Detailed checks of clearances should be made when exact machine requirements are known.
(Reprinted from 'The Design of Polytechnic Institute Buildings' by permission of
Unesco.© Unesco 1972.)

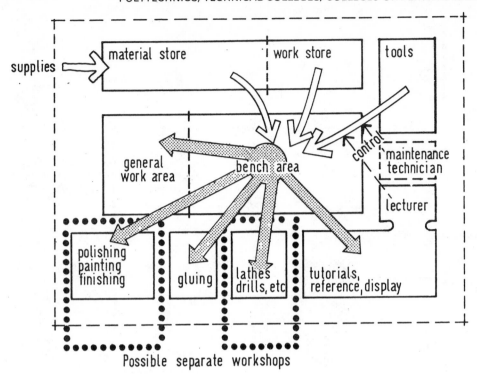

Fig. 3.33 Diagrammatic layouts, showing functional requirements of typical workshops (Reprinted from 'The Design of Polytechnic Institute Buildings' by permission of Unesco. © Unesco 1972.)

GENERAL WOODWORK SHOP

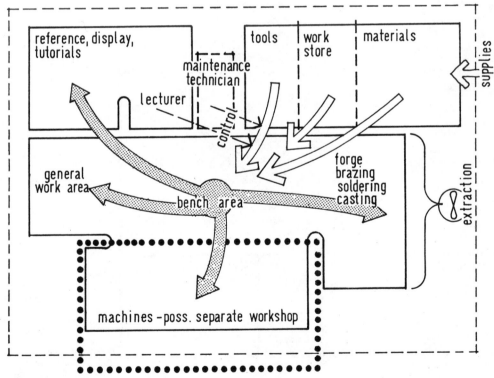

GENERAL ENGINEERING/METALWORK SHOP

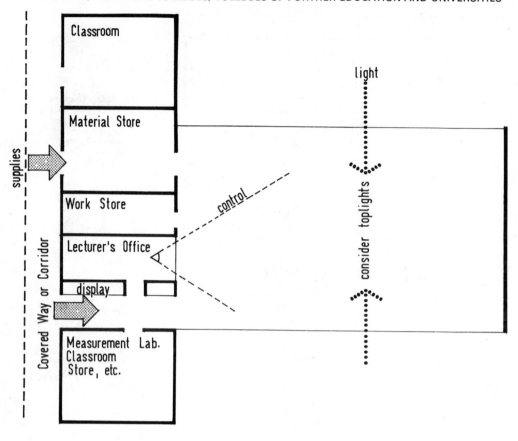

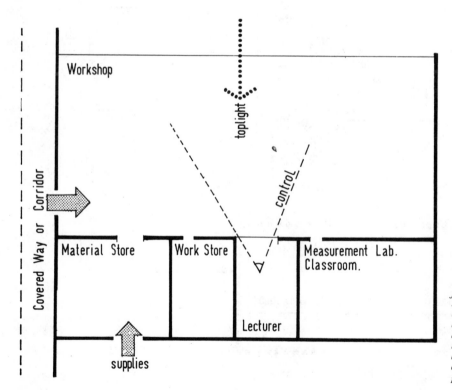

Fig. 3.34 Alternative arrangements for main workshop areas and ancillary spaces. Where workshops are planned as part of a larger unit top lighting is essential. Both plans indicate good access for materials and supervision of the workshop floor by the staff in charge. (Reprinted from 'The Design of Polytechnic Institute Buildings', by permission of Unesco. © Unesco 1972)

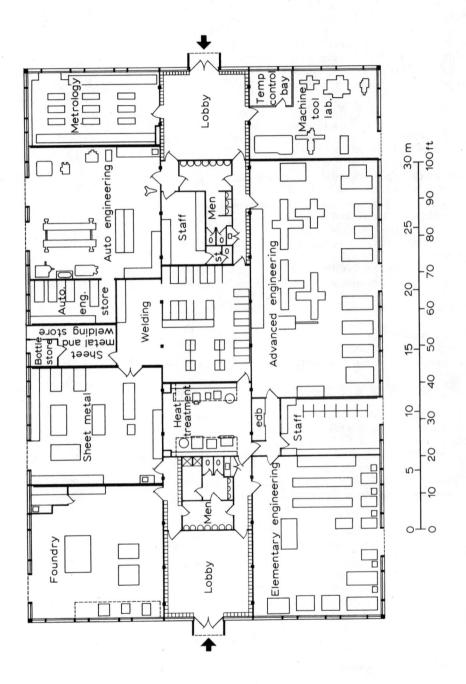

*Fig. 3.35   Mechanical engineering workshop—Harris College, Preston
(Architects Co-Partnership Inc.)*

STATUTORY REQUIREMENTS

(This information is correct at July 1974).

There are numerous Statutory Acts, and Statutory Instruments and Regulations made under these Acts, which make provisions with regard to the planning, construction and usage of educational buildings. The most important of these Acts is the Education Act 1944. Section 10 empowers the making of regulations prescribing the standards to which the premises of schools maintained by local education authorities are to conform.

Section 63(1) amends Section 71 of the Public Health Act 1936 with regard to the exemption from the provisions of the building regulations any educational establishment erected or to be erected in accordance with plans approved by the Secretary of State for Education and Science.

With regard to the regulations made under the Act, Statutory Instruments Nos. 1959–890, 1968–433, 1971–1553 and 1972–1255 set out standards of educational amenity and of health and safety for school premises. They include requirements on site and teaching areas, structural stability, fire precautions, lighting, heating, ventilation, washing and sanitary accommodation.

Regulations made under Section 100 of the Act, and Section 3 of the Local Government Act 1958 contain requirements on the use of premises and specify that the approval of the Secretary of State must be obtained before premises can be provided or altered.

The following regulations are also applicable:
Direct Grant Schools Regulations (SI 1959–1832).
Handicapped Pupils and Special Schools Regulations (SI 1959–365).
Handicapped Pupils (Boarding) Regulations (SI 1959–362).
Schools Regulations (SI 1959–364).
Training of Teachers Regulations (SI 1967–792).
Further Education Regulations (SI 1969–403).

In addition, the Department of Education and Science publishes advisory literature from time to time, of which its Building Bulletins and Safety Series are just two examples.

A list of the relevant Acts under subject headings is given below.

ACCESS

To buildings by disabled persons	Chronically Sick and Disabled Persons Act 1970.
For vehicles	Restriction of Ribbon Development Act 1935, S.17.
For removal of refuse	Public Health Act 1936, S.55.
To premises from highway	Highways Act 1971, Ss. 29, 40.

ASSEMBLY BUILDINGS

Ingress and egress	Public Health Act 1936, S.59.
Fire certificates	Fire Precautions Act 1971, S.1.

BUILDING(S)

At corners of highways	Highways Act 1959, S.81.
Forecourts to	Public Health Act 1961, S.46.
In conservation areas	Town & Country Planning Amendment Act 1972, S.8.
Line	Highways Act 1959, Ss. 72, 73.
Projections from	Highways Act 1959, S.131.
Sanitation generally	Public Health Act 1936, Part II.
Within inner London	London Building (Construction) By-Laws 1972.

CAR PARKS

Multi-storey or underground	Petroleum (Consolidation Act), 1928.

CHILDREN

Homes, community	Children & Young Persons Act 1969.
Homes, voluntary	Childrens Act 1948, S.29.
Nurseries	Nurseries & Child Minders Regulation Act 1948.
Nurseries	Health Service & Public Health Act 1963, S.60.

CHIMNEY(S)

Height of	Clean Air Acts 1956, S.10 and 1968, S.6.
Flue pipes	Building Regulations, Part L

CLOAKROOM

Requirements	Offices, Shops & Railway Premises Act 1968, S.12.

COOKING APPLIANCES

Installation of	Building Regulations 1972, Part M.

DRAINAGE AND SEWERAGE

General	Public Health Acts 1936 and 1961.
Regulations	Building Regulations 1972, Part M.

ELECTRICITY

Supply	Electricity Acts 1947 and 1957.
Works by undertakers	Electric Lighting Act 1882.

FIRE

General	Fire Precautions Act 1971
Means of escape	Public Health Act 1936, S.60.
Means of escape in London	London Building Act (Amendment) 1939, S.34.
Structural precautions	Building Regulations, Part E

FOOD

Catering, storage, etc.	Food & Drugs Act 1955, S.13.

BOILERS

Details	Clean Air Acts 1956 and 1968.

GAS

General	Gas Act 1972.

HANDICAPPED PERSONS

Facilities in buildings	Chronically Sick & Disabled Persons Act 1970.

LIGHTING

In offices	Offices, Shops & Railway Premises Act 1963, Ss.8, 42–43.
Emergency	See under FIRE.

OFFICES

Drinking water, floors, passages and stairs, heating, overcrowding, sanitary conveniences, washing facilities and ventilation	Offices, Shops & Railway Premises

PETROL

Garages and storage	Petroleum (Consolidation) Act 1928.

SMOKE CONTROL

Areas	Clean Air Acts.

REFUSE DISPOSAL

General	Building Regulations, Part J.
Access for	Public Health Act, S.55.

STAIRCASES

Offices	Offices, Shops & Railway Premises Act 1963, Ss.16, 42–43.
Within inner London	London Building Act (Amendment) 1939, S.34.
To a 'high' building within inner London	London Building Act (Amendment) 1939, S.20.

TOWN & COUNTRY PLANNING

General	Town & Country Planning Acts 1971 and 1972.
Buildings in conservation areas	Town & Country Planning Act 1971, S.28.
Listed buildings	Town & Country Planning Act 1971, Ss. 54–58.
Tree preservation orders	Town & Country Planning Act 1971, S.60.

VENTILATION

General	Building Regulations, Part K.
Offices	Offices, Shops & Railway Premises Act 1963, S.7.

EXAMPLES

A number of examples from Europe and North America are published in:

1. Entwurf und Planung 12, Hochschulbauten, Institutsgebäude, Finger, H. Herausgegeben von Peters, P. *Verlag Georg D. W. Callwey, München,* (1973).
2. Universities, *L'Architecture d'aujourd'hui,* (April–May 1968).
3. Hochschulplanung 1, Linde, H., *Werner Verlag,* Dusseldorf (1970).
4. Bauen and Wohnen, November 1969 (several articles).

BIBLIOGRAPHY

Mills, E. D. and Kaylor, H., *The Design of Polytechnic Institute Buildings,* UNESCO Paris, France (1972).

Fairweather, L. and Sliwa, Jan A., *AJ Metric Handbook,* The Architectural Press.

Duncan, C. J. (Ed.), *Modern Lecture Theatres,* Oriel Press (1973).

Divisible Auditoriums, Educational Facilities Laboratories, New York (1966).

The Design of Research Laboratories, Nuffield Foundation, Division for Architectural Studies. Oxford University Press London (1961).

Harris College Preston, Building Bulletin 29, Department of Education and Science, HMSO, London (1966).

Schramm, W., *Chemistry and Biology Laboratories: Design/Construction/Equipment*, Pergamon Press (1965).

Robert Matthew, Johnson-Marshall & Partners, *The Proposed University of Bath. A technological University*, Development Plan. Report No. 1, Robert Matthew, Johnson-Marshall & Partners. Bath University Press (1965).

Bullock, N., Dickens, P., and Steadman, P. H., *A Theoretical Basis for University Planning, Land Use and Built Form Studies*, Report No. 1, University of Cambridge School of Architecture (1968).

Neufert, E., *Neufert Architects' data*, Crosby Lockwood & Son Ltd., London (1970).

The Architects' Journal Information Library

Developing a range of adaptable furniture and services for laboratories.		16.8.72
Design Guide: Laboratories	Part 1	1.11.67
	Part 2	8.11.67
Laboratory buildings	Technical Study	15.11.67
Briefing Guide: laboratory spaces, fixtures and equipment.		13.1.65
		27.1.65
The design of laboratory spaces.		6.1.65
		3.2.65
		10.2.65
York University		23.2.72

Polytechnics: Planning for Development, Design note 8, Department of Education and Science, HMSO.

Furniture and Equipment Dimensions: Further and Higher Education (18 to 25 age group). Building Bulletin 44. Department of Education and Science HMSO (1970).

Papers published by the Laboratory Investigation Unit London.

Paper 1 An approach to laboratory building, (1969)

Paper 2 Deep or shallow building. A comparison of cost in use, (1970).

Paper 3 Growth and change in laboratory activity, 1971).

Paper 4 The economics of adaptability. A comparative study of the initial and life costs of partitions, (1971).

Paper 5 Conversions of buildings for science and technology, (1971).

Paper 6 Adaptable Furniture and Services for Education and Science, (1972).

Notes on Procedure 1973, Capital Grants, University Grants Committee.

Planning Norms for University Buildings, Norms revised February 1974, University Grants Committee.

Notes on Procedure for the Approval of Polytechnic Projects, Department of Education and Science.

Notes on Procedure for the Approval of Further Education Projects, (not including Polytechnics), Department of Education and Science.

Jordan, John, *Dip, Arch. (Birm.) RIBA is a director of Architects' Co-Partnership Incorporated where he takes a particular interest in educational building and brief preparation. He did some original development work on CLASP, has been in charge of ACP offices in Nigeria and Bristol and has practical experience of projects in several countries. Held a research lectureship at the Birmingham School for two years and has subsequently published numerous articles on educational work and system building and is a regular consultant to UNESCO.*

Mooij, Dirk, *M.Sc. (Delft) has been employed with Architects' Co-Partnership, and his main field of work is educational facilities planning. He was a Unesco expert for three years, in the Educational Facilities Section, and in this capacity worked in a number of educational building projects, both in the U.K. and elsewhere, in addition to consultancy services to IBRD and UNESCO.*

4 LIBRARIES

B. W. LOREN, R.I.B.A.
A. G. Sheppard Fidler and Associates

INTRODUCTION

To be successful, the design of a library demands more than most projects, the closest collaboration at all stages between the appointed architect and the client—in this case the librarian, who should become a member of the design team from the initiation of the project. Not only will the librarian have given much preliminary thought to the library and its facilities but will be formulating the initial brief to the architect in the light of his experience and research.

There is, of course, a wide variety of library provision but, at all levels, the aim of a well designed library building is to form an environment which will provide access to books, information and audio-visual material in conditions of comfort, economy, efficiency and security.

Library buildings may broadly be classified by their size and their relationship to the communities or organisations they serve. There is, therefore, a wide variety in function and requirements ranging from a national library which is a special project in every sense (and is because of circumstances and expense a rarity) down to a small specialised library in an office or home.

There are, however, three broad classifications as follows:
1. *Libraries for Education.* These vary greatly in size according to the type of institution, e.g. university and polytechnic libraries, college and school libraries etc. All these categories of libraries form an integrated part of a larger complex and are thus active participants in the process of teaching and learning.

School libraries can vary in size within wide limits from a few books housed in a single room to a larger unit approaching the size of a college library. In most cases school libraries will form an integral part of the school building and will be very rarely located in a separate building.
2. *Public Libraries.* These types of libraries will vary considerably in size depending on the communities they serve. As well as lending and reference functions, in recent years the development of new media and technology has brough great changes and affects the basic planning of library buildings.

Public library buildings can be divided into three categories:
  (a) Central libraries (for large communities).
  (b) County libraries (also serve as administrative and distribution centres).
  (c) Branch or local libraries.
3. *Research and Special Libraries.* The function and purpose of this wide group of libraries varies to an unlimited extent and broad divisions are as follows: Libraries in research associations, learned institutions, Government departments, commercial and industrial firms and associations. Library facilities are also required in hospitals and prisons where pioneering work is also being done.

THE SITE

In most cases the library will form a part of a large organisation or complex of buildings. Designers of a master plan for a complex which includes a library should therefore consider its location with great care, bearing in mind its needs, functions and characteristics. Experience has shown that the location of the site of any library is one of the greatest factors in ensuring its success in use.

In view of its function, the location of a public library is dependent on the ability to attract users and readers. Whether the library is located in a separate building, or forms a part of other building complexes, it should be easily accessible and located near the centre of activity such as shopping, entertainment etc, and conveniently related to transport. Thus it will be convenient for regular users and potential readers.

It is, of course, important for the architect to study the nature of the area from which potential library users are to be drawn and to design his building to attract them to it.

A pleasant environment is the ideal setting for a library and accessibility is of vital importance. In most central sites where land is scarce and expensive it is not possible for libraries to have their own car parks, but ease of access for car users is an important element in making the library the vital point it should be in any community.

PLANNING

RELATIONSHIPS OF OPERATIONAL AREAS

One of the imperative decisions in planning the library building will be the relationship in space between various operational areas and the priority of access routes between them. These decisions cannot be imposed rigidly by the client, nor insisted upon by the architect. Precommitment by the librarian can have hampering effect on the architect, who must approach this problem with a completely open mind, in order to develop a decision. A good working partnership between librarian and architect is necessary to solve all these problems.

In a multi-storey solution a statement must be obtained from the librarian, not only as to which areas need to be close together, but also which action areas need to be on the same level. These should be listed in order of priority. Architects are advised to study the methods as described in 'Architectural practice and management' issued by the RIBA Part 3.525: User Requirement Study.

Fig. 4.1 illustrates possible relationships between the operational areas of a small library.

Areas most used by readers should be located near the entrance and control point. At the same time, it must not be forgotten that 'serious' readers, students and users of reference libraries are not reluctant to use upper floors, if easy access is provided. This could include adequate lifts, staircases, or, ramps for disabled persons.

Example of possible division of operational areas in multi-storey buildings for a medium sized library.

Main Floor	Entrance
	Control
	Exhibition
	Cloakrooms
	Prams
	Adult lending, workrooms
	Childrens lending, workrooms
	Periodicals
	Record lending
	Picture lending, etc
Other Floors	Reference library with carrels
	Study rooms
	Local history
	Museum
	Technical library
	Closed stack (if not on the same level a hoist to be provided)
Goods Entrance Floor	Goods reception
	Despatch
	Accessions area
	Bindery etc.

During the decision making on sizes and juxtapositions of the operational areas, it must be remembered that the efficiency of the library will depend on good communication and no interference between routes of readers and materials (see Figs. 4.2 to 4.5).

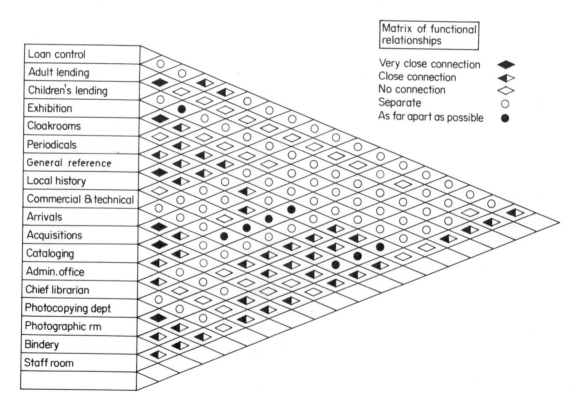

Matrix of functional relationships

Very close connection
Close connection
No connection
Separate
As far apart as possible

Loan control
Adult lending
Children's lending
Exhibition
Cloakrooms
Periodicals
General reference
Local history
Commercial & technical
Arrivals
Acquisitions
Cataloging
Admin. office
Chief librarian
Photocopying dept.
Photographic rm
Bindery
Staff room

Fig. 4.1   Relationship between sections of medium sized central library

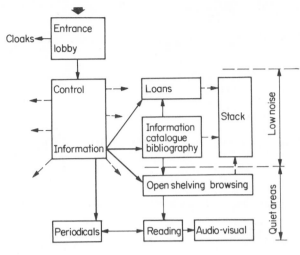

Fig. 4.2   Progress of readers through a public library

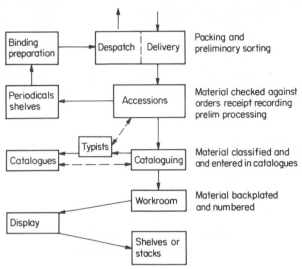

Fig. 4.4   Progress of materials

Following the example (Fig. 4.1) of possible space relationships between operational areas, the positions of all departments in relation to each other must be established. Each operational area must be studied very carefully and its size decided after the briefing is completed.

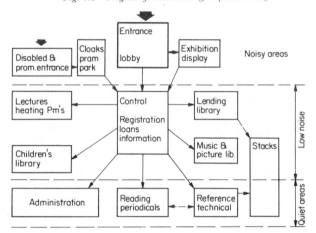

Fig. 4.3(a)   Progress of readers through a research library

PATTERN OF OPERATIONS

Following the space relationships established with the help of Fig. 4.1, it will be necessary to establish pattern of operations for book and reader services.

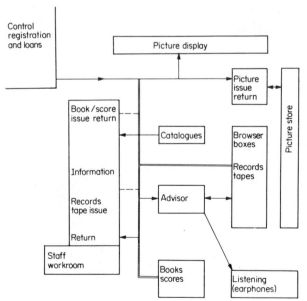

Fig. 4.3(b)   Flow diagram—music, records, picture lending departments

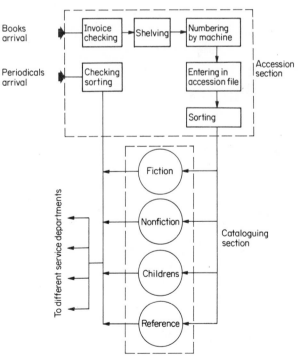

Fig. 4.5   Material intake through processing sections

4–3

SPACE REQUIREMENTS

There are two methods of preliminary assessment of sizes of areas to plan library buildings.

The first and best method is to establish the preliminary functional areas from the number of users, and number of staff and sizes of equipment, but, in some cases the designer may find it necessary to find a quicker way of establishing the preliminary areas.

Standards are issued by the International Federation of Library Associations, the Department of Education and Science and the Library Advisory Council.

'RULE OF THUMB' ASSESSMENT OF AREAS

When assessing the amount of space given to a particular area, it is important to remember that each individual case is different and that the question should be fully discussed with the client. The figures given below give a rough guide of typical space conversion factors.

Some typical measurements

Books per single sided 900 mm tier, ¾ full; 5 shelves high	120 to 130
Depth of single sided tier	200 mm
Height of wall shelving	2 m (adults); 1·5 m (children)
Height of island bookcases	1350 mm
Height of bottom shelf from floor	380 mm
Distance between freestanding bookcases	2 m to 3 m
Overall capacity	65 vol/m² 17 to 65 books/m³
Space per reader (other than at tables)	0·465 m²

Special areas: Reference, etc.

Space per reader (min)	0·93–1·3 m²
Space allowance for one carrel user	3·7 m²
Space allowance for one research worker	3·25 m²
Public reference libraries	
per 500 population served allow	1 seat
per 1000 population served allow	7 m²
Open stack 2·3 m high shelved ¾ full	130 books/m² 50 books/m³
Books under 300 mm tall in these conditions	180 to 220 books/m² 78 to 80 books/m³
Compact book storage	330 to 440 books/m² 120 to 170 books/m³

General

Work space per head of staff	11 m²
Cataloguing staff	13·5 m²
Capacity of catalogue drawer	1000 cards (300 files)
Weight of shelf of books; 900 mm long ¾ full	12 to 14 kg
Weight of shelf of directories or bound periodicals	22 to 25 kg
Percentage of students who will require seats in an academic library	30%

DATA

ASSESSMENT OF SIZE OF OPERATIONAL AREAS AND NECESSARY DATA

As mentioned in the beginning of the paragraph 'Space requirements' the only accurate method of establishing the areas is from the number of users, staff and equipment.

The areas of library are very strongly related to activities

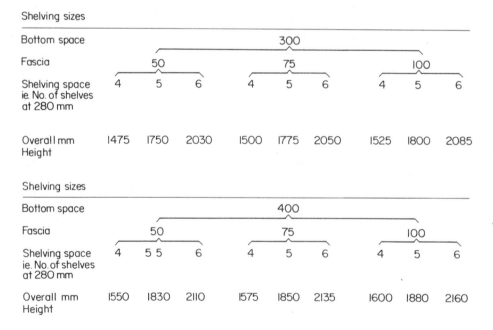

Fig. 4.6 Shelving sizes

and equipment contained—or materials to be used. In the foreseeable future the bulk of holdings of libraries will still be in book form, or boxes which can be shelved as books, although the use of audio-visual material must constantly be increasing. Books must be housed in an acceptable way for those who use them, bearing in mind the economics of space and finance.

BOOKSHELVES

Books are edited in various sizes, but it has been established that at least 90% of books are less than 230 m deep.

Special libraries holding large volumes of bound newspapers, music or art books, will have a different problem which would have to be studied specially. Libraries could standardise on 230 mm wide shelving, with special runs of shelving (limited number) 300 mm wide for books over 230 mm wide (see Fig. 4.6).

Manufacturers offer three lengths of shelving in their systems, 750 mm, 900 mm and 1 m, which may fit the building module if required.

Wall shelving should never be higher than 2 m (preferably 1·8) island shelves in lending libraries should not be higher than 1·5 m and 1·375 m is preferred. No shelf in public areas should be lower than 300 mm from the floor and preferably 400 mm in island shelving (Fig. 4.7).

In junior schools and parts of children's libraries the bottom shelves can be as low as 75 mm (Figs. 4.8 and 4.9).

Fig. 4.7 Shelving sizes—adult library

Fig. 4.8 Shelving sizes—junior library

Fig. 4.9 Shelving sizes—children's library

Type of book	No. per 300 mm run of shelf	No. per 900 mm run of shelf
Childrens books	10–12	30–35
Loan and fiction public libraries	8	24–25
Literature, history, politics and economics	7	21
Science, technology	6	18
Medicine, public documents and bound periodicals	5	15
Law	4	12
AVERAGES	7	21

Fig. 4.10 Number of books on shelf

CLOSED STACK

This type of book stack will form a major part of book housing in large libraries—national, city, county, etc.

The shelving should provide the maximum storage of books with minimum use of space. This will mean island double sided stacks, with single sided along the perimeter walls. The distances between stacks will be dictated by access of book trolley. The bottom shelf in closed book stack can be as near to the floor as possible (75 mm) with top shelf not higher than 1·9 m, thus, preferred total height of stack 2·3 m (7 shelves total). See Fig. 4.11.

Housing of outsize books will need separate consideration. It is advisable to allow this on single sided shelves along walls, where little additional space will have no effect on planning.

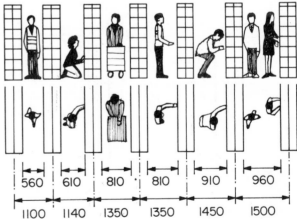

Fig. 4.11 Closed stack—critical sizes

OPEN STACK

In open stack book storage more room must be provided for readers for browsing and cross traffic. This type of shelving is used widely in universities, colleges and organisations where readers have access to book storage. Provision of cross-aisles is important. Bottom shelf height should not be less than 150 mm from floor, top shelf not higher than 1·9 m. The

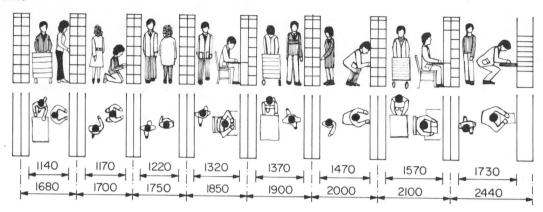

Fig. 4.12 Open stack—critical sizes

maximum height of stack recommended is 2·3 m (7 shelves). Separate space allocation must be made for higher or deeper books. See Fig. 4.12.

If very heavy use is expected or the stack area is very large, main aisles should be minimum 1·5 m wide. In the case of a large library design, the reader is advised to refer to 'Planning and design of library buildings' by Godfrey Thompson.

OPEN ACCESS

This is a most space consuming arrangement of book storage, providing for large numbers of browsing readers, forming large part of public lending, school or hospital libraries. Space must be provided for browsing readers, traffic and trolleys, also areas for reading.

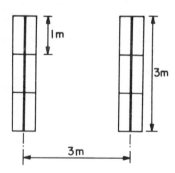

Fig. 4.13 Recommended standard shelving unit

It is recommended to provide approx. 900 mm browsing space in front of shelves and a space of approx. 760 mm beyond this as passage space—a minimum of 2560 mm between shelves. With a stack width of 440 mm (double) it will make up space of 3 mm c/c of stacks. See Figs. 4.14 and 4.15.

The height of island stack should not be more than 1600 mm, and with wall fixed shelving up to 1850 mm, shelf thickness 20 mm, the height of bottom shelf should be 400 mm from the floor (Fig. 4.16). The shelving recommended should have five shelves in 1850 mm and four shelves in 1600 mm

high stack. The vertical distances between shelves will be approximately 270 mm.

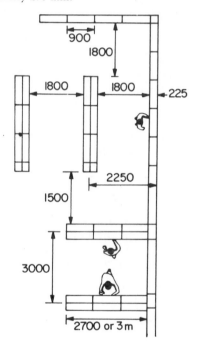

Fig. 4.14 Minimum dimensions in open case book stack

STUDY/READING AREAS

Depending on the aims of a library there will be a fundamental difference between browsing and serious study areas.

The study areas will form a major part of a university or college library and an important part of a public reference library. The space will be determined of course by the number of readers and books to be housed in this area. The most economical layout is one with reading tables in centre, surrounded with shelves round the walls (Fig. 4.17).

In university libraries the stacks (which may be divided by subjects on separate floors) will be surrounded by reading areas. Tables may often be spaced within as well as outside the books stacks (Figs. 4.23 and 4.24).

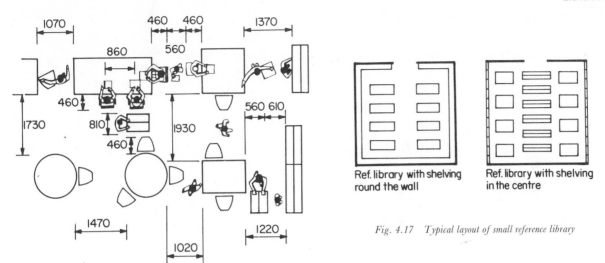

Fig. 4.15   Minimum clearances in reading rooms

Ref. library with shelving round the wall

Ref. library with shelving in the centre

Fig. 4.17   Typical layout of small reference library

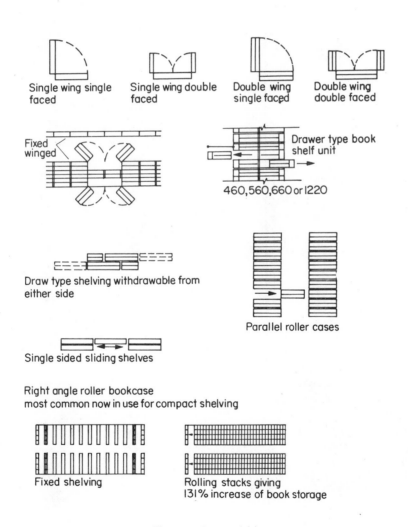

Single wing single faced

Single wing double faced

Double wing single faced

Double wing double faced

Fixed winged

Drawer type book shelf unit

460, 560, 660 or 1220

Draw type shelving withdrawable from either side

Parallel roller cases

Single sided sliding shelves

Right angle roller bookcase most common now in use for compact shelving

Fixed shelving

Rolling stacks giving 131% increase of book storage

Fig. 4.16   Compact shelving

CRITICAL SIZES IN READING AREAS

The recommended size of each individual table is 900×600 mm. If tables are arranged in rows this size will have to be increased to 900×900 mm. Each reader allowance in reading area should be $2 \cdot 3$ m² giving him the share of circulation within the room.

A long table can accommodate up to twelve readers: the width of such a table should be 1200 mm. Seating should not be allowed at ends of tables. It is recommended that long tables should have central division, which can accommodate individual lighting and points for audio-visual equipment. (In this case, side divisions are recommended)

Typical arrangements showing minimum space and table requirements are shown in Figs 4.19 to 4.26.

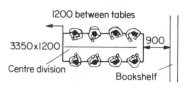

Fig. 4.20   Eight person reading table

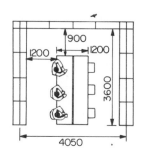

Fig. 4.21   Reading space for alcove

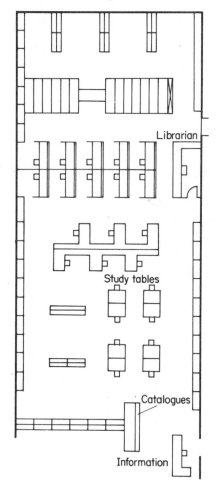

Fig. 4.18   Reference library in medium size branch library

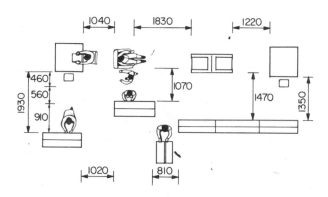

Fig. 4.22   Recommended minimum clearances round tables

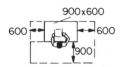

Fig. 4.19   Recommended minimum size for one person table and space

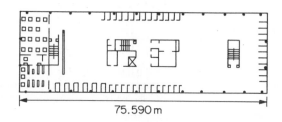

Fig. 4.23   Typical floor of Warwick University library

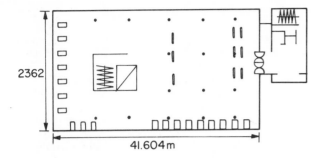

Fig. 4.24   Typical stack at Essex University library

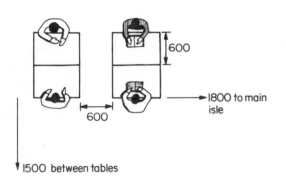

Fig. 4.25   Recommended minimum allowance for one person reading area

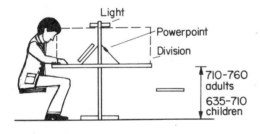

Fig. 4.26   Recommended sizes for reading tables

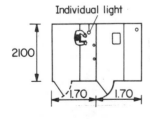

Fig. 4.27   Recommended single person reading carrel, open top or totally enclosed

STUDY CARRELS AND STUDY ROOMS

In addition to open reading areas, provision for study carrels will be necessary for servicing long term readers. Long term may range from a few hours in a small public library to a whole term in a university.

The provision and type of such carrel will vary with degree of separation and privacy needed, and type of equipment needed by the user of this facility. Typewriters, tape recorders and audio-visual equipment may be used in the carrels.

Carrels should be equipped with ample provision of power points, lockable cupboards, coat hanging facilities and in some instances wash basins. Some carrels will have to be soundproofed.

Depending on amount and use of this facility, different types of study carrels (Figs 4.27 to 4.30) are employed, i.e.

Individual tables with screens.
Individual tables in recesses or alcoves.
Individual tables against walls.
Staggered tables with screens.
Semi enclosed carrels.
Enclosed carrels.
Individual rooms.
Double or quadruple carrels.

Several types of carrels are offered by library furniture manufacturers. These types, in most cases, are moveable and are a very valuable addition to standardised type of special library equipment on the market.

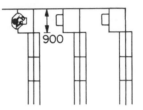

Fig. 4.28   Open carrel for stack area

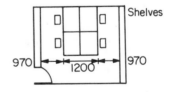

Fig. 4.29   Minimum dimensions for four person carrel room

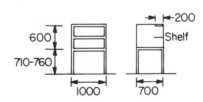

Fig. 4.30   Typical open carrel

READER SERVICE AREAS

All reader areas will be served by staff centres who will: supervise all reader activities, give bibliographical assistance to readers, control the issue and return of books or other material on loan. In very small libraries all these services will be conducted from a centrally located desk.

In very large establishments the issue and return counter may be separated, with remaining services located in other reader areas.

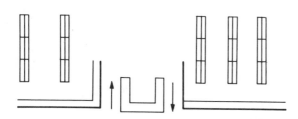

Fig. 4.31   Bottle neck counter—one person control in quiet period

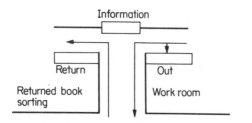

Fig. 4.32   Bottle neck counter—three person (minimum two) at all times

The detail design of counter for return and issue is of very great importance (see Figs 4.31 and 4.32). It is advisable to conduct a study of changing, return, sorting, etc. The range of tasks is small, but they will be repeated annually millions of times, large numbers of books will be handled at peak periods.

The operation of receiving books and placing them for checking and disposal must be conducted without disturbing the flow of readers.

Disposal of books may be arranged by means of trolleys, trolley shelves, book hod trolleys, or conveyor belt connecting the counter and sorting room (Fig. 4.33), or a chute/hoist to lower level.

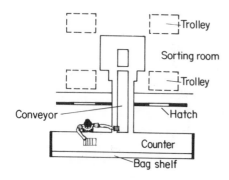

Fig. 4.33   Plan of counter—with conveyor belt to sorting room

INFORMATION

In small libraries this service will be provided at the reception desk. The duty of an information service is to give bibliographical assistance to readers requests. In view of this service, certain books must be close to this service point.

Positions and numbers of such information stations will depend on the size and type of library, but essentially it must be close to cataloguing (whether card or microfilm control) and bibliographical stocks. In large libraries the staff will be consulted by the readers, conduct reservations for books on loan, receive books from closed stacks and hold reserved books —return books to stacks. These activities show that there must be an efficient relationship between information station(s) and other parts of the library, i.e. stack retrieval system, book transfer, document copying, etc.

CATALOGUES

In research libraries or libraries with very large tiered stacks, the catalogue department will be a major bibliographical section on its own.

At present, the majority of libraries will use card cataloguing systems which is space and time consuming and requires large numbers of staff to prepare this type of information (see Figs 4.34 and 4.35). Some libraries have already introduced less space consuming systems, e.g. computerised systems, which require less space and are economical in staffing.

A system of microfilm cataloguing will also save considerable amount of space, but of course this saving will have to be offset by necessity of provision of several microfilm readers. This system is already operational, and used by many libraries throughout the country.

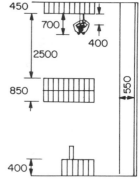

Fig. 4.34   Recommended plan dimensions in card cataloguing area

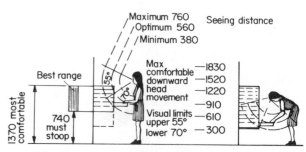

Fig. 4.35   Recommended drawer heights in cataloguing area

ACCOMMODATION

ARCHITECT'S BRIEF

The information given to the architect should normally be in a form which enables him to assess at an early stage the size of departments and of the building in relation to its site. It is important that the architect can carry out this early exercise so as to determine whether a multi-storey building is required to meet the planning problem.

In order to assess the size of the building the following information is essential:

(a) It is necessary to assess the maximum expected number of readers and the times at which the peak periods occur.

(b) The total number of books to be housed in each area of the library.

(c) It must be established what methods will be used for housing the books in the departments i.e. how long the book shelves should be, how many book shelves to each stack, etc. to work out the area required for each book shelf and how many books to each shelf.

(d) It must be decided at the initiation of the project what sort of equipment will be installed in the library.

(e) The client, or the librarian, must make a very early decision as to which services in the building will be provided for the readers, i.e. reading areas, browsing areas, study carrels, study rooms etc. etc. It will be necessary to establish the life expectancy of the building and possibilities of extension and growth, not only of certain areas in the building but also the building itself.

All the information enabling the architect to proceed with his work should be limited and expressed in two values only:

1. Numbers of persons both users of the building and staff serving the users, with very thorough descriptions of their activities.

2. Description of all equipment to be housed in the building.

(All this information should enable the architect to see the library clearly as an operational unit with the environmental conditions to meet the desired aims).

The preliminary brief should also contain a very clear description of the role the library is to play in the community or the parent organisation.

MATERIALS IN THE LIBRARY

The great bulk of material housed in the library will be in the form of books of all sizes, documents, maps, records, audio-visual material, periodicals, newspapers, photographs, prints, broadsheets, cuttings, catalogues, pamphlets, etc. Generally, the books will be housed in two areas of the library:

(a) *Open Areas.* Those which are accessible to the public and certain users of the library.

(b) *Closed Areas.* Those which are not accessible by the public but only used by staff.

The books used in the open areas could be very briefly divided into the following categories:

1. Bibliographical.
2. General reference.
3. Special reference.
4. Adult lending.
5. Children lending.
6. Local history.
7. Music.
8. Arts.
9. Others.

Books which are kept in the closed areas and are accessible by staff, are the surplus books or stored books and may be divided as follows:

10. Local stacks for 3–9 above.
11. General stacks.
12. Compact shelving stacks.
13. Special collections.
14. Extension services stacks.

ACTIVITIES IN THE LIBRARY BUILDING

The activities which are conducted in a library automatically fall into two divisions:

1. Those which are conducted by the public and the users of the library.

2. The ones which are conducted by the staff serving the users.

An exact knowledge of the above activities is necessary to the designer in order that he may assess the size of the areas required. The estimates and forecasts must be made on proportions of users engaged in all sorts of different library activities and information must be obtained as to when these proportions may vary. The designer must obtain the information as to times of opening of the building, the expected peak hours of the use of certain areas, information regarding peak days in a week and in the year, (this will apply particularly to educational institutions).

One of the most important pieces of information will be the number of readers in each section or area in the library at normal and peak hours. It is also of some validity to obtain the information on length of time of stay in different departments of the library and the required number of places for seating and reading.

ASSOCIATED ACTIVITIES

At present, library buildings provide not only for the essential activities of lending and reading books but also for many associated activities, which can be conducted in the library buildings and provide educational and information facilities.

The architect must obtain the information whether it is necessary to provide areas for the following functions:

Story hour room. The size of this area to be assessed from the number of children attending.

Creative activity rooms.

Language learning areas.

Meeting rooms, for committees and associations.

Lecture rooms, with facilities for transparency and film showing.

Areas for musical recitals.

Art and trade exhibitions.

FACILITIES FOR READERS

Depending on the size of the library establishment, it will be necessary not only to provide the facility of lending and reading, but also to provide more sophisticated facilities for obtaining information, which would involve in some cases very complicated and sophisticated electronic equipment. This information must be decided upon from the initiation of the brief. These facilities may be as follows:

(a) Document copying by means of photographing equipment or Xerox which would need not only room for equipment but also will affect the supply of electricity.

(b) The building may be equipped with telecommunication facilities, i.e. cameras and television screens.

(c) It may be necessary to provide video tape reproduction facilities which may not only be visual but also audio and in this case special areas would have to be assigned for this facility.

(d) Microfilm viewing equipment although not very bulky would require electrical supplies.

(e) The information must also be obtained whether any sales would be conducted in the building, i.e. scripts, soft backs, copies of documents, etc. and what area provisions may be necessary for this facility.

(f) *Display.* It is also necessary to obtain information as to whether there is intention to provide facilities for art and poster displays and exhibitions, which would include for example displays of posters for local activities.

PUBLIC FACILITIES

These facilities do not differ in requirements from any other kind of building in which large numbers of people gather. In some cases it may be necessary to supply further facilities for refreshments, minimum requirements being provision of vending machines, to snack bar or cafeteria.

If it is envisaged that the users of the library will stay in the building for longer periods it will be necessary to provide cloakrooms, for storage of outdoor clothing and belongings, and of course, lavatories. This provision should be in accordance with an appropriate Code of Practice but it is advisable in larger libraries to have this facility not only at the entrance but also scattered throughout the building, adjacent to large concentrations of readers/users. In some cases it will be necessary to provide first aid rooms and/or ladies rest rooms.

Pram Parking. In the case of a public library which may be used by a wide variety of people it is most advisable to provide parking facilities for prams and bicycles, as well as car parking for staff.

Shops. In some cases the library may want to conduct selling of documents, copies etc. In this case, the decision whether to provide shop facilities must be established at a very early stage.

Access for disabled persons. An early decision must be made as to which activities are accessible for disabled persons, other than statutory provisions.

STAFF ACTIVITIES

Staff on duty serving the reader. The number of staff on duty to serve readers and users of the library must be determined early in the formulation of the brief. This will mean the establishment of numbers engaged at the security points through-out the library, and number of staff engaged in issuing and receiving the returned books. It will also determine the number of staff engaged at information points or desks and also at enquiry desks. There may also be other staff engaged on different undefined activities serving the readers.

Staff engaged in external activities. With the exception of very small branch libraries there will be a number of staff engaged in other activities than serving the readers. This will apply to central libraries, county libraries, university libraries etc.

There may be a number of staff engaged in:

School library services;

Welfare library services;

Hospital library services, etc.

In the case of a very large library there may be areas for privileged readers which would have to be staffed specially. Some of the larger libraries may have mobile library services (for old people or housing estates). In some libraries there will be areas for readers with special technical services which also have to be served by specialised staff.

STAFF ACCOMMODATION

In addition to staff directly serving the users, there may be a number of staff engaged in areas in a variety of activities. The number of staff should be established and based on peak time requirements. Separate administration offices must be provided for clerical staff, administration and machine operators.

There will be a number of executive offices and secretarial offices. It must be established how many staff will be engaged in the following areas:

Acquisition areas	Which will employ staff in the checking of materials against orders and execute the preliminary processing of materials.
Cataloguing areas and typists	Raw materials will be classified and entered in the catalogues.
Processing areas	Where the material is plated and numbered.

Post room.
Telex room.
Telephone room.
Work rooms.
Photographic laboratory.
Bindery and repair room.
Printing.
Art studio.

SECONDARY STAFF ACCOMMODATION

Having established as precisely as possible numbers of staff engaged in the proposed library building, it will be necessary to establish the accommodation required for staff facilities and additional staff who will be engaged in activities not connected directly with the library function. It will also be necessary to establish the number and size of cleaners' stores throughout the building. In addition it is important to finalise the methods of security and provision for the security staff.

From the total numbers of staff it will be necessary to assess provision for rest accommodation, separate facilities for male and female clerical staff and male and female porters and cleaners. It is customary to provide rest rooms, tea rooms and kitchens for all staff engaged in the library. Provision of lavatories and locker rooms has also to be established from the total number of staff.

In view of the nature of the library building it must be remembered that provision of store rooms is very important, especially if the library caters also for other cultural activities, such as meeting/lecture rooms etc.

STATUTORY REQUIREMENTS, LEGISLATION AND AUTHORITIES

There are no special statutory requirements concerning libraries. The buildings will be classed depending on its location and ownership, public buildings, educational or offices, if attached to commercial organisations etc. The architect or the designer of the library is advised here to follow the recommendations as listed in the 'Architects Job Book Stages A–F' (current issue), published by the RIBA.

Consents Building Regulations B2b/4
         Undertakings B2b/5
         Party Walls B2b/6

The latest information on trends and recent developments can be obtained from,

The Library Association,
7 Ridgmount Street,
London WC1E 7AR

The Department of Education & Science,
Library Advisors, Library Division,
Art and Libraries Branch,
38 Belgrave Square,
London. SW1X NR

The Department of Education & Science,
Architects and Buildings Branch,
38 Belgrave Square,
London SW1X 8NR

EXAMPLES OF RECENT LIBRARY BUILDINGS

Library and Public Hall, West Norwood, London
    Lambeth Borough Council Department of Architecture & Planning. *Arhcitects Journal* (17 September, 1969).
University of Hull Library
    Castle Park Dean Hook. *Architects Journal* (27 January, 1971).
Library at Trinity College, Dublin
    Ahrends, Burton & Koralek. *Architects Journal* (11 October, 1967) and 26 July, 1972.
Library at Glasgow University
    William Whitfield. *Architects Journal* (16 April, 1969).
Library at the University of Durham
    George C. Pace (Consultant Architect). *Building* (29 November, 1968).
Extensions to Cambridge University Library
    Gollins, Melvin Ward Partners. *Architects Journal* (23 August, 1972).

Library for Kent University
    Farmer & Dark. *Architects Journal* (23 August, 1972).
Wallsend Borough Council Library
    Williamson, Faulkner Brown & Partners. *Architect & Building News* (8 February, 1967).
Library at the University of Edinburgh
    Sir Basil Spence, Glover & Ferguson. *Architects Journal* (19 June, 1968).
Library at the University of York
    Robert Matthew, Johnson-Marshall & Partners. *Architects Journal* (8 May, 1968).
Library at Sunbury-on-Thames for Surrey County Council Education Committee
    B. L. Adams in association with Raymond Ash (County Architect). *Architects Journal* (3 January, 1968).
Finsbury Library, London E.C.1
    Franck & Deeks. *Building* (21 April, 1967).
Horley Central Library for Surrey County Council
    Howard V. Lobb & Partners. *Building* (16 December, 1966).
Library at West Byfleet for the Surrey County Council in conjunction with Norwich Union Insurance Societies
    Scott Brownrigg & Turner. *Architect & Building News* (24 August, 1968).
Library at the University of Warwick
    Yorke Rosenberg & Mardall. *Architects Journal* (23 November, 1966).
Bourne Hall Library & Social Centre for the Borough of Epsom & Ewell
    A. G. Sheppard Fidler & Associates. *Building* (17 April, 1970) and *The Architect* (19 March, 1970).
Great Missenden Library, Haddenham Library, Burnham Library
    Buckinghamshire County Architects Department, (County Architect, Fred Pooley). *Architects Journal* (20 February, 1974).

BIBLIOGRAPHY

LIBRARY PLANNING—GENERAL

Brawne, Michael, *Libraries: architecture and equipment*, Pall Mall Press (1970).
Library Association, *Better Library buildings: architect/librarian co-operation in their design*, London and Home Counties Branch (1969).
Library Association, *Library buildings: design and fulfilment*, London and Home Counties Branch (1967).
Library Association, *Design for reading: papers given at the Annual Weekend Conference, 1969*, S.W. Branch, 1969.
Library buildings, 1965, Library Association (1966).
Library buildings, 1966, Library Association (1967).
Library buildings, 1967/68, Library Association (1969).
Library buildings, 1972, Library Association (1973).
Marples, David L. and Knell, K. A., *Circulation and library design: the influence of 'movement' on the layout of libraries*, Cambridge (Engineering Department Cambridge University (1971).
Orr, James M., *Designing library buildings for activity*. Deutsch (1972).

LIBRARIES

Reynolds, John D., *The Future of library buildings: a feasibility study for a research project*, Library Association (1968).

Thompson, Anthony, *Library buildings of Britain and Europe*, Butterworth (1963).

Thompson, Godfrey, *Planning and design of library buildings*, Architectural Press (1973).

UNIVERSITY AND COLLEGE LIBRARIES

Department of Education and Science, *The design of libraries in colleges of education*, HMSO (1969).

Langmead, Stephen and Beckman, M., *New library design: guide lines to planning academic library buildings*, Wiley (1970).

Library Association, *Libraries in the new polytechnics*, Library Association Record (September 1968).

PUBLIC LIBRARIES

Berriman, Sidney G., and Harrison, K. C., *British public library buildings*, Deutsch (1966).

Danish State Library Inspectorate, *Public library buildings: standards and type plans for library premises in areas with populations of 5000–25 000*. Library Association (1971).

Galvin, Hoyt R. and Van Buren, M., *The small public library building*, UNESCO Paris (1959).

Loren, B. W. *(A. G. Sheppard Fidler & Associates). Completed Architectural Studies in Polish University in Liverpool and London in 1951. Elected RIBA in 1962. Experience with GLC and private practices in London, 1951–1964. Joined A. G. Sheppard Fidler & Associates in 1964, Associate in practice 1970. Responsible for part of practice dealing with council housing, libraries—Bourne Hall Library and Social Centre for Epsom and Ewell Borough Council, and Central Library for Borough of Lewisham.*

5 ANIMAL HOUSING (BREEDING AND RESEARCH)

C. E. BAGWELL-PUREFOY, A.A. Dip., F.R.I.B.A.

INTRODUCTION

GENERAL

The demand for animals for use in medical and scientific research is considerable and calls for high standards of accommodation and environment.

Animal house design involves the closest team working with the client and on no account should design work proceed until sufficient and common agreement has been reached. A considerable onus falls on the client to prepare a clear brief, and the architect and consultants should be given the earliest opportunity to partake in discussions as members of the design team. Suggestions for the structure of a suitable planning group to deal with animal house designs, are given in '*The Laboratory Animal*' (Academic Press) in Chapter 6, 11B, see Bibliography.

It is equally important to refer to the specialist publications available (see Bibliography). The information and advice which these contain provides essential background material and should be familiar to any architect and consultant concerned with the design of an animal house.

CATEGORIES AND STANDARDS OF ANIMAL HOUSES

Animal houses may be divided into three main categories:

(i) *Breeding and holding units.* Where animals are bred and then held in readiness for experimental purposes elsewhere.

(ii) *Experimental animal units.* Where experimental work is carried out on animals received from breeding and holding units.

(iii) *Combined breeding, holding and experimental units.* This is a common arrangement but, where space and siting conditions permit, it is always better practice to house breeding and holding units and experimental units in separate buildings to reduce the risks of cross-infection and because environmental and other requirements may be very different.

A basic function of an animal house is to enable a 'barrier', partly physical, partly environmental and also assisted by other controls, to be created around the animals. This is to protect them from those infections commonly present in other animals and which prove a hindrance to effective experimental work.

The barrier principle, which will become familiar to architects at an early stage of design discussions, is represented by the whole spectrum ranging from the basic protection offered by four walls and a roof to the relative sophistication of a germ-free isolator (See 'SPF Units' below). In practice most animal houses fall well within this spectrum and these may be broadly classified under two headings: conventional and SPF (Specific-Pathogen-Free).

The following notes apply particularly to breeding units, although the barrier and operational principles described for conventional animal houses apply equally to experimental units. In both types of unit the highest standards of general animal health are aimed at together with the exclusion of extraneous infection.

CONVENTIONAL ANIMAL HOUSES

The following characteristics apply, all of which contribute to the barrier:

(i) The maintenance of the inside of the building, particularly the animal rooms, at a positive pressure to the ambient air. This is fundamental practice in any animal house and is the chief means of preventing the entry of infection, although for infected or smelly animals the pressure will be negative. High rates of air change will also be provided. These assist the barrier and provide the means of reducing animal odour. Some filtration of the supply air will be necessary.

(ii) The arrangement of the plan and circulation to avoid the proximity and cross flow of 'clean' and 'dirty' animals and goods.

(iii) The need for staff and visitors to change into protective top clothing. Visitors having no good reason to enter the animal house will be discouraged.

(iv) The provision of adequate cage and bottle washing and sterilising facilities.

The development of SPF animals represents the major advance in animal breeding techniques during the past twenty years. The International Committee on Laboratory Animals (ICLA, 1964) has defined SPF animals as 'animals that are free of specific micro-organisms and parasites, but not necessarily free of the others not specified', and their function and needs are fully described in the UFAW Handbook and other publications listed (see Bibliography).

The barrier features for maintaining such animals will be more rigorous than for conventional animals and may be summarised as follows:

(i) In addition to positive air pressures and high air-change rates, the supply air will be finely filtered.

(ii) A rigorous 'clean' and 'dirty' discipline must be observed in terms of planning and general operation. All animals and goods will be passed into and out of the SPF zone via air locks, dunk tanks and autoclaves or gas chambers.

(iii) Staff and visitors will be rquired to take a shower and change into clean clothing on entering the SPF zone. Visitors will only be allowed inside in exceptional circumstances.

(iv) Similar cage and bottle washing facilities will apply to those in a conventional animal house. Cages and bottles, etc., will be sterilised in the autoclaves linking the SPF and outer zones.

Two refinements should be noted which effectively bring the barrier close to the animal; these are filter racks and germ-free isolators. Filter racks (see *The Laboratory Animal*, Chap. 6V A, pp. 131–2 and *UFAW Handbook*, Chap. 6, p. 79; see Bibliography) incorporate their own filtered and treated air supply which is passed over or through each cage. Germ-free isolators (*UFAW Handbook*, Chap. 11) provide the only absolute barrier around the animals. These are sealed plastic or metal containers with their own sterile and treated air supply and which incorporate gloves for internal manipulation. SPF units are normally stocked initially with animals which have been caesarian derived within such isolators.

A mystique has undoubtedly grown around the term SPF, although doubts are now frequently expressed about the effectiveness of the SPF barrier in the absolute terms which were originally aimed at and which the term itself implies. It must be realised that hazards will always be present no matter how many precautions are taken and perhaps the greatest of these is the human factor.

Although SPF remains a controversial definition, the need for clean animals has become the generally acceptable standard and it is perhaps true to say that the margin between conventional and SPF animal houses is becoming blurred. Animal houses which aim to achieve SPF conditions are now sometimes described simply as Barrier Maintained Units and this label may be preferred, being less presumptuous in terms of what is likely to be achieved.

It may be appropriate to comment that, particularly in times of inflationary building costs, attempts to achieve a totally effective physical barrier in building and constructional terms may prove to be excessive. If the efficiency of this aspect of the barrier is, in any case suspect, clients and architects may be well advised to adopt a less rigorous approach to this type of building.

The most commonly used laboratory animals may conveniently be divided into two main groups; small and large. These two groups will include the following species:

Small animals	*Large animals*
Mice	Sheep
Rats	Pigs
Guinea Pigs	Goats
Hamsters	Other farm animals
Rabbits	Cats
Ferrets	Primates
etc.	etc.

Small animals will be housed in cages arranged on either wall-mounted or mobile, floor-standing racks. It is possible for the majority of small animal rooms to be planned identically and it is clearly helpful that they should be arranged in the interests of flexibility. Their shape will be governed by the preferred cage-rack layout, i.e. lining the walls, in peninsular or island form or a combination of these and will be directly influenced by the need to achieve consistent and draught-free air movement relative to all the cage positions.

Large animals will normally be housed in individual pens and a number of these may be included in one room. It is therefore equally possible for at least some of the large animal rooms to be planned identically. Although the majority of animal accommodation will comprise these two categories of animal rooms, certain species will require specialist accommodation. The most common of these are as follows.

Primates (see page **5**–7, (iii))

Primates, in common with all other mammals, are subject to strict quarantine regulations under the Rabies (Importation of Mammals) Order, 1971 and are also associated with infection risks to humans which are not all yet fully understood. Primate units must therefore be planned to be self-contained and self-supporting in terms of cage washing etc., and will also incorporate security features to prevent escape.

Cats (see page **5**–7, (iv))

Although it is possible to house cats in standard small animal rooms, larger cat colonies will require special accommodation which will allow them to roam freely within larger areas.

Dogs (see page **5**–7, (v))

Where larger quantities of long-stay dogs are required a special unit must be provided, including an exercise area. The accommodation must be acoustically treated to avoid disturbance from barking to internal and external surrounding areas.

Other animals

It is conceivable that accommodation may be required for any species of animal and, in the case of rarer species, guidance can only be obtained from the client. The UFAW Handbook contains accommodation data for a wide range of species of laboratory animals and it will nearly always be possible to house these in standard animal rooms.

FARM ANIMALS

The Agricultural Research Council and other authorities have established a number of units for research on farm animals. In these and similar cases, where there is little or no risk of infection, normal farm conditions and accommodation needs will be suitable (see *Planning: Buildings for Habitation, Commerce and Industry*). Laboratories and other research facilities for such units will normally be housed in separate buildings.

At the Animal Virus Research Institute, Pirbright, however, where research is carried out on foot and mouth and other animal virus diseases, the most stringent security precautions are applied, calling for specialised planning and environmental control (see Examples and Bibliography at the end of this section).

SITING

Ideally, independent animal units should be sited in open, rural areas well away from sources of atmospheric pollution. This is partly to reduce the risk of outside infection and also to ensure maximum life for the air filtration plant but it should be realised that air pollution can be heavy even in the country, especially down wind from towns.

Many animal units have been developed on farm sites and these undoubtedly provide the most satisfactory location in terms of environment and amenity.

Where animal houses form an integral part of a medical school, hospital or large research establishment, such a complex may well be located in an urban area where the disadvantages will be obvious but unavoidable. In these cases it may be possible to locate the accommodation at the top of one of the higher blocks, although this may call for planning on more than one level. A better solution, particularly where the need for animals is a large one, would be to provide the accommodation at basement level. Either a high- or low-level location has the advantage of more efficient isolation, but at basement level it should be possible to provide a greater spread of single-level accommodation.

Wherever an animal house is situated, provision must be made for regular bulk deliveries of food and bedding requiring access for lorries up to 8–12 tons in weight.

The siting of the access area, which will presumably include the animal, goods and staff entry points, needs careful consideration, particularly on congested sites. The animal entry point must be sited as discreetly as possible and on hospital sites there must be maximum separation between hospital and animal house traffic. In rural areas the location of entry points will present less of a problem although, if the animal house is overlooked by private houses or other buildings, the arrangement of the entrances must be equally discreet.

The problem of smell has obvious siting implications, particularly on congested sites, although this will largely be a matter of efficient ventilation design and careful location

of the extract grilles. Because the ventilation system relies on fine filtration of the supply air, it is also important to site the air intake grilles carefully in relation to obvious sources of airborne particles such as incinerator and boiler flues. It should be remembered that an animal house may well be located near to an incinerator in order to reduce the movement of carcasses and soiled goods for disposal.

In rural areas a high perimeter fence will probably be needed to exclude foxes and other animals.

PLANNING

Figs. 5.1 and 5.2 show by means of flow diagrams the essential circulation required for a conventional animal house and an SPF or barrier maintained unit. In addition the *UFAW Handbook* (Fig. 5.2) and *The Laboratory Animal— Principles and Practice* (Figs. 5.5, 5.6 and 5.7) should be consulted. The Architects Journal Information Sheet No. 1597 is also devoted to experimental animal housing and includes (see Fig. 1) a diagram indicating the circulation requirements of a barrier maintained unit based upon a two corridor system (see below).

The following points should also be taken into account:

(a) The circulation must be arranged to minimise contact between 'clean' and 'dirty' animals and goods, thereby reducing the risk of cross-infection. A two-corridor system to serve the animal rooms is sometimes adopted whereby clean animals and goods enter at one end and leave via a dirty corridor at the other end. Such duplication, however, is extravagant and must be justified in terms of operational efficiency. In a one-corridor system all animals and goods enter and leave the animal rooms by the same doors and the risk of cross-infection is reduced by avoiding the coincidence of clean and dirty traffic movement. So far there is no convincing evidence to show that this is less satisfactory than a two-corridor system.

An effective compromise is sometimes adopted whereby dirty material is passed outside the building through airlocks at the ends of the animal rooms and then moved via an external covered way.

(b) Operational efficiency will be improved by deep planning and by arranging the accommodation on the fewest number of storeys. Ideally, an animal house should be planned on one level (excluding plant rooms) although site restrictions and the size of unit will not always make this possible. The minimal need for windows will also assist in deep planning.

(c) Accommodation which presents potential infection hazards, i.e. Quarantine Rooms, Post-mortem Rooms, Infected Animal Rooms, etc., should be located away from the other animal rooms and should be directly associated with the 'dirty' circulation route to the cage cleaning and disposal areas.

(d) Unnecessary movement of large animals within the animal house should be avoided and their accommodation should be closely related to the Operating Theatre suite.

(e) Animals should be protected from either continuous or sudden sources of noise, both of which will affect their breeding performance and general health. This factor should be taken into account when planning. Background music has been provided at the new SPF unit for the National Institute for Medical Research at Mill Hill, partly as a staff amenity and partly as a means of lessening the effects of sudden noise upon the animals.

(f) There may well be conflict between the achievement of the barrier in terms of planning and the provision of adequate means of escape. It is therefore essential to consult the Fire Authorities at a relatively early stage of planning.

(g) In order to limit the spread of potential infection it is preferable to think in terms of a large number of small rooms for animals rather than a small number of large rooms. It should be possible to accommodate the majority of the animal population of an animal house in rooms of standard size, no matter how varied the species.

EXPERIMENTAL ANIMAL HOLDING UNIT

The principles illustrated in Fig. 5.1 apply equally to conventional breeding units.

It is desirable for the entry points for animals, staff and goods to be planned separately, although these can be grouped into a common area.

The staff entry may be designed to form part of the peripheral barrier and, in addition to locker rooms and toilets, may include showers and certainly an area for changing into protective top clothing. Showers may in any case be needed as an amenity, even if not part of the barrier.

Animals will be examined in the Reception Area and, if necessary, be kept in the Quarantine Area. They will then be passed from either of these areas directly to the Animal Holding Rooms.

Goods will be delivered directly into the Storage Area and food and bedding may be required to be sterilised before being passed through to the Animal Rooms. The cages will also be washed and sterilised before use and there is therefore an important relationship between the Storage and Cleaning Areas.

The Animal Rooms will be closely related to the laboratories and Operating Theatres and carcasses and soiled goods from these areas will either be passed to a local disposal area or removed for disposal elsewhere. The disposal area or exit point should be planned well away from the entry area.

Dirty cages from the Animal Rooms will be taken directly to the Cleaning Area and then back to the Animal Rooms. Whether a one- or two-corridor system is used, the circulation between the Animal Rooms and Cleaning Area and within the Cleaning Area itself should be arranged so that 'clean' and 'dirty' traffic is effectively segregated. In the Cleaning Area this may be achieved by adopting a one-way system progressing from 'dirty' to 'clean'.

When animal drinking bottles are to be washed and sterilised in bulk, they will follow the same route as the dirty cages, although these are often washed in the Animal Rooms themselves.

In addition to the principal areas described, an Office and Mess Room will certainly be required and a Workshop will be needed if workshop facilities are not available elsewhere.

All the accommodation shown in Fig. 5.1 is related to a Common Area which could either represent a system of corridors or a concourse which might be planned on a semi-open basis to include the Storage and Cleaning Areas.

SPF OR BARRIER MAINTAINED UNIT

The same planning principles illustrated in Fig. 5.1, likewise apply to Fig. 5.2, but the requirements are intensified by the

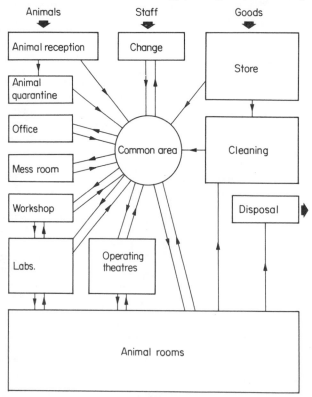

Fig. 5.1   Experimental animal holding unit

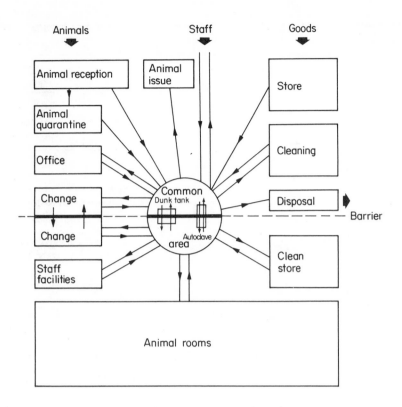

Fig. 5.2   SPF or barrier maintained unit

need to maintain the Animal Rooms, the Clean Storage Area, Staff Facilities, etc., behind a much more rigorous barrier. Basically this involves providing a physical barrier incorporating double-ended autoclaves or gas chambers and a dunk tank. All animal goods, bedding and cages are sterilised in the autoclaves on entering the clean zone and other articles are bagged and passed through the dunk tank which contains disinfected liquid and a baffle plate. Details of a dunk tank are shown in *Laboratory Animal Symposia, etc.,* p. 93, Fig. 2; see Bibliography.

Animals for issue are passed out of the clean zone via air locks and dirty cages, soiled bedding, refuse, etc., are passed out through the autoclaves after each run.

Staff are required to pass through a special changing and shower area which forms an essential part of the barrier. Here they strip off on the dirty side, shower and then change into sterile clothing on the clean side. On leaving the clean zone the process is reversed without the need for a shower.

In order to reduce the entry and exit of staff it is normal to provide a small Mess Room and toilet facilities within the clean zone.

SPACE REQUIREMENTS

INTRODUCTION

The Client will wish to offer direct advice about detailed planning requirements and their interpretation, particularly for the animal rooms. The following notes therefore offer guidance on the approach to planning each of the areas described rather than specific dimensional advice. Reference

should be made, however, to *the UFAW Handbook* and to the *Guidance Notes on the Law Relating to Experiments on Animals.* Both publications set out recommended areas and dimensions for a wide variety of laboratory animal accommodation.

ANIMAL ROOMS

(i) *Small animal rooms*

These will form the greater part of the animal accommodation in any animal house and should therefore be planned on standard lines. Although there may be a requirement for some variation in size most, if not all of the small animal rooms can be planned identically. The main considerations are:

(a) Rooms should be relatively small to limit the spread of infection.

(b) Cage racks should be arranged to achieve adequate and consistent ventilation to all cages.

(c) Dimension between cage racks must allow a technician with a trolley to manoeuvre freely in order to service cages and animals; i.e. cleaning, watering, feeding, etc.

(d) The inclusion of a sink for bottle washing and filling and, ideally, a bench for minor operative procedures on smaller animals.

(e) The height of the room should allow for the proper functioning of the ventilation system relative to the animal cages. A minimum of 2743 mm is recommended. Figs. 5.3 to 5.6 show different arrangements of small animal rooms.

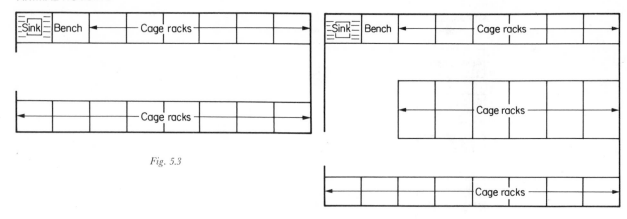

Fig. 5.3

Fig. 5.4

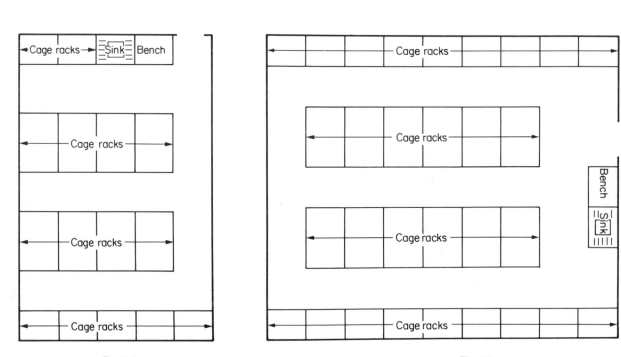

Fig. 5.5

Fig. 5.6

(ii) *Large animal rooms*

Large animals will normally be housed in individual pens divided by in-situ, half-height partitions and served by a central corridor. Rooms containing up to twelve pens are suitable and can conveniently be included in animal houses containing mixed accommodation. The main considerations are:

   (a) The service corridor must be wide enough for the animals to be manoeuvred on trolleys.

   (b) The pen partitions should be of solid construction and these and all surfaces should be capable of being regularly washed down. Tubular steel gates are suitable and allow animals in opposite pens to see each other. This is important with common species. It may be desirable, however, to divide some pairs of pens with removable partitions in order to create larger pens for larger animals.

(c) Drainage will normally be via a continuous floor channel in the corridor with a removable grating. This can either be served by gulleys with removable baskets or by flushing gulleys for the direct disposal of faeces. An 'asian' closet at floor level in a separate bay may assist the disposal of larger quantities of faeces.

(d) Falls to animal pen floors for drainage may be required but these are not always satisfactorily achieved and are superfluous if the floors are regularly swept and squeegeed.

(e) Low temperature underfloor heating may be desirable, perhaps with a raised section of the floor to act as a bed. These are strictly matters for client decision.

(f) Ceiling or high level wall fixings may be required over each pen for infra-red heaters and power points should be provided regularly at approx. 2500 mm above floor level for automatic shears, cleaning equipment etc.

(g) Rooms which are to accommodate short-stay dogs should be acoustically treated to reduce noise transmission internally, and externally.

(h) A writing surface (perhaps a hinged flap) may be required in the animal rooms but sink and bench facilities will be more suitably located in an adjacent common area.

(iii) *Primate suites*

Primates are subject to quarantine and security controls under the Rabies Order and, if they are to be included as part of a general animal house, their accommodation must be planned as a self-contained suite.

(a) Entry points to the suite must be protected by pairs of doors controlled with electrical interlocks.

(b) It is usual for primate rooms to be comprehensively fitted out by specialist firms, including cages, drainage and animal watering systems. The cages may be arranged in one or two rows and can either be suspended from the ceiling or, more usually, bracketed from the walls. Wall fixings must be taken into account when designing walls and partitions.

(c) Primate cages will be washed in a special dip tank or washer (see data on page 5–9) which can either be accommodated in a cage cleaning room or, more economically, in a bay forming part of the general circulation.

(d) The cages will normally be transported between the rooms and the dip tank or washer by means of a fork-lift truck. The truck will require a parking space and door opening sizes, corridor widths and, in particular, the space in front of the cage racks must be carefully considered to allow the truck to be manoeuvred freely. It is equally important to ensure that ventilation trunking and diffusers do not interfere with the truck when loaded and in the raised position.

(e) Primate suites will normally include independent laboratory facilities and separate staff changing rooms. Toilets, including showers, should also be provided. Separate food storage may be required but it is acceptable for primate food to be kept in the central food store.

(iv) *Cat breeding units*

Accommodation for cat breeding is still experimental and examples of this building type are few. The *UFAW Handbook* (4th ed.) Chap. 28, provides a comprehensive survey of accommodation needs, including dimensional data and diagrams based upon two existing units. *Laboratory Animals Symposium* 1, pp. 97–112, should also be consulted.

A major unit for a cat breeding colony under barrier maintained conditions has recently been completed for the National Institute for Medical Research at Mill Hill. This is a relatively advanced type of building and may set the pattern for future cat units (see Examples at the end of this section).

Where cats are to be housed in general animal accommodation, they may be held in standard rooms although these should be provided with opening windows protected with wire screens. If possible, the windows should be located to permit the cats to have an external view. Ideally, such rooms should have access to external runs.

(v) *Dog units*

Reference should be made to *Laboratory Animals Symposium* 1, pp. 97–112, and the Architects Journal Information Sheet No. 1599. Both of these publications provide comprehensive data for dog accommodation.

Where dog units are situated near to residential areas, care must be taken to ensure that barking does not cause a nuisance, particularly at night. In such cases, not only must the building, including external doors and windows, be acoustically designed, but air intake and extract louvres must be fitted with sound-attenuating filters. If dog pens are to be included as part of general animal accommodation, the rooms containing them must be separated acoustically from the rest of the building by providing thicker walls and soundproof doors.

The problem of noise has been carefully studied at the National Institute for Medical Research at Mill Hill where the Dog House has been designed as a self-contained unit, including an Operating Theatre and ancillary rooms (see Examples at the end of this section).

(vi) *Other animal rooms*

Reference should be made to the *UFAW Handbook* for accommodation data for all other species of animals.

OTHER AREAS

Animal reception and examination room

Animals will be examined in this room on arrival and will then either be moved into the Quarantine area or direct to the animal rooms. Recommended features are:

(a) Wall benching and a sink.

(b) A peninsular bench or free standing table for all-round examination and shearing of larger animals. Electric shears can be fed from a ceiling power point above.

(c) An in-situ animal pen with flexible shower fitting for washing large animals.

(d) A ceiling ring for hoisting large animals.

(e) Washable surfaces and floor drainage.

Animal quarantine

The Quarantine area must be divided into a series of small rooms for flexibility of use and to limit the spread of infection. The requirements are:

(a) The Quarantine area should have direct external as well as internal access. Both entries should be arranged as air locks with electrically interlocking pairs of doors.

(b) A lobby should be provided containing a lavatory basin and space for changing into protective top clothing.

(c) Animal rooms should include a cold water point for filling drinking bottles, etc.

Air locks

Air locks will be required at entry points to certain types of accommodation (Primate Units, Quarantine Area, etc.)

and as part of the barrier in SPF or barrier maintained units. Pairs of doors enclosing air locks will sometimes require to be controlled by electrical interlocking devices to ensure that only one door is ever open at a time. The size of air lock will be governed by the largest piece of equipment which will have to pass through it, i.e. trolleys, mobile cage racks, fork lift trucks. The air lock may sometimes include a lavatory basin and hooks for protective top clothing.

Storage areas

The storage rooms should open from a delivery area designed to receive goods directly from goods vehicles.

Separate store rooms will be required for food, bedding and cages and these must be duplicated in the 'clean' areas where goods have been sterilised. Size will depend on the quantity of food and bedding, etc., to be held in stock at any time and the client must clearly specify these quantities (see page 5–13 for recommendations).

Bulk deliveries of bedding and pelleted diet are sometimes made by special vehicles which blow the goods via a flexible hose pipe directly into the store rooms. In such cases the rooms will incorporate points in the external wall to receive hose fixings and, because of the considerable pressure which builds up within the room during delivery, internal access points should be protected by air locks.

Food preparation

Although the majority of laboratory animals will be fed on pelleted and other commercially prepared bulk foods, separate food preparation facilities must be provided if cats, dogs and primates are to be held. These animals may require a minced and cooked diet and a suitably equipped work top with either a separate cooker or built in cooking rings will be necessary. A sink will be required and, in addition to storage cupboards, shelves and a refrigerator, a freezer cabinet will assist the bulk storage of meat and other perishable food. The size of room and equipment will depend entirely on the size of animal unit to be served.

Some animal units prefer to manufacture their own pelleted diet but the necessary equipment is costly and space consuming and other units having experience of this procedure should be consulted before taking a decision.

Cage cleaning area

In a conventional animal house, the cage cleaning area will include sterilisation and washing facilities for cages and size will depend upon the type of equipment to be used and the frequency and extent of washing (see *The Laboratory Animal etc.*, Chap. 6 IIA, 3c and IIIB, g, for guidance). The autoclaves may also be used for sterilising food and bedding if this is a requirement and the cleaning area may include washing facilities for animal drinking bottles if these are to be washed centrally rather than in the animal rooms. In

SPF units sterilisation of cages, bottles, food and bedding will take place in the pass-through autoclaves linking the SPF and outer zones.

The following points should be noted:

(a) The cage cleaning area should be arranged so that used cages progress from a 'dirty' to a 'clean' end, the latter including or having direct access to a clean cage store.

(b) The most effective arrangement can be achieved by using a tunnel cage washer built into a partition which divides the area into a clean and dirty zone. Double ended autoclaves can be arranged to feed into the dirty zone from an adjacent area allowing a complete sterilisation and washing cycle to be followed. Similarly the sterilisation procedure can be by-passed. The autoclaves can also be used independently for sterilising food and bedding.

If tunnel cage washers are used, some cages may have to pass through twice because they are still dirty. A return hatch for this purpose may be necessary.

(c) Where a cabinet cage washer is to be used this should be located to achieve an equally effective dirty and clean flow.

(d) It is usual to include a cage hosing bay in the dirty zone to enable encrusted dirt to be removed prior to passing cages through the washing machine.

(e) If central bottle washing facilities are to be provided, these may either be included in the general cage cleaning area or be closely associated with it. Routine use of the autoclaves may also be needed for sterilising the bottles.

Various bottle washing machines are available and planning and location will depend upon which of these is selected. In many animal houses manual bottle washing and rinsing in a suitably sized sink is preferred. Whichever method is chosen, a general purpose sink should be provided in the cleaning area.

Bottles may be partially or completely replaced by automatic washing which will need its own plumbing.

Pass-through showers

Pass-through shower suites form an essential part of the barrier between SPF or barrier maintained zones and the outer or 'dirty' zones.

The suites comprise shower cubicles arranged to form links between 'clean' and 'dirty' changing areas and the number of suites will depend upon total staff numbers and the division between the sexes. Suitable design of shower suites can greatly increase their capacity for passing staff through quickly.

Corridors

Corridor widths will depend upon the estimated traffic flow and the dimensions of trolleys and equipment which will regularly be moved along them. It is suggested that, generally, the clear width of corridors should not be less than 2 m.

DATA

It is impossible to be precise about types and dimensions of equipment. The choice of equipment will always be a specific matter for the client who will have had wide experience of other units and have firm views in this respect. It must be emphasised to the client, however, that much of the detailed planning cannot proceed until certain initial choices have been made. The chief of these are as follows.

Cage racking and approved layout	This is fundamental and will be decisive in establishing the building layout, planning grid, etc.
Mobile equipment, i.e. standard service trolleys, General animal trolleys, Other trolleys, Fork lift trucks, Mobile X-ray equipment	This will effect circulation widths and heights, and determine vertical, trunking and diffuser heights.
Autoclaves	Double ended autoclaves allowing access to dirty areas may have as much as 1800 lit. capacity for bulk sterilisation and will sometimes be arranged in pairs to provide a 'stand-by' facility.
Cage washer	A fully equipped double washer may require a clear length of 10 m or more, including handling space at either end.
Primates cage dipping tank or front loading washer	It is essential to allow sufficient headroom above the tank to allow cage loading from a fork-lift truck. Front loading washers will require enough space in front for manoeuvre.

The following schedule provides a suggested check list of fixed and loose equipment which would normally be required for an animal house and which will have an impact on planning and space requirements. Only animal rooms and strictly related areas have been included; other areas such as Laboratories, Operating Theatres, Offices, Staff Rooms, etc. are dealt with in other sections of Planning.

Fixed	*Loose*
Cage racking, wall mounted or ceiling hung	Cage racking, mobile
Autoclaves, double ended	Cages, various
Autoclaves, single ended	Germ free isolators
Cage washer, tunnel type	Filter racks
Cage washer, cabinet type	Trolleys, standard
Cage washer, Primates (dipping tank or front loading washer) Bottle Washer	Trolleys for transporting larger animals
Dunk or pass-through tank	Trolleys, hydraulic for pigs
Power outlets, wall mounted	Rodent barriers, and slots.
Power outlets, ceiling level for clippers and dryers	Under bench cupboards
Vacuum points (see remarks in following section on Accommodation)	Fork lift truck and charger
Header tanks for automatic watering systems	
Operating and inspection lamps, wall and ceiling mounted.	
Work tops, shelves and wall cupboards	
Chalk boards and notice boards	
Infra-red lamps (or provision for) above large animal pens	
Ceiling rings for pulleys, and weighing machines.	

ACCOMMODATION

ACCOMMODATION SCHEDULE

The following Schedule includes a comprehensive selection of the accommodation commonly found in experimental or breeding units or a combination of the two. The Schedule applies equally to independent units for primates, cats, dogs, etc., and to quarantine units, all of which need to be self-supporting in terms of sections (iii) to (viii). Variations between different types of animal buildings and their function will therefore occur in Sections (i) and (ii).

(i) Animal Rooms and Associated Areas

Entrance lobby
Animal reception and examination room

Animal quarantine suite
  (a) Quarantine rooms
  (b) Washing and changing lobby

Under the Rabies Order 1971, primates and all other imported mammals must be quarantined for 6 months (vampire bats for life) in specially authorised premises. The suite referred to here provides temporary isolation facilities within the animal house for most or all in-coming animals (unimported).

Animal despatch room
Small animal rooms
Large animal rooms

Primate suite

Primates for research and vaccine production are not normally bred in this country and their accommodation will usually only be included in experimental animal houses. Where large numbers are involved, primates will be housed in an independent building. The importation and holding of primates are both strictly controlled under the Rabies Order involving a statutory period of quarantine in an independent unit and permanent accommodation within the animal house itself.

  (a) Primate rooms
  (b) Laboratory
  (c) Cage cleaning room

  (d) Storage rooms

(The central animal house storage and food preparation facilities may also be used.)

  (e) Staff toilets, changing rooms and showers.
Dog rooms

These animals will only be included in general animal house accommodation where small numbers of short stay animals are required. Larger colonies of these animals will be housed in independent buildings designed to include special rooms with open runs.

Other animal rooms
Infected animal rooms

Radioactive animal suite
  (a) Animal rooms
  (b) Laboratory
  (c) Dispensary and store

This accommodation and the arrangements for the disposal of contaminated material and effluent must comply with the Radioactive Substances Act 1960. The *Guidance Notes on the Law relating to Experiments on Animals*, Section G3–7 item 12(c), should be consulted.

Gnotobiotic animal rooms

The animals are reared in germ-free isolators (see 1, D). These may be accommodated in standard small animal rooms.

SPF animal rooms

SPF Suites are sometimes included as part of general animal accommodation, although in such cases risks to the barrier are considerable.

(ii) EXPERIMENTAL AND SPECIAL AREAS

Laboratories

Conventional chemistry or bio-chemistry laboratory facilities will be appropriate. As minor operative procedures on small animals will take place in the laboratories, bench tops should be finished with an impervious material, i.e. laminate, stainless steel, etc.

Operating theatre suite
  (a) Theatres
  (b) Wash-up room
  (c) Lay-up room
  (d) Anaesthetic room
  (e) Recovery room
  (f) Changing rooms including showers and WCs

The Operating theatre suite will be used for surgery on primates and large animals. The extent and standard of the Suite will depend upon the particular surgical requirements of the animal house. Where complex surgery is envisaged, full hospital standards may be required, although in many cases normal laboratory standards will be sufficient.

Post-mortem room	Standard hospital post-mortem facilities will aplly where large animals are involved. Post-mortem work on small animals may be carried out in the Laboratories or on benches in the small animal rooms.
Cold Room	A standard $+4°C$ cold room may be needed in connection with the post-mortem room including freezer cabinets for cadavers.
Radiology suite	
(a) Radiology room	It is probable that a mobile X-Ray unit will be used in order to reduce movement of the animals. Radiology is therefore more likely to take place in the theatres and in the animal rooms rather than in the Radiology Room which would then simply provide a base for the unit together with bench and sink facilities. Space for record keeping should also be included.
(b) Dark room	Standard dark room facilities will apply. An X-ray processing machine will probably be included and the dark rooms will also provide processing facilities for other photographic work carried out in the animal house.

(iii) Storage Areas, etc.	To calculate sizes see table on page 5-13.
Delivery bay	
Food store	
Food preparation room	
Bedding store	
Cage store	
Equipment and general store	
Cleaning equipment room	
First aid store	
Workshop	
Disposal area	

(iv) Cage Washing Area, etc.	
Cage washing area	
Autoclaves (i)	For central sterilisation of cages, etc.
Autoclaves (ii)	Pass-through autoclaves linking SPF or barrier maintained zones with outer areas.
Clean cage store	In a conventional breeding unit or an experimental unit this might well form part of the 'clean' end of the cage wash room. In SPF units it will be necessary to include a clean cage store on the clean side of the barrier.
Bottle washing area	

(v) Central Staff Changing Areas	
Staff entrance	
Locker rooms	
Changing rooms	
Toilets	
Showers	
Pass-through shower suites	These will apply particularly to SPF and barrier maintained units.

(vi) Administration	
General office and reception Superintendent's office Chief Technician's office	These rooms should be provided with windows.

(vii) Staff Facilities	
Mess room Rest room	These rooms should be provided with windows.

(viii) Plant Rooms

THE BUILDING

Any sound method of building construction will be suitable for an animal house, including some of the better pre-fabricated systems. It is essential, however, when clients are aiming to achieve stringent barrier conditions, that the natural limitations of traditional building methods and materials are recognised. Much can be done to reduce openings and risks of cracking in the periphery of the building, but the barrier, in terms of a seal between inside and outside, can never be absolute. The positive air pressure within the building must be relied upon to overcome any weaknesses in this respect.

Except for offices, staff rooms and some animal rooms (primates, cats, etc.) windows are unnecessary, although some clients find this a difficult point to accept. Where windows are provided in animal areas they should be located to have the least effect on temperature control.

FINISHES AND DETAILS

Finishes should be robust, washable and easy to maintain and, although the cost of achieving these qualities can be high, this is an element of the building where savings are frequently sought. Some general points regarding finishes and other details are:

(i) Gloss paint finishes for walls and ceilings are often preferred, although matt finishes, including high-quality emulsion paint, will be equally serviceable and will avoid streaking in areas where condensation is likely to occur.

(ii) There is a growing interest in the use of sprayed plastic film, particularly in prefabricated buildings where there may be a likelihood of movement in the external walls and partitions. Such material cocoons the internal surfaces and is relied upon to provide a seal across cracks which may occur.

(iii) The walls in the rooms at the Isolation Unit at The Animal Virus Research Institute, Pirbright (completed in 1973) are finished with reinforced fibreglass which has also been successfully applied in abattoirs. This is exceptionally durable material and its high cost was justified where low maintenance and regular washing down were essential in maximum disease security conditions.

(iv) Welded sheet p.v.c. has proved successful as a general floor finish in animal houses, although it becomes slippery when wet and is sometimes criticised for this reason. This material can also be continued up the walls thus enabling wet areas to be effectively tanked. Repairs are simple to carry out by welding in new pieces of material.

(v) Epoxy resin is ideal as a general floor finish but is costly. Epoxy based floor paints, however, are significantly cheaper and have been successfully applied in factories. A decision has been taken to use this material in the new experimental animal house for Cambridge University where it will be applied directly to power-floated concrete.

(vi) Where a deep plan has been adopted with minimal external openings, drying out will be almost impossible without further mechanical assistance. This is an essential point to take into account where impervious finishes are to be used. Experience shows that the only effective means of drying out is to use the permanent ventilation system

at a sufficiently early stage during the construction period. This often causes contractual difficulties, but these can be overcome if the requirements are clarified at tender stage.

(vii) Ledges where dust and dirt can collect should be avoided and all surfaces must be accessible for cleaning, i.e. exposed ventilation trunking should either be fitted closely to ceilings and walls with the joint sealed or have sufficient clearance to allow adequate cleaning. Exposed electrical conduit should be fixed on distance pieces. False ceilings should be avoided in animal rooms.

(viii) Where plant rooms occur directly over animal accommodation careful attention should be paid to detailing where ventilation trunking passes through the floor slab. Flooding can occur in plant rooms and leakage into 'clean' areas presents an extraneous infection hazard.

(ix) External doors and many of the internal doors and corridors will be fitted with removable barriers to prevent the entry and movement of wild rodents. *The Laboratory Animal*, etc. (See Bibliography) illustrates an example of a suitable barrier (Fig. 5.11) and Chapter 6, VI advises generally on the methods of pest exclusion.

DRAINAGE

Liberal washing down is now discouraged in most animal houses because it is realised that this is an effective means of spreading infection. The use of sprayed disinfectant removed with a squeegee or mop is preferred and enables floor drainage to be significantly reduced or omitted altogether from the general animal areas.

Areas where floor drainage is either desirable or essential are listed below:

Large animal rooms	Floor drainage in these rooms may
Primate rooms	also be used as a means of waste disposal by incorporating flushing or macerating systems.

Cage wash and other wet areas
Animal reception and examination room
Animal quarantine rooms
Infected animal rooms
Operating theatres
Post-mortem room

ENVIRONMENTAL CONTROL

Effective mechanical ventilation and air treatment play an essential part in the efficient operation of an animal house providing high rates of air change, differential air pressures and fine filtration of the supply air. The ventilation system is therefore a vital feature of the barrier and, even in the simplest animal house, it is fundamentally good practice to maintain the inside of the building at a positive air pressure. In addition, densely stocked animal rooms create a significant problem in terms of heat gain and humidity levels and it is only possible to achieve the required environmental conditions and control for small animal rooms by the use of full air-conditioning i.e. with cooling and humidity control.

Detailed recommendations for the environmental control of animal houses are to be found in the specialist publications listed in the Bibliography. These also indicate the temperature ranges, humidity levels and recommended air change rates for different species of animals, although it will be up to the client to provide a clear brief about his requirements. The consulting engineer should be invited to take almost as early a role in the design team discussions as the architect.

It is important to emphasise the need for a generous space allowance for the mechanical and associated plant. The building may be divided into a number of zones each of which will require its own plant. The fan motors will be large to overcome the high impedance offered by the air filters and the filter banks themselves will be space consuming. In addition it is common practice to duplicate or split much of the air handling plant to provide a standby facility in case of plant failure.

OTHER SERVICES

Automatic animal drinking watering systems are commonly installed in animal rooms. A header tank is normally required in each room to be served and adequate space must be allowed. Tubing or piping is then run from the tank to supply a valve in each cage or pen.

A central vacuum plant is sometimes installed to feed points arranged at regular intervals in the animal rooms and other areas for cage and general cleaning. The distribution of pipework and outlets will have an impact on planning and it is essential for the whole installation to be readily accessible for maintenance and rodding. The main plant must either be located well away from the animal areas or in a sound-proofed plant room so as to avoid disturbance to the animals. Such installations frequently break down because of wet waste clogging up the vacuum lines and this risk can only be reduced by minimising the number of bends in the pipework distribution. It is because of these problems that users often prefer mobile vacuum equipment. A regular distribution of power outlets will be required for this and other purposes.

Central disinfectant installations serving points throughout the animal house are also common and will require adequate space within the plant room. Where a sterilised water supply is required for animal drinking, there will also be additional space demands in the plant room.

TABLE 5.1

The following table has been based upon information prepared by Dr. Lane-Petter and indicates approximate estimates of staff numbers, storage capacity and cage washing need per 100 m² of small animal room floor area.

	Mice	Rats	Guinea-Pigs	Rabbits
Staff	5	4–5	2.5	1.8
Storage of Consumables (m³)				
food	5	7.5	7	2.5
hay	–	–	12	5
bedding	5.5	5	5	5
Cage-washing weekly (m³)	25–30	45–50	50	50

LEGISLATION

Premises where experiments are carried out on animals are subject to the Cruelty to Animals Act, 1876. The Act is administered by the Home Office with whom such premises must be registered and registration will only be granted when the Home Office Inspector is satisfied that the general proposals do not conflict with current acceptable practice and guide lines laid down. These guide lines are set out in the Home Office Notes on Animal Houses (see Bibliography) which should therefore be given the closest attention.

The Act does not refer specifically to areas concerned with animal breeding but it is normal practice and a matter of courtesy to consult the Home Office about these as well as experimental areas. The Act is described in detail in the I.A.T. Manual, Chap. 1 'The Law and Laboratory Animals' and also in the Research Defence Society's 'Guidance Notes on the Law relating to Experiments on Animals' (see Bibliography).

In addition, primates and other imported mammals are subject to the Rabies (Importation of Mammals) Order, 1971 administered by the Ministry of Agriculture, Fisheries and Food. The Order calls for special security features to be observed when planning and administering the accommodation for these animals (see Sec. 4, B(iii)). Application for authorisation under the Rabies Order should be made to the Animal Health Division of the MAFF.

It is the Client's responsibility to obtain approval of the plans and these should be discussed with the above authorities before the design has been finalised.

EXAMPLES

The MRC Laboratory Animals Centre, Woodmansterne Road, Carshalton, Surrey, will advise generally on animal house design and will offer guidance about good examples of this building type. In addition the Medical Research Council and the Agricultural Research Council operate animal breeding and research units throughout Britain and will be willing to put architects in touch with these establishments. Many of the commercial pharmaceutical and scientific research organisations also operate such units and are always willing to offer advice and to arrange visits.

Chapter 11 of 'The Laboratory Animal, etc.' (see Bibliography) gives details of other laboratory animal centres in Europe and overseas and these organisations should be contacted for similar advice in these countries.

The following list includes a short selection of recently completed animal houses in the UK.

Building	Client	Architect
SPF Unit	The Medical	Cusdin, Burden
Dog House	Research Council,	and Howitt
Cat breeding unit	National Institute	
Primate quarantine unit	for Medical Research, Mill Hill	
SPF unit	The Agricultural Research Council, Institute for Research on Animal Diseases, Compton, Berks.	Triad (Ref. *Architect's Journal*, **156,** No. 41 (11.10.72)

Experimental animal house (1975)	University of Cambridge, Hills Road, Cambridge	Cusdin, Burden and Howitt
Isolation unit for cattle	The Agricultural Research Council, Animal Virus Research Institute, Pirbright, Surrey	Cusdin, Burden and Howitt
Leahurst veterinary field station	Liverpool University	Alan Reiach, Eric Hall & Partners, *Building* (22 Oct. 1971)
Barrier maintained unit	Fisons Ltd., Pharmaceutical Division.	Engineer, Fisons Ltd. Fertilizer Div., Building Projects Group, Felixstowe. (M. F. Woodward, Projects Manager)
Laboratories for the Department of Pathology.	Institute of Animal Physiology, Agricultural Research Council, Babraham, Cambridge.	John Musgrove, *Architects Journal* (29.11.67).
Research Building Edinburgh	Animal Breeding Research Organisation	Sir Basil Spence, Glover and Ferguson, *Architect and Building News*, 6/10/65.

BIBLIOGRAPHY

The publications listed below are particularly recommended and each contains its own bibliography.

Guidance notes on the law relating to experiments on animals, Research Defence Society, London (1972).
　　Essential reading. This publication includes the Home Office Notes on Animal Houses referred to in Section 7, as well as extensive recommendations for accommodation and environmental needs for different species of animals. The Bibliography section is particularly comprehensive.

The UFAW Handbook on the care and management of laboratory animals (4th ed.), Churchill Livingstone (1972).
　　This is the most comprehensive of the books on this subject. Chapter 6 deals specifically with Animal House design and equipment and the chapters on individual species each give details of accommodation needs.

The Laboratory Animal – Principles and Practice, W. Lane-Petter and A.E.G. Pearson, Academic Press.
　　An excellent publication. Chapter 6 is devoted to animal house design, equipment and environmental control in addition to specific information. This book is valuable for the opinions expressed. A comprehensive Bibliography is included and there is much general information of considerable interest.

The design function of laboratory animal houses, R. Hare and P.N. O'Donoghue, Laboratory Animals, London (1968).
　　Contains specific information, suggested layouts, special details, etc.

The I.A.T. Manual of Laboratory Animal Practice and Techniques, D.J. Short and D.P. Woodnott, Crosby Lockwood, London (1969).
　　A well established and much respected publication. Chapter 2 deals specifically with animal house design.

Laboratory Animal Handbooks 7: Control of the Animal House Environment, (ed. T. McSheehy), Laboratory Animals, London (1975).

The following publication, which is not included in any of the above bibliographies, should also be noted.
Lokaler för Försöksdjur. KBS-Rapport Number 34. Stockholm. Kungl. Byggnadsstyrelsen. (Swedish text), (1969).
　　An exceptionally well produced and comprehensive publication containing extensive diagrammatic material.

Report of the Working Party on the Laboratory use of Dangerous Pathogens, Department of Health And Social Security, HMSO., London (1975).

Technical Study No. UDC 727.6 Laboratory Animal Houses, published by The Architects Journal (dated 29.5.68).
　　This includes Information Sheet Nos. 1597–9 which are concerned with floor layouts and accommodation details for rabbits, rodents, cats, dogs and primates.

ACKNOWLEDGEMENT

The author would like to acknowledge the help and guidance he has received from Dr Lane-Petter, Superintendent of the Animal Holding and Breeding Unit, University of Cambridge.

Bagwell-Purefoy, Christopher Edward, *A.A.Dip., F.R.I.B.A. (Principal Associate of Cusdin Burden and Howitt). Educated at Bradfield College and The Architectural School of Architecture. In 1956 joined Easton and Robertson, Cusdin, Preston and Smith. Continued with Cusdin Burden and Howitt as Associate on formation of new practice in April 1965, where he now specialises in Laboratories and Animal Houses. Job Architect for various departments in the University of Cambridge including Department of Pharmacology and Animal House. Also the new Amenity Building and Specific Pathogen Free Animal Breeding Unit for the National Institute for Medical Research, Mill Hill, London and the Exotic Virus Research Laboratory for the Animal Virus Research Institute, Pirbright. He also has conducted research into all categories of experimental animal breeding buildings with special emphasis on specific pathogen free and germ-free techniques.*

6 RESEARCH LABORATORIES

Cusdin Burden & Howitt

INTRODUCTION

GENERAL

The purpose of this section is to provide guidance to architects engaged in the design of research laboratories by stating essential principles and objectives. Special emphasis has been laid upon briefing procedures and the approach to the design concept, while more detailed sub-sections provide a means of checking that all aspects of laboratory design have been adequately considered.

It is not intended to duplicate comprehensive planning and dimensional data already published and this section should therefore be regarded as partly introductory and partly complementary to such material. Details of these publications are included in the Bibliography.

This section applies to conventional research laboratories, i.e. chemistry, biochemistry, biology, physics, including radiochemical and bio-hazardous laboratories, which are to a large extent interchangeable. Laboratories for more specialised research are not dealt with, although much of the advice about planning principles and the recommended briefing procedures will apply equally to these.

BRIEFING

Effective briefing is of paramount importance. Although the responsibility for this lies with the Client, the architect has much to contribute at this stage by ensuring that a clearly understood method for exchanging and recording information exists. It is equally important for the Client to adopt an efficient discipline for decision taking.

Architects and Clients are strongly recommended to adopt either the following or similar procedures to achieve maximum working efficiency during the design stage and a satisfactory end product:

1. The setting up (by the Client) of a Planning Group or Committee which will be responsible for decision taking and matters of policy. The Committee will present the initial brief to the architect and will be responsible for approving the final scheme.

2. The appointment of a Working Party which will be answerable to the Building Committee and be responsible for developing the brief in detail. An important function of the Working Party will be to act as a filter for the other users' accommodation and technical requirements to ensure that these are reasonable and not excessive.

3. User-Client representation can most effectively be achieved by appointing one scientist and one technician to act as spokesmen for the other users, and as the channel of communication for the architect in matters of detail.

4. The earliest agreement by the Working Party to the basic disciplines which will be applied as standards throughout the project and which will fundamentally influence the planning and structure of the building, i.e.:

(a) A planning grid arising from the arrangement, spacing and width of benches.

(b) The method of services distribution.

(c) The composition and frequency of the bench or work 'place'.

(d) The frequency and location of fume cupboards.

(e) The degree of flexibility required.

(f) The basic environmental requirements, i.e. air-conditioning, etc.

5. Use should be made by the Working Party of the Room Data Sheet principle whereby the detailed requirements and content of each room are specifically recorded by the users and ultimately drawn by the architect for approval (see under 'Room Data Sheets' below).

6. The production by the professional team of a Design Concept document which will state the planning principles, the basic disciplines referred to above and include brief specifications for the services installations and the structure.

7. The adoption of a programme of work at the earliest possible stage. This should be prepared by the architect and include time scales for items of Client responsibility. The programme should follow the sequence and procedure set out in the RIBA Plan of Work.

8. Client approval on completion of the Scheme Design Stage should be reached on the basis of clearly agreed documentation. This should include:

(a) The sketch plans.

A. GENERAL AND BUILDING	File Ref. No. .... /	Sheet No. ....

I. FUNCTION & DESCRIPTION OF ACTIVITIES (See Note 1)

8. ITEMS FOR REPROCESSING:
Items: ....
Within Department / Other Department: ....
Transfer Method: ....
Requirements: ....

9. DOORS:
Open in / Open out / Double Swing / Sliding / Lightproof.
Solid / Fully glazed / Half glazed / Small panel / Clear / Clear wired /
   Obscured / Obscured wired.
Furniture: Closer / Hold open / Latch / Lock / Indicator Bolt / Kick Rail /
   Trolley Rail.
Width: Daily use .... Maximum ....

2. POPULATION AND TIME
Normal number: .... Time: ....
Intermittent (max.) number: .... Time: ....

3. CRITICAL DIMENSIONS: (See Note 2)

10. WINDOWS:
To open / Not to open / Limited opening / Sash.
Clear glass / Obscured / Double glazing / Solar control film.
Blackout / Curtains / Sun blind / Venetian blind.
Roof Light / Ventilated Roof Light.
Other : ....

4. RELATIONSHIPS:
(a) Separation essential from ....
        desirable from ....
(b) Proximity essential to ....
        desirable to ....

11. CEILINGS:
Special requirements: ....

5. SPECIAL RISKS:
(a) Protect from: Noise / Vibration / Smell / Damage / Radiation /
     Magnetic fields / Dust / Infection.
(b) Liable to create: Noise / Vibration / Smell / Radiation /
     Magnetic fields / Dust / Infection / Steam / Heat / Noxious gases.
(c) Fire.
(d) Theft.

12. WALLS:
Normal finish / Washable / Splashback.
Buffer rail / ....
Exceptional weight fixed to wall: ....kg.

13. FLOOR:
Normal / Heavy duty.   Carpet.   Non-slip.
Spillage risk: State liquid ....
Anti-static: .... Floor Drain: ....
Exceptional Floor Loading: ....kg/m^2.

6. ITEMS TO BE SUPPLIED AND STORED:
Hardware / Stationery / Food / General Stores / Instruments / Pharmacy /
Inflammable Liquids / Clothing / Animal Food / Animal Bedding /
Animal Cages / ....

14. INSULATION:
Special requirements: ....

7. ITEMS FOR DISPOSAL:
Burnable / Non-Burnable.
Disposal by: Paper Sack / Truck / Macerator / Incinerator.

15. SPECIAL PROVISIONS:

B. EQUIPMENT

Item	No.	L	W	H	Details	Contract	Client supply / Contractor fix
Hatches					Sliding / Hinged		
Benches					Laminate / Teak		
Cupboards					Underbench / Wall / Floor Proportion with drawers		

Shelves
   Reagent
   Storage
					Fixed / Adjustable		

Blackboards					Soap dispenser		
Plastic writing					Curtain fittings		
Pin notice boards					Coat hooks		
Glass covered pin boards							
Mirror							

Loose furniture and equipment (supplied by the client and put in place outside the General Contract) having a **significant effect on space and / or services**

Item	L	W	H	Weight	Details (inc. services required)

Fig. 6.1   Room data sheet
(Courtesy Medical Research Council)

C. ENGINEERING SERVICES	File Ref. No. .... /	Sheet No. ....

I. MECHANICAL ENGINEERING:

HEATING:

Temperature required: .... °C.

Radiators / Ceiling htg / Other ....

VENTILATION:

Natural / Extract only / Local Extract / Plenum / Air Conditioning.

Air Changes: .... / hr.   Temperature Tolerance: ± ....

Humidity: .... %.   Tolerance: ± ....

Filtration: Supply micron level ....

Extract micron level: ....

Fume cupboards: No. ....   Fume hoods: No. ....

Temperature alarms: High level / Low level.

Refrigeration

GASES:

Oxygen: .... twin, ... single.

Suction: .... twin, ... single.

Compressed Air: .... twin, ... single.

Town Gas: .... twin, ... single.

Wall mounted / Pendant / Bench / Services spine.

2. SANITARY FITTINGS:

Washbasin: No. ....   Shower: No. ....

Urinal: No. ....   W.C.: No. ....   Drink Fountain: No. ....

.... : No. .... : No. ....

Spray tap / Normal tap outlet.   Wrist / Elbow / Foot operated.

Separate h. & c. / Mixer / Unitap.   Shower mixer: Wall spray / Handset.

SINKS: *(For standard sizes see separate schedule.)*

Large: No. ....   Medium: No. ....   Small: No. ....

Special: No. ....   Size: ....

Stainless / Porcelain /

In bench / Bench top / Wall / Free standing.   Drip cups.

Drainer: Single / Double / Integral / Bench.

h. & c. / c. only.   Single taps / Mixer / Special.

Filter on cold water? ....

Drinking water.

Controlled outlet temp.? .... °C ± .... °C.

DRAINAGE:

Abnormal fluids: Solvents / Acids / Alkali / Radioactive / Very hot water.

Floor drainage: With / Without channel.

3. ELECTRICAL ENGINEERING:

LIGHTING:

General: Fluorescent / Tungsten: .... lux.   Dimming.

Colour: White / Colour corrected / ....

Emergency: Grade ....

Time switching: ....

Photosafe: ....

Warning lights: ....

Special: ....

POWER:

13 amp. sockets: .... twin, ... single.

13 amp. ceiling sockets: No. ....

Floor sockets: ....

Sparkless / Hoseproof: Isolated earth / Switched.

Emergency: All / 75% / 50% / 25% / ....

Portable X-Ray equipment: ....

Voltage stability: ....

Trunking: ....

Low voltage sockets: .... twin, ... single.

Voltage: .... V.   Current Rating: .... A.

3 Ph. & N. sockets: ....   Rating: .... A.

DDA cupboard alarm: ....

Warning light: ....

Special:

COMMUNICATIONS:

Telephone: Internal: ....

External: ....

Secretarial facilities on internal / external to: ....

....

Clock: Impulse / Synchronous / Battery / Sweep second hand /

Time elapse / Digital.

4. SPECIAL PROVISIONS:

Electrical screening / Lifts / Hoists / ....

5. CONNECTIONS TO EQUIPMENT:

Item: ....

Air: Supply / Extract.   Rate: .... l/s.

Steam: Pressure .... b.   Rate: .... kg/h.

Water: Pressure: .... b.   Rate: .... l/s.

Water: Maximum weekly consumption: ....

Cooling water: Mains / Recirculating.

Maximum weekly consumption: ....

Softened supply / Deionised / Distilled.

Maximum weekly consumption: ....

Filtered: Temperature: .... °C. ± .... °C.

Maximum weekly consumption: ....

Drainage: ....   Gas(es): ....

Compressed Air: Pressure: .... b.   Rate: .... kg/h.

Electricity: I Ph. / 3 PH. / 3 Ph. & N.   Rating: .... kW.

Item: ....

Air: Supply / Extract.   Rate: .... l/s.

Steam: Pressure .... b.   Rate: .... kg/h.

Water: Pressure: .... b.   Rate: .... l/s.

Water: Maximum weekly consumption: ....

Cooling water: Mains / Recirculating.

Maximum weekly consumption: ....

Softened supply / Deionised / Distilled.

Maximum weekly consumption: ....

Filtered: Temperature: .... °C. ± .... °C.

Maximum weekly consumption: ....

Drainage: ....   Gas(es): ....

Compressed Air: Pressure: .... b.   Rate: .... kg/h.

Electricity: I Ph. / 3 PH. / 3 Ph. & N.   Rating: .... kW.

Item: ....

Air: Supply / Extract.   Rate: .... l/s.

Steam: Pressure .... b.   Rate: .... kg/h.

Water: Pressure: .... b.   Rate: .... l/s.

Water: Maximum weekly consumption: ....

Cooling water: Mains / Recirculating.

Maximum weekly consumption: ....

Softened supply / Deionised / Distilled.

Maximum weekly consumption: ....

Filtered: Temperature: .... °C. ± .... °C.

Maximum weekly consumption: ....

Drainage: ....   Gas(es): ....

Compressed Air: Pressure: .... b.   Rate: .... kg/h.

Electricity: I Ph. / 3 PH. / 3 Ph. & N.   Rating: .... kW.

6. FIRE SERVICES:

Hosereel / Hydrant / Dry Riser / Foam Inlet / CO_2.

Smoke / Heat Detector / Sprinkler.   Fire Alarm Contact.

Bell / Indicator Light / ....

Alarm relayed to: ....

Fig. 6.1   Room data sheet (continued)   **6**–3

(b) A design concept (see 6 above).

(c) Completed Room Data Sheets (see under 'Room Data Sheets' below).

ROOM DATA SHEETS

Room Data Sheets provide a means of checking that the planning and spatial requirements as well as the detailed content of each room are properly taken into account. Although Room Data Sheets are widely used by architects, one of the most comprehensive versions has been developed by the Medical Research Council. Fig. 6.1 shows this in full in order to clarify their function in detail.

The normal procedure is for the Client to submit completed sheets for each room as part of the brief. These are updated as necessary during the Scheme Design Stage in consultation with the architect and, when agreed, translated into drawing form to include wall elevations as well as a plan. If the drawn sections of the Room Data Sheets are prepared in sufficient detail, they also serve a valuable co-ordinating role during the construction stage.

The design of the mechanical and electrical services forms an essential part of the general laboratory design and the services consultants will therefore play almost as early a role as the architect. Likewise costs will influence the approach to design and the quantity surveyor's advice will be required at an equally early stage. Consequently, when the architect is referred to in this section, the professional team is often implied.

Siting

The main factors in the siting of laboratories are seen to be a balance between Technics and Humanities. The various factors which have to be considered under these headings are as follows.

Technics	*Humanities*
Support and communication with other departments	Staff access
	Outlook
Supplies access	Catering
Main services	Pollution, Waste, Noise
Disposal access	
Air handling	
Sun defence	
Future expansion	

PLANNING

GENERAL

The planning and form of the building is dictated by the laboratory requirements to a greater extent than is often realised. The services content may well be over 50 % of the built cost and their correct distribution and functioning is fundamental to laboratory work. The scientific disciplines involved set the relationship of rooms and these must be established with the users; they vary with each discipline. A detailed understanding of the pattern of use particularly with regard to special techniques and equipment is necessary and this, once again, emphasises the essential importance of adequate briefing.

Where research laboratories are to be financed by the University Grants Committee the space standards included in the UGC 'Notes on Procedure' must be followed and will form the basis for cost allowances. For further details, see Bibliography.

Major factors which have a direct influence on form and planning are given in the following paragraphs.

PLAN FORM

A fundamental decision is whether the buildings are to be of shallow width, in which every room can receive natural light and ventilation, or deep plan, in which only the outer rooms have natural light and ventilation, The selection depends on the functions involved in relation to the funds and site space available. If it is established that artificial ventilation is a user requirement then a deep plan becomes suitable, using the centre core for rooms where daylight is unimportant or not required.

Heat gains within the building, from a quantity of connected apparatus, the use of noxious substances and needs for a constant environment, set the pattern for ventilation as much as for the comfort of the occupants. The degree varies with the discipline and the costs, from full air-conditioning downwards, but the decision affects the planning of the rooms. Daylighting standards are often of little consequence, as artificial lighting tends to be used permanently during working hours, with venetian blinds set to reduce glare from outside, whether bright or dull. It follows that the role of daylighting and normal ventilation is most appreciated where the work is not direct laboratory work, such as in writing spaces and ancillary rooms, where a contrast in environment should be sought.

MODULE

Laboratories are particularly suited to modular planning; the problem is to obtain compatibility of the bench module (see Fig. 6.2) with the building module, which is frequently 3000 to 3300. A 3000 module can be made to fit both benches and building in most circumstances, but where the benches are larger or where the lengths of benches are greater, a 3300 module becomes more applicable. An important criterion is the ability to pass another working place without risk of collision; there is a hazard to safety if spaces are too close.

Architects are strongly advised, however, to acquaint themselves with the latest studies carried out into modular and general laboratory planning and to visit research establishments to explore the Architect/User approach to these questions. Scientists generally welcome the opportunity for such discussions with architects and to point out, often all too frankly, inherent weaknesses which may exist in completed projects.

Although the standard works of reference listed in the Bibliography give guidance to planning principles, thinking has advanced considerably since much of this material was produced in the early 60's. Amongst significant developments are:

1. The adoption of square, as opposed to rectangular,

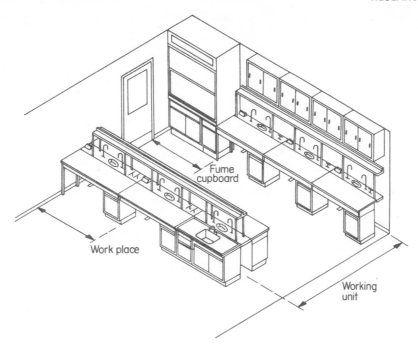

Fume
cupboard

Work place

Working
unit

Fig. 6.2   Typical laboratory layout

laboratory modules which allow far greater flexibility in terms of bench arrangement and permit the introduction of island bench units and free-standing equipment. Where this module has been used, the gain in flexibility is regarded as more advantageous than the slightly greater bench run provided by the rectangular module.

2. The application of laboratory benching as a series of 'loose-fit' table tops in standard unit lengths. In such cases the services and power outlets will be provided in an independent services spine. Such a system allows considerable variations to be made to the layout of the benching with minimum inconvenience. Bench framing can also be manufactured to permit height adjustment to be made to the working tops.

3. The arrangement of heavy equipment, fume cupboards, wash-up facilities, etc., in a common central area. This system has been successfully adopted at the Department of Zoology, Edinburgh University, where the central area also provides through circulation. The central area, however, undoubtedly raises problems in connection with means of escape and fire protection and calls for early consultation with the Fire Authorities.

THE WORK PLACE

The planning of individual laboratories normally starts from a determination of the work place which can be taken as a unit length of benching, provided with piped and electrical services and drainage. Arranged in modules or bays, as described above, the resulting group of work places forms a

work unit. This will require back-up facilities such as fume cupboards, sinks, etc.

Bench tops in research laboratories are ideally removable in unit sections (see above), normally corresponding to the work place, to permit the introduction of floor standing equipment. Fig. 6.2 illustrates these features. For detailed information about storage and shelving and other standard laboratory content (see page **6**-8).

OFFICE RELATED SPACE FOR RESEARCH

Paper work plays as important a role as bench work in research, calling for a close association between the work place and office space. There are various planning solutions:

1. Desk height bench spaces, either adjacent to the work place or near to the windows, where they can be designed to provide a change of working environment, possibly separated by a glazed screen.

2. Offices adjacent to laboratories: Each office is directly related to one laboratory (see Fig. 6.3).

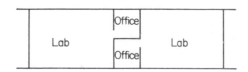

Fig. 6.3   Office space related to laboratory

3. Offices on opposite side of a corridor, either for shallow or deep plan buildings. The offices need not be directly related to particular laboratories (see Fig. 6.4).

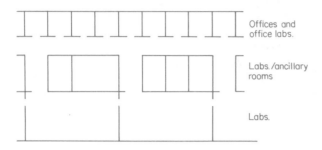

Fig. 6.4   Typical arrangement of offices and laboratories

SERVICES DISTRIBUTION

The arrangement of services can either be off a series of vertical ducts, serving individual, or pairs of laboratories at each level; or horizontal ducts, serving a group of laboratories on each floor. The second method is generally cheaper initially, but does not have the same adaptability, and involves many floor penetrations.

Service runs require careful detailing in order to avoid flooding caused by leakage which is one of the major hazards in laboratories. The practice of sealing floors and servicing horizontally from vertical ducts is increasing on this account.

Horizontal services distribution suspended from floor slabs gives a strong bias to a flat slab structure, particularly if services are exposed. If beams are used as a structural economy, it is desirable that all services including ventilation ductwork, fume cupboard extract ducts and electrical trunking should run below beams, and their general co-ordination should be an important factor in the determining the floor height.

ADAPTABILITY

The pace of change is accelerating, and laboratory requirements and techniques will almost certainly be varied long before the economic life of the building is over. The concept of adaptability must be taken into account in planning, even to the extent of resisting a highly specialised brief from a dedicated research worker, which may become obsolete before the building is even occupied. Adaptability is achieved in various ways:

1. *Structural.* A standardised grid of holes through the structure for services, vertical and horizontal, allows for extensions to be made to services.

2. *Servicing.* Each piped service where possible should have a stopped off T-connection point for possible future runs of services. Ideally, there should be complete access to concealed services for both maintenance and future alterations and additions. To permit installation of new pipework in economic lengths, ceilings should be at least partially demountable and vertical ducts should have full height access.

3. *Extendibility.* Each department should have an 'open end' so that individual extensions can be made, without affecting other departments. Where the site permits, each block should also be extendible.

4. *A range of room sizes.* Experiments are done with groups of various sizes requiring differing room sizes. These may, of course, be classified as 'activities', all taking place in a large open plan laboratory. However, compartmentation to contain any outbreak of fire and reduce smoke damage should be considered. The upper limit of the volume and area permitted by legislation should be checked with the Local Authority.

5. *Standardised laboratories.* Comparative analysis of a number of specialised research activities shows that provided the services are available and there is space for equipment, the activity can be fitted within a standardised layout. There are obvious benefits in adaptability, particularly in the long term, in comparison with a series of individually laid out rooms and therefore standardised planning is greatly to be encouraged.

6. *Areas of anticipated change.* Demountable cross wall partitioning can be restricted to pre-determined zones where change is most likely to be required. Services should be kept off these partitions as far as possible to allow for alterations.

A judgment of the suitability of a laboratory will frequently be 'How convenient is it to install a new piece of equipment?' The provision allowed in the plan under the above headings will ensure that a reasonable answer can be given. It should be stressed that it is the ability to adapt that is important

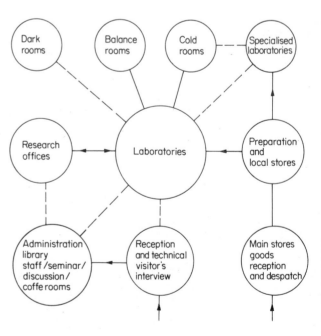

Fig. 6.5   Planning of basic ancillary rooms

rather than the initial provision of expensive services connections and demountability to meet contingencies that may never arise.

COST

Laboratory buildings are expensive, and the investment in hem high. The plan form can influence both the initial cost and the cost effectiveness over a number of years. The cheapest initial cost will seldom be the best value over a period of years. In particular the plan should have the benefit of 'loose-fit'—that is, capable of absorbing changes in patterns of use without major disruption. In addition, total energy conservation may have to be taken into account. For instance, whereas in the past prodigal waste of heat and water has been accepted, in the future, means of recycling must be planned for and costed at the outset. These are fundamentals that are difficult and expensive to alter after the building is erected.

ANCILLARY ROOMS

Fig. 6.5 shows the planning relationship of the basic ancilliary rooms to the laboratories. The detail requirements for specialised rooms are set out under 'Space Requirements' below.

SPACE REQUIREMENTS

Most laboratory buildings, whatever their primary research use, may be expected to contain rooms and spaces in four main categories.
A. Standard laboratories for the normal primary research work.
B. Ancillary specialised rooms as direct research adjuncts usually requiring to be in close proximity to category A rooms.
C. Work support and other rooms in close proximity to category A and B rooms.
D. Work support and other rooms not necessarily requiring close proximity to category A, B and C rooms.

Typical rooms in these four categories are described or listed below, attention being drawn to special environmental conditions and services likely to be required. These are followed by notes applicable to certain more specialised types of research where, although their general content can be divided into the categories A, B, C and D above, special conditions attach to the building as a whole.

A. STANDARD LABORATORIES

These rooms may contain one or a multiple series of similar work units (see page **6**–5). The layout, services and fixed equipment for individual units in a multiple series room will not differ significantly from those in a separate room for one working unit only. Standardisation of the work place and the work unit is in fact always desirable and is certainly in the long term interests of the building. There may be more than one user to a work unit. Attention is again drawn to the need to provide related office space for research (see pages **6**–5 and **6**–6) for suggested planning solutions.

Bench layouts

There are many possible combinations and arrangements of benches and only the Client can determine what is most suitable for his needs in this type of room. However the present tendency is for free floor space requirements to increase either for floor-mounted experiments or for floor-mounted instruments or a combination of both. The manufacture and use of instruments and equipment mounted on wheels which can be brought into the room and connected to the appropriate service is generally increasing.

Where most of the research work is carried out on benches present practice in most types of research is for 40% of the total bench space to be used for working and 60% for instruments. For most purposes a clear bench width of 600 mm is adequate, though physics work may need more. For flexibility of use it is preferable that all benches in this type of room should be independent of the services racks or spines. The Client should confirm the working heights of all benching. Attention is again drawn to related comments on page **6**–4.

Circulation spaces, Doors

The practical minimum clear space between benches is about 1500 mm. Other internal room circulation space should allow for the passage and manoeuvring of equipment and trolleys, door swings, and standing at fume cupboards and wash-up sinks. The clear opening of single doors should generally be about 950 mm minimum.

In large multiple unit rooms opening off a main corridor, doors at each end are recommended for convenience and escape in emergency. One of these doors should have a minimum total clear opening of 1350 mm to allow for the passage of equipment. However, clear door openings and gangways between benches should be confirmed by the Client. The latter are crucial to the establishment of the size of these rooms and may have an important bearing on the structural grid of the building as a whole.

Generally, agreement with the Client on the design of the standardised rooms should have high priority in planning the building.

Services

In discussing the question of services it is assumed that the general environmental conditions, e.g. full air conditioning, or mechanical ventilation without cooling, or none at all in rooms without fume cupboards, have been determined and only services actually necessary to the research work are described below.

Each work space should be provided with one or more standard sets of service outlets, depending on the total length of the benching, and these should be preferably mounted on an independent service rack or spine, which should be designed to permit the easy maintenance of pipework, access to stopcocks, valves and liquid waste receivers or traps, and also allow for future alterations and additions.

For most research purposes a quite limited range of services to benches is adequate, the selection usually being made from 13 A power, cold water, town gas, laboratory vacuum and laboratory compressed air. This range would also apply generally to fume cupboards and laminar flow cabinets. Hot water is not normally required except to wash-up sinks and hand basins. With the increasing use of electrically operated or electronic instruments it is important that sufficient power sockets are provided for them without having to resort to adaptors. Other typical services may include a telephone, slave clock and clock with sweep second hand. Where long-term work may be otherwise effectively lost, it may be necessary for apparatus and instruments to be connected to power outlets on stand-by electrical supply to permit continuity in the event of main power failure. It is desirable in a work unit where this precaution applies for all or some of the lighting also to be on stand-by supply.

Fixed equipment and facilities

The following are commonly installed:
1. Fume cupboards or laminar flow cabinets.
2. Wash-up sinks and drainers—these are not always required in single work unit rooms. In multiple-unit rooms they are often shared. For example a three-unit room would probably need only one, but a four-unit room is likely to need two. The services required are generally a hot and cold mixer tap, a separate cold water tap, and possibly also separate deionised water.
3. Small sinks let into bench tops and provided with cold water.
4. Most biological research rooms will need a separate hand basin with an elbow operated hot and cold mixer tap.
5. Chalkboard or writing board.
6. Pin-up board.
7. Coathooks, if cloakrooms are not reasonably nearby.

Storage and shelving

1. *Underbench cupboards and drawers.* These should be in easily removable units to facilitate access to services, and sufficient clearance should be allowed behind them for stopcocks and waste receivers or traps. Varying widths of cupboards, and drawer sizes and depths are desirable. These units may be specially designed or of proprietary manufacture and independent from the bench or acting as sole support to the bench top in which case they should have adjustable feet. If no separate desk or office area is provided in the room the units should be arranged to provide knee-hole space for each user. Reference has been

made above to the working heights of benches, and this will reflect on the sizes of cupboard and drawer units. Their provision and design should be specified by the Client.
2. *Reagent bottle shelving.* This is usually over benching, and is often fixed above service racks and spines. Since its potential loading is high, approximately 22·5 kilos per metre run, it needs strong supports at not more than 900 mm intervals.
3. *Wall-mounted cupboards and other shelving.* These may be required for books and apparatus.

Other fittings

1. Space should be allowed for a paper hand towel dispenser, soap dispenser and disposal bin where a hand basin is provided.
2. Draining racks may be required at wash-up sink positions.

Other factors

Rooms where work involving mercury in quantity is done should have integral floor and skirting surfaces. Bench tops should be in tray form. Inaccessible places into which the mercury may run should be avoided. Waste traps and receivers should be of transparent material.

B. COMMONLY REQUIRED ANCILLARY SPECIALISED ROOMS

Dark room

Fig. 6.6 illustrates a typical layout for manual processing where only one technician will be working. If automatic processing is required, the room will need to be slightly larger and the processor itself will need cold water and 13 A power services and waste drainage.

Wall mounted safelights and 13 A socket outlets should be mounted above the bench at frequent intervals at a uniform height for various processes such as enlarging. Illuminated viewing boxes if required can be wall or bench mounted. A red warning light to indicate that dark conditions are operating should be provided outside the room above or near the door.

Instrument Room

One or more rooms may be necessary for microscopes, balances and other optical and analytical instruments. The Client's brief will indicate the type of instrument in each room and its size will depend on the number of working places, 750–900 mm of bench length for each place is usually adequate and each place should be provided with a 13 A socket. The width of the room should be sufficient for bench widths of approximately 600 mm, sitting space and circulation.

Most modern instruments are not affected by structure-borne vibration, heat or humidity, and do not need specially rigid benches or special environmental conditions in the room generally. However, some optical instrument rooms

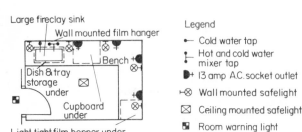

Legend

← Cold water tap

↳ Hot and cold water mixer tap

▶+ 13 amp A.C. socket outlet

⊢⊗ Wall mounted safelight

⊠ Ceiling mounted safelight

▪ Room warning light

Fig. 6.6 Typical layout of small dark room

may need to be completely light-tight, and will therefore need mechanical ventilation. This point should be checked with the Client, who should also confirm the specification as to the rigidity and inertia of the materials used for the bench tops.

Hot Rooms

The room size will depend on the Client's requirements but it will normally contain serviced working benching and shelving 400–500 mm deep (Fig. 6.7). Allowance should be

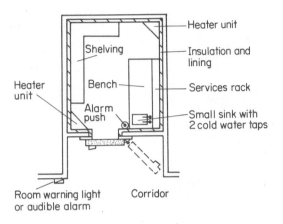

Fig. 6.7   *Typical layout of hot room*

made in planning for wall, floor and ceiling insulation thickness and for the internal heater units. Each room should have an emergency alarm push connected to a warning light or audible alarm whose sound should be distinct from a fire warning.

The Client should confirm the working temperature required and its permissible fluctuation limits at an early stage.

Cold Rooms

The room sizes will depend on the Client's requirements. Temperatures of e.g. $+4\,°C$ will permit working in them for short periods. Very low temperature, e.g. $-20\,°C$, rooms are suitable only for storage. In the latter rooms, to minimise temperature loss when the door is open, they should open on to an air lock or a higher temperature cold room (Fig. 6.8).

Space considerations should allow for internal cooler units, and for floor, wall and ceiling insulation thickness. In very low temperature rooms, insulation thickness can be as much as 200–250 mm or more.

The Client will give requirements for shelving widths. These are generally slatted and of galvanised steel or wood battens. Gangway space between shelving should allow for trolleys. Ideally the refrigeration plant is best placed immediately above the cold rooms with working space around it for access and maintenance if the structural height will permit it. If not a small separate plant chamber at general laboratory floor level will be required with easy access. In both cases the heat generated by the plant should be con-

sidered and may be required to be dissipated by mechanical ventilation. It is recommended that the location of the plant is discussed at an early stage of general planning with the local Fire Brigade, since some Fire Officers may insist on the plant space, or a separate chamber for it, being directly ventilated to open air.

Each room should have an emergency alarm push connected to a warning light or audible alarm whose sound should be distinct from a fire warning.

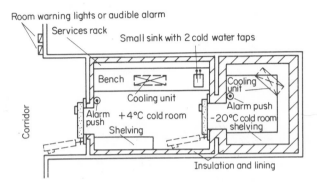

Fig. 6.8   *Typical layout of* $+4\,°C$ *and* $-20\,°C$ *cold room suite*

Insulated doors to hot or cold rooms function most efficiently when they can be closed at the bottom against a threshold step. This can be naturally formed because of the thickness of floor insulation and finish. The acceptability of a step should be decided on the amount of trolleying anticipated to and from the room. If it is not acceptable, either the structural floor must be dropped locally or a ramp up introduced which may need increased clear floor space sdjacent to the entrance. The door can be provided with a sweeping gasket at the bottom but this may need periodic replacement, and is not as a rule as efficient as closure against a step. Doors opening onto a main corridor should be recessed.

The Client should confirm the working temperatures required and their permissible fluctuation limits at an early stage.

Centrifuge Room

Large centrifuges give off heat and also produce noise at a level sufficient to make their location in general research rooms unsuitable. It is preferable that all the larger centrifuges which the laboratory may use are concentrated in a separate room.

Some serviced benching may be required, but in general the room space should be free with wall-mounted socket outlets at suitable intervals to serve the centrifuges. 13 A outlets are adequate for most types of centrifuge, but one or two outlets of higher capacity, such as 30 A, may be required. The Client should confirm the capacity and spacing of outlets. Additional mechanical ventilation may be necessary to dissipate the heat emitted by the centrifuges, and walls and doors may need to be lined with sound-absorbing material depending on the location of the room. Clear door widths should be a minimum of 1350 mm.

Deep Freezers

These do not necessarily need a separate room if there are a number of large freezers to be accommodated close together and frequent use may make an open area adjacent to a main corridor equally suitable, although in this instance access space to the freezers and trolley standing should be clear of the corridor.

Additional mechanical ventilation may be necessary to dissipate the heat emitted from the refrigerating machinery.

Electron Microscope

Before determining the room size and height, the manufacturer's recommendations and requirements should be obtained together with services needs.

Fluorescent Microscopy

The size of the room will depend on the Client's requirements. It is usually in association with electron microscopy with which it may need to communicate, or both rooms may communicate with a small shared dark room, the latter generally using manual processing. (See above for a typical small laboratory dark room layout).

Tissue Culture

The following applies to single rooms or a small group of such rooms within a laboratory.

The size of the room will depend on the number of working places. However, even if it is for only one or two places the clean conditions necessary will require it to be entered from, and supported by, its own preparation room (see Fig. 6.9). Both types of room should have mechanical ventilation under positive pressure. The degree of air filtration in both should be specified by the Client. This is usually of the order of 0·2 microns. Windows should be sealed.

Counting Rooms

These are a necessary adjunct to radio-chemistry work, but are sometimes required for other types of research. Typical fittings are a small amount of serviced benching with sink, a counting bench with a socket outlet at each working place with some shelving above. Free wall space with socket outlets at intervals may be required for floor mounted equipment. The size of the room will depend upon the number of working places and free floor space.

Fire-resisting Rooms

These are sometimes referred to as 'overnight' rooms. They have two main uses:

1. For work using mechanical apparatus such as an oven, which needs to be run for longer periods than a normal working day, and is consequently unattended for periods. Failure of the control apparatus, for example a thermostat,

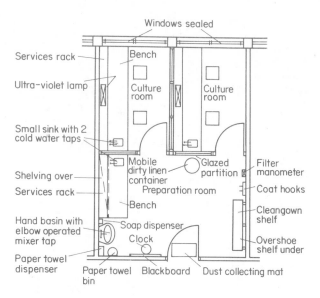

Fig. 6.9   Typical layout of tissue culture suite

may lead to the risk of explosion and fire or flooding.

2. Heavy use of inflammable liquids or solvents such as ether for research work or in supporting processes such as distillation.

The size of the room will depend on the Client's requirements. Special structural precautions will be necessary, e.g. solid floor and ceiling slabs, and the room should be on an external wall. All partition walls should be taken up to the underside of the ceiling slab or roof structure and be of brick or concrete blocks. The floor finish should be laid to fall away from doors. Doors should be fire resisting, and self-closing and a secondary means of escape provided.

The standard of fire resistance of the room and its doors should be agreed at an early planning stage with the appropriate Local Authority who will also give guidance on automatic smoke or heat detection and automatic extinguishing installations, such as CO_2 appropriate to the use of the room. Each fume cupboard should be separately exhausted with fire resistant ductwork, and their exhaust fans should automatically cut out in the event of fire. Refrigerators in such rooms should be of the sparkless type.

Processes such as high-voltage electro-phoresis which use large quantities of inflammable liquids are particularly specialised and do not come within the scope of this section, although many of the structural and other precautions for fire resisting rooms as described above will also apply.

C. COMMONLY REQUIRED WORK SUPPORT AND OTHER ROOMS IN CLOSE PROXIMITY TO CATEGORY A AND B ROOMS

Central wash-up

The size of the room will depend on the equipment required and the daily work load. As a rule, one or more large stainless steel sink units will be necessary. The daily through-put of items to be treated will determine the possible need for an automatic washing machine in addition. If this is necessary. it should have space round it for maintenance access as well as sufficient space in front for loading and unloading.

Other equipment should include electric drying ovens, shelving or cupboards and benches for stacking and pre-liminary cleaning. The latter may need tops resistant to heat or to various acids used in preliminary cleaning. There should be space for manoeuvring and parking of large trolleys. A slop hopper is sometimes required.

The rooms should have good extract ventilation. Clear door widths should be 1350 mm minimum.

Preparation Rooms

The basic content of these rooms is usually serviced benching, wash-up sinks, and storage units and the size will vary ac-cording to the Client's requirements and number of techni-cians normally working in the rooms.

Some research may require preparation under special conditions needing abnormal ventilation and air filtration, and direct access from the main circulation corridor may be unsuitable.

Tissue culture preparation rooms are not included under this particular heading and have been described in Category B.

Clear door widths to central preparation rooms should be 1350 mm minimum.

General Laboratory Store for a floor, or group of Research Laboratories

The size of this room will depend on the Client's requirements but it would not normally be used for chemical storage or for very large equipment or apparatus. It should have adjustable shelving in widths between 300 and 600 mm. Gangways should allow for trolleys.

Autoclaves

These are commonly in separate rooms in association with or opening off central wash-up rooms. The size will depend on the number of autoclaves, the space required in front of them for loading and unloading, and other working and circulation space. Good extract ventilation is necessary.

The plant should be enclosed in a separate chamber mechanically ventilated with sufficient working space for maintenance. It is preferable for the chamber to be entered from a main corridor. The door opening should have a kerb to contain possible flooding due to condense leakage. It is desirable for each autoclave to have an adjacent floor gulley for draining down steam condense pipes, and also to dispose of water from leakage (Fig. 6.10).

Cleaner

A small cleaner's room is desirable on each floor of a multi-storey building, containing a bucket sink, shelf for cleaning materials, broom or mop pegs, coat hooks and space for a vacuum cleaner or floor polisher. For a large single-storey building, more space may be needed for cleaning equipment.

Lavatories and Cloakrooms

The total provision for the whole building should conform to the requirements of the Offices, Shops and Railway Premises Act, 1963. In a multistorey building it may be considered desirable for there to be lavatories for both sexes on each floor. The provision of research staff cloakrooms at each floor will depend on the Client's policy on this point.

D. COMMONLY REQUIRED WORK SUPPORT AND OTHER ROOMS NOT NECESSARILY NEAR A, B AND C CATEGORY ROOMS

Seminar room

The size will depend on the maximum number of staff likely to be using it at any one time. They should, however, have reasonable sight lines to a chalkboard and projection screen, if provided. If film or slide projection is required, and the room is not internal, then blackout provisions will be neces-sary and in any case mechanical ventilation is desirable. One or two socket outlets will be required. Space for a pin-up board and chalkboard is recommended.

Research staff conference room

The size of the room will depend on the Client's requirements. A chalkboard and pin-up space may be useful.

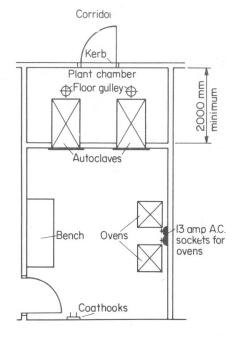

Fig. 6.10   Typical layout of Autoclave suite

RESEARCH LABORATORIES

Office for senior technician

This should be large enough for a desk and desk chair, serviced bench about 1800 mm long, filing cabinets, and chairs and space for one or two visitors, with some storage units. A room about 7·5 m² should be adequate.

Office for director of research

The size will depend on the Client's requirements, but it could be expected to contain a large desk and desk chair, a coat cupboard, chalkboard or writing board, pin-up board, filing cabinets, bookcase, and space for visitors and chairs for them. Space for a table and additional chairs may be also necessory if there is no separate Staff Conference Room.

Other administrative and secretarial rooms

The extent and sizes of these will depend on the Client's administrative policy and organisation. A large laboratory may have a Manager or Superintendent in addition to the Director of Research, and both may have personal secretaries, or share one. There may also be additional secretarial staff or clerks. The secretarial unit should include space for stationery, filing, records and duplicating. Whether any of these are in separate rooms will depend on the Client's needs.

Library

The size of this room, if separate, will depend on the Client's needs. Provision for a large number of periodicals is common, including storage space for back numbers.

Computer Unit

Computer suites, which are installed by specialist firms, require special ventilation, provision in the structure for heavy loading, acoustic treatment, and areas of special flooring with continuous access for electrical services below. These conditions will need early consideration in the building design.

Full information on the design of computer centres is given in Section 7 which also gives guidance on the simpler requirements for terminal links.

Heavy laboratory workshop

The size of the room will depend on the number and type of machines used. These would generally be floor mounted and include millers, lathes, grinders, power saw, guillotine, etc. Moving parts should not encroach into circulation spaces or gangways. Most machines will require 3-phase power, compressed air for blowing out dust and an inspection lamp mounted on the machine itself. The services should be arranged to permit easy installation of new or additional machines. The room should contain a sink with hot and cold water, space for tool storage and some benching with power, town gas and compressed air outlets.

The provision of materials storage in a separate room will depend on several factors, e.g. scope and volume of work, available frequency of deliveries from outside, and normal amounts held in stock. Whether or not a separate room is provided, materials storage will need strong racking and shelving, free wall space for stacking sheet material and drawers or pigeon holes for smaller items.

It may be necessary to provide a separate carpenter's workshop with strong benching and space for floor mounted wood-working machines.

Other workshop processes such as welding, brazing and paint spraying may require separate rooms or spaces.

Instrument and electronic workshops

These rooms would be used for delicate or precision work and the repair and maintenance of instruments and electronic equipment. Their size will depend on the number of working bench places, any special benches and storage cupboards and shelving for materials and tools. A sink with hot and cold water should be provided. Other services would generally include power for bench-mounted machines and adjustable bench lamps, town gas and compressed air.

Central stores

This room would be expected to be for bulk chemical storage, excluding solvents, and some equipment and apparatus. It should have an issuing hatch with lockable shutter and counter with drawers and cupboards below, and space for Head Storekeeper's desk and chair and filing cabinets. Some free floor space should be provided for large or heavy apparatus and such items as carboys. There should be a supplies delivery and checking and unpacking area if this is not a separate room.

Shelving will be required in various widths to suit different sizes of chemical bottles; 300 mm is a useful and common width for smaller sizes and these should preferably be adjustable. Other sizes, such as large Winchester bottles, will need 400–450 mm. For equipment and apparatus, widths will be usually in the 450–675 mm range. There may be a need for security cupboards or racking.

Gangways between bottle shelves can be fairly narrow, about 1 m, others for equipment and apparatus may need to be wider.

A secondary means of escape may be required depending on the size of the room but at least one internal access door should be of the order of 1800 mm clear.

The appropriate Local Authority should be consulted at an early stage with regard to fire precautions. A smoke detector system may be required.

Store for very large or heavy equipment if required to be separate from central store

This should contain very strong shelving from 600–900 mm deep. The extent and vertical intervals should be confirmed with the Client. The door should be about 1800 mm clear width opening on to a free space large enough for the unpacking of a large crate.

Supplies and goods reception area

Ideally this should be separate from, but adjacent to, the central stores. If sufficient height is available, a runway beam capable of carrying 1 tonne should be provided to project over a large goods delivery vehicle such as a 5 tonne lorry.

In a multi-storey building a goods lift to open off the delivery area will be necessary. The maximum carrying capacity and clear car size and car door opening should be given by the Client at an early stage. A small hoist may be convenient in addition to serve upper floors and may discharge into central preparation rooms. The reception area should also include unpacking space.

Glass-blowing

Except in very large establishments with a heavy demand for non-standard glassware, glass-blowing rooms are not necessary and such work can usually be subcontracted elsewhere. However, the Client will confirm whether this provision is needed and will indicate the special requirements.

Special gas cylinder storage

Some gases may require to be piped to laboratories from a central cylinder bank. In other instances the actual cylinders may need to be taken from storage for use in the research rooms. It is recommended that the Fire Officer is consulted at an early stage and that he is informed, for each gas, of the number of cylinders in a bank, or held in store, which would be necessary for research requirements. The external or internal location of cylinder banks or stores will depend on the Fire Officer's recommendations.

Special gas plant

On economic grounds, consumption rates in the laboratories may warrant either manufacture within the building itself or external storage in a large commercial vessel. A common installation is for liquid nitrogen.

Manufacture within the building may need consideration of special ventilation, and noise and vibration since compressors are necessary.

If vessels are employed, they should have easy access for tanker vehicles to recharge them, and be reasonably near the laboratories for staff access.

Solvent and inflammable liquid storage

It is usual for these materials to be kept in a store entirely separate from the main laboratory building with easy access for delivery vehicles. The door threshold should ideally be at tailboard level, with a ramp up from normal road level for the convenience of technician staff fetching materials when they would generally be using trolleys.

The store should be of strong construction with fire-resisting doors and permanent ventilation. In the event of accidental explosion, the explosive force should be able to be taken up by 'blow-out' panels, preferably in the roof. These could be roof-lights or ventilators. All shelving should be of fire-resisting construction. The Local Authority and Fire Officer should be consulted.

Radioactive material storage

In most normal research laboratories, i.e. other than those exclusively for radiochemistry work, radioactive material such as isotopes is brought in and circulated in lead-lined containers. However, radioactive waste material will need to be held in a separate store until safe disposal is possible.

Research staff common room

Staff cloakrooms and lavatories

Technician staff common room

Technician staff cloakrooms and lavatories

Staff canteen—Teamaking facilities—Automatic beverage vending

Visitors' reception and waiting space

Telephone exchange
  (a) Manual
  (b) PABX, PMBX
  (c) Automatic internal telephone system.

Clean laboratory linen storage

Dirty laboratory linen and laundering—Collection; Disposal.

Laboratory and domestic refuse—Collection; Disposal.

Special waste and refuse—Solid Radioactive waste; Biohazardous waste; Workshop swarf; Waste for incineration.

SOME MORE SPECIALISED TYPES OF RESEARCH WHERE SPECIAL CHARACTERISTICS AND CONDITIONS APPLY TO THE RESEARCH UNIT AS A WHOLE

These are briefly described below as a general guide.

Radiochemistry

(a) Statutory regulations covering the protection of personnel against radioactivity are referred to in a later section, together with the relevant Code of Practice. In addition if the research unit directly abuts, or is above or below other building parts its actual structure may need to incorporate protection for the adjoining areas, for example solid barium concrete floor slabs and walls. The degree of structural protection necessary should be established at any early design stage.

(b) Structural precautions such as barium concrete walls in addition to floor and ceiling slabs may be necessary within the unit itself for counting rooms and radio-active material stores.

(c) Precautions must be taken against contamination of adjoining areas through accidental flooding. Floodwater must be contained by raised door thresholds or steps or ramps within the unit.

(d) Disposal of radioactive liquid waste into the public drainage system is subject to control by Local Authorities at a specified level of radioactivity and holding tanks may be required. If such is the case sufficient access space should be provided adjacent to the tanks should the level of radioactivity become so high that their contents will require to be removed in an Atomic Energy Authority tanker vehicle.

(e) Other radioactive waste material will need to be stored within the unit until it can be safely removed.

(f) Provision must be made immediately outside the unit entrance for staff changing rooms with showers. Space should also be allowed for the storage of protective clothing.

(g) Surfaces of rooms generally must be able to be cleaned down easily in the event of contamination or strippable paint must be used. Floor coverings must be integral with coved skirtings and should be able to be easily removed if contaminated.

(h) Fume cupboards for radio-chemistry work usually require exceptionally high extract rates, and will need to be of special design to facilitate cleaning. Extract fans should be in a separate plant room which will require cold water and compressed air supplies for the cleaning down of plant and extract ductwork. Changing of air extract filters must take place within the plant room.

Bio-hazardous research

The term 'bio-hazardous' covers work using pathogenic organisms such as anthrax, cancer cells, smallpox and other dangerous viruses, and general hazards arising from the field of genetic engineering.

The following are the most important points of function and design.

(a) The research unit must be entirely self-contained, and must include all supporting ancillary rooms. It must function under clean conditions, and must be entered only through an air-lock, with ultra-violet lighting, leading to special changing rooms, showers and lavatories.

(b) All work using pathogens must take place, using aseptic techniques, either in special bio-hazardous laminar flow cabinets or on benches in separate rooms with ultra-violet lighting and special ventilation with positive pressure and air filtration down to about 0·2 microns. In all other circumstances the pathogens must be kept in sealed containers.

(c) Liquid laboratory waste should be treated with ultra-violet light before passing in to the main drainage system.

(d) Walls, ceilings and floors must be able to be easily

washed down. A special domestic cleaning routine will be required.

(e) Linen must be sterilised in an autoclave before leaving the unit for laundering.

(f) Special symbols must be used at the unit entrance and on doors to rooms using pathogens.

(g) The unit or room should not be sited next to a known fire hazard or be in danger of flooding from another source.

It is important to be familiar with the Report of the Working Party of the Laboratory use of Dangerous Pathogens prepared by the Department of Health and Social Security, 1975 (see Bibliography) which is likely to become the basis of future legislation.

DATA

The final choice of equipment must lie with the Client. However, some items with space and servicing implications must be decided on in principle if not in complete detail at an early planning stage, for example fume cupboards, whose numbers, space requirements and exhaust rate will have an important effect on ventilation plant and room planning. With some other items, provided the Client gives information in good time on their approximate space requirements, space required round them and services if any, his ultimate choice of the actual instrument should have no other effect. An example of this type of item is a large floor mounted centrifuge or a group of them.

The weights of the larger items of equipment should be checked with the Client, with particular references to items which maybe abnormally heavy and have only a comparatively small base area, at an early design stage since they will have an effect on the general floor loading and hence the structure. With most laboratories it will be necessary in any case to use a higher general live load than, for example office blocks, in assessing the structural requirements.

The following schedule gives a suggested check-list of fixed and loose equipment commonly found in research laboratory buildings and which will have an impact on planning and space requirements.

Fixed

Fume cupboards: normal work*
  work using perchloric acid*
  work using radiochemistry*
Laminar flow cabinets*
Bio-hazardous laminar flow cabinets*
Manipulative glove boxes*
Stills*
Autoclaves*
Glassware washing machines*
Electron microscope*
Wash-up sinks*
Computer*
Workshop machines*
Benching and service racks*
Emergency drench showers*
Shelving including reagent shelving
Workshop storage racks
Central stores racks
Wall cupboards
Chalkboards and pin-up boards

Loose

Centrifuges*
Auto-analysers and other floor mounted instruments*
Deep freezers*
Refrigerators* (including under-bench types)
Water baths*
Glassware drying cabinets*
Ovens*
Under-bench cupboards and drawers

> *Items marked with an asterisk will require one or more services.

ACCOMMODATION

SCHEDULE OF ACCOMMODATION

The earlier subsection on 'Space Requirements' dealt comprehensively with the room types to be found in Research Laboratories and the headings given may be used as an accommodation check-list. No separate Schedule of Accommodation has therefore been provided.

FINISHES AND SPECIAL DETAILS

Finishes should be standardised as far as possible to simplify maintenance and replacement.

(i) *Floors*

Flooring materials should have the usual properties of durability and ease of maintenance but, in addition, they should be resistant to most chemicals likely to be spilled and should be easily washable. As there is a high risk of flooding in laboratories, floors should ideally be jointless or have as few joints as possible. In this connection it should be remembered that if piped services rise through the floor to serve island benches, etc, careful consideration should be given to the detailing at this point to avoid seepage to the subfloor or ceiling void below.

A continuous finish can be achieved most economically by the use of a sheet p.v.c. with inset coved skirtings, all having welded joints. Obviously, the effectiveness of such a floor relies on the quality of the welds and in the past a number of failures have occurred, but welding techniques have now improved and with good supervision satisfactory results can be achieved. Truly jointless floors can now be provided by epoxy resins but these are costly and are normally limited to special areas where exceptional conditions are required.

There is still a marked preference among laboratory users for traditional flooring materials such as linoleum and wood block. 4·5 mm linoleum laid in sheet form with close butt joints and treated with a suitable plastic sealer provides a satisfactory finish for most purposes. Wood block is a suitable material for use in Geology and Physics Laboratories but is expensive and capital budgets today do not normally allow their use.

A number of other finishes such as p.v.c. tiles, vinyl asbestos tiles, clay or vitreous tiles, mastic asphalt, rubber-latex cement, etc, may be used in various areas depending on the type of research being undertaken. These can be established once the brief has been finalised.

(ii) *Laboratory worktops*

The traditional material for laboratory worktops is solid timber. The most commonly used is teak but other timbers which may be used successfully are Iroko, Afrormosia and Kokrodua. Solid teak bench tops are still preferred by many users but increasing costs are dictating the use of cheaper alternatives. Blockboard or particle board with either timber or laminated plastics veneers are now increasingly used. Laminated plastics have only a limited resistance to acid attack but have good resistance to organic solvents and are often used in areas where a high degree of cleanliness is required.

Asbestos cement (30 mm thick), may be used very successfully and is available in various grades depending on the degree of chemical resistance required.

Linoleum provides a very satisfactory finish for worktops in physics laboratories and in special instrument rooms. It has also been used in some chemical laboratories where it can be easily and cheaply replaced when stained or damaged.

As with floors, many different materials such as p.v.c., polythene, clay or vitreous tiles, stainless steel, epoxy resins, etc, may be used on benchtops depending on the type of work being carried out.

(iii) *Walls and ceilings*

Walls and ceilings generally require no special protection and a good quality emulsion paint is satisfactory in most areas. However, some areas which may need a high degree of cleanliness or to be washed down from time to time will require gloss paint or may have a sprayed plastic finish.

SERVICES

Reference has already been made above to the importance of the services provision being considered in the early design stages, and also to the high proportion of services costs in relation to the total building cost. The following is intended as a check-list for consideration of general and particular points which commonly apply to laboratories.

General points

1. Coordination of services at design stage.
2. Type of building heating system and scope of mechanical ventilation generally.
3. Confirmation by the Client of diversity factors for piped services and electrical outlets.
4. Accessibility—within rooms, in ceiling voids, in main ducts.
5. Flexibility for future changes or additions, including consideration of installing tees in main piping runs to assist in future alterations.
6. Scope of provision of shut-off valves for piped services

to particular fittings, runs of benching and whole floors or parts of floors to allow maintenance, repairs, or alteration work to proceed with minimum disruption to research work.

7. General piping, or piping from a local source within rooms, for certain services, e.g. town gas, vacuum, compressed air.

8. Spare capacity in main switch rooms and floor fuseboards, with particular reference to 3-phase provision.

9. Avoidance of cramped plant rooms.

10. Ventilation of plant rooms where the plant emits heat, e.g. calorifier rooms.

11. Choice of materials, including piped services, waste pipes, waste stacks, taps, bench and other outlets, fume cupboard extract ducts. Consideration of solvent disposal in the choice of waste system materials.

12. Typical bench services, including consideration of prefabrication of service pipe and conduit installations and pre-installation of outlets. Services to fume cupboards.

13. Ceiling mounted services gantries or pendants, or floor ducts, for isolated work areas or equipment.

14. Manufacture of special gases within the building, e.g. liquid nitrogen.

15. Location of plant producing noise, e.g. compressors, ventilation fans.

16. Location of fume cupboard extract outlets to avoid noxious or corrosive fumes entering fresh-air inlets.

17. Automatic shutting-off of ventilation and fume cupboard extract fans in the event of fire.

Types of service

1. Town gas.
2. Compressed air.
3. Vacuum.
4. Special gases.
5. Cold water
   (a) domestic, and supply to laboratories from normal down service from storage tanks.
   (b) boosted service to laboratories from storage tanks if there is insufficient head for the required working pressure.
6. Hot water.
7. Deionised water: consideration of central or local source.
8. Distilled water.
9. Drinking water.
10. Emergency drench showers.
11. Steam: autoclaves, pilot plants.
12. 13 A AC.
13. Non-standard low amperage AC, e.g. 5 A, 15 A.
14. Stabilised AC: consideration of location of stabilising equipment.
15. Non-standard voltage AC.
16. DC.
17. 3-phase AC for research work.
18. Standby supply AC
    (a) Laboratory socket outlets.
    (b) Fire alarm system.
    (c) Automatic fire prevention systems with electrical operations.
    (d) Equipment.

19. Standby supply AC for lighting
    (a) Fire escape routes.
    (b) Laboratories.
20. Special lighting, e.g. ultra-violet.
21. Fire alarm system.
22. Automatic fire-prevention systems.
23. Wet fire main, hosereels.
24. Dry fire riser: consideration of external Fire Brigade access.
25. Localised alarm systems, e.g. in connection with personnel trapped in hot and cold rooms.
26. Telephone system: manual exchange, PABX, PMXB, PAX.
27. Other intercommunication systems
    (a) Talkbox systems.
    (b) Personal bleepers: consideration of aerials and location of central transmitting equipment.
28. Master and slave clock system, clocks with sweep second hands.
29. Data transmission and computer link.

Laboratory waste system

1. General
   (a) Normal.
   (b) Bio-hazardous: treatment of effluent by ultra-violet light before entering main waste pipe or stack.
   (c) Radioactive: Local Authority requirements.
2. Bench waste system: consideration of drip cups, bottle traps, interception and dilution of waste by running traps or receivers before entering main waste pipe or stack.
3. Floor gulleys.
4. Effluent sampling points, for inspection for contamination by Local Authority. Consideration of accessibility.

Fume cupboards and special safety cabinets

1. Requiring extract ducting to outside air
   (a) Special design or proprietary type for fume cupboards for normal research work.
   (b) Special design or proprietary type for fume cupboards for radiochemistry work.
   (c) Special design or proprietary type for fume cupboards where the work involves the use of perchloric acid.
   (d) Manipulative glove boxes.
   (e) Exhaust rates required for each fume cupboard or glove box.
   (f) Individual provision for each fitting of exhaust ducting and extract fan.
2. Not requiring extract ducting to external air
   (a) Laminar flow cabinets.
   (b) Special laminar flow cabinets for bio-hazardous work.
   (c) Portable bench mounted air filtration cabinets for work involving hazardous material e.g. mercury in the process of cleaning manometers for which this type of cabinet is appropriate.

STATUTORY REQUIREMENTS, LEGISLATION AND AUTHORITIES

A check should be made on up-to-date legislation since amendment may involve more stringent requirements.

Reference should be made to 'Building Design and Construction: Guide to Statutory Provisions', Dec., 1972 Department of the Environment Welsh Office, London HMSO (1973), or to later editions. This publication refers to general Acts having application in England and Wales. It does not extend to Local Acts or Acts applying to Inner London, neither does it deal with Local Byelaws. It does not claim to be completely comprehensive and advises that Local Authorities will be able to supply information about any Local Acts of relevance and water undertakers will be able to provide information about water byelaws in their areas.

Codes of Practice are regarded as meeting the deemed to satisfy provisions of legislation, without necessarily being referred to in the legislation. Early agreement should be reached with the clients regarding approaches to be made to the various authorities. Although by agreement such approaches are often made on behalf of the client it is important to recognise that the client will finally be responsible for continuing the compliance with regulations.

Much legislation is related to minimising hazards to life and property. An early appraisal should therefore be made of all the hazards, taken singly and in combination, which are likely to arise. Many of these are not peculiar to research laboratories, whereas certain hazards require specialised knowledge to evaluate the risks.

By nature, research laboratories may undergo changes in use affecting hazards or introducing new ones. Compliance with legislation is also inherent where changes occur.

Consultation with the appropriate authority knowing what it is intended to use, and how, can do much to reduce the hazards. It may also influence the users' approach to the problem.

Many of the present requirements are intended to cover most situations in full awareness that special circumstances may exist which are not covered specifically. It is therefore desirable to grasp from the written word the basic requirements to be satisfied and thereafter to identify those aspects not so covered. Early consultation with the authority administering the legislation is particularly valuable where special aspects are involved or where unspecified alternatives are offered in the legislation.

In very limited circumstances there is scope for obtaining a waiver to a normal requirement where compliance would be unduly onerous and where such a waiver would not be completely counter to the spirit of the legislation.

Conversely there is a case for conforming to legislation intended for other categories of accommodation where this results in better practice, although not required legally.

Parliamentary consideration of the Bill for 'Health and Safety at Work, etc' is likely to produce some rationalisation of building legislation, incorporating some of the 'Proposals for a Building Bill' issued by DOE as a consultative document in July 1972. In particular it is intended to introduce, by Statutory Instruments, a better indication of how the existing legislative requirements can be met.

It is evident that for some time it will still be necessary to supplement the written word with enquiry to the authorities administering the legislation, to establish the full requirements in a particular case. This enquiry serves to cross link the various parts of legislation. This need will tend to diminish if the Building Regulations are modified to include as many as possible of the controls in other legislation as intended in Proposals for a Building Bill.

BIBLIOGRAPHY FOR STATUTORY REQUIREMENTS

The Building Regulations, 1972.
Clean Air Acts, 1956 and 1968 (DOE, WO).
Cruelty to Animals Act, 1876 (HO).
Electric Lighting Acts, 1882 and 1888 (DTI).
Electric Lighting (Clauses) Act, 1899 (DTI).
Electricity Acts, 1947 and 1957 (DTI).
  Electricity Supply Regulations, 1937.
Factories Act, 1961 (DE)
Highly Flammable Liquids and Liquified Petroleum Gases. Regulations (SI 1972 No. 917).
Fire Services Act, 1947 (HO).
Gas Act, 1972 (DTI)
  Gas Safety Regulations, 1972 (SI 1972, No. 1178).
Offices, Shops and Railway Premises Act, 1963 (DE).
Petroleum (Consolidation) Act, 1928.
Public Health Act, 1936 (Mainly DOE and WO: DOE and HO for Section 59 and 60).
Public Health (Drainage of Trade Premises) Act, 1937 (DOE).
Radioactive Substances Acts, 1948 and 1960 (DOE, WO).
Code of Practice for the Protection of Persons Exposed to Ionising Radiations in Research and Teaching (DE).
Water Act, 1945 (DOE, WO).
Bio-hazards in Biological Research, Cold Spring Harbour Laboratory, U.S.A., 1973.

EXAMPLES

It is impossible to quote individual examples of this widespread building type. Reference should be made to the two Architectural Periodical Indexes quoted in the Bibliography for recent examples. The universities, research councils and commercial scientific research organisations will also normally be willing to give advice and arrange for visits to their own establishments.

BIBLIOGRAPHY

The major sources of reference for up-to-date information on research laboratories will be found in the architectural press and periodicals. There are two indexes from which references can be obtained. These are:

1. *RIBA Architectural Periodical Index*. Available from RIBA Publications Ltd, 66 Portland Place, London W1.
2. *The Avery Index to Architectural Periodicals*. Available from Columbia University, Central Office, 562 West 113 Street, New York 10025.

Both these indexes can be referred to at the RIBA Library, and (for members only) the Architectural Association library.

Very little significant new material has been published about research laboratories in recent years and the first four books quoted below remain the standard works on the subject. Most of the books mentioned contain their own Bibliographies.

1. Munce, J. F., *Laboratory Planning*, Butterworths London (1962).

2. *The Design of Research Laboratories*. The Report of a study carried out by the Division for Architectural Studies of the Nuffield Foundation, Oxford University Press, London (1961).

3. Schramm, W., *Chemistry and Biology Laboratories*, Pergamon Press, Oxford (1965).

4. Lewis, Harry F., *Laboratory Planning for Chemistry and Chemical Engineering*, Reinhold Publishing Corp., New York (1962).

5. Ferguson, W. R., *Practical Laboratory Planning*, Applied Science Publishers Ltd, London (1973).

This is the most recent specialised publication to appear. Examples are drawn from Australia, USA and W. Germany and no bibliography is included.

6. *An Approach to Laboratory Building*, Laboratories Investigation Unit, Department of Education and Science and the University Grants Committee (1969).

7. *Report on Laboratory Design*, The University of Edinburgh. Edinburgh (1970).

8. *Report of the Working Party on the Laboratory use of Pathogens*, Department of Health and Social Security, HMSO, London (1975).

Revised 'Notes on Procedure' dated 1974 are now available direct from the UGC and are to be implemented for all new projects. These are based upon the application of unit area alowances and will form the basis for negotiating project costs with the UGC. They are not to be published, however, until the new procedures have been sufficiently tried. Details of the planning norms which are referred to in the new Notes on Procedure are also available separately from the UGC.

This section has been contributed by the following members of Cusdin Burden and Howitt.

C. E. Bagwell-Purefoy, AA. Dip., F.R.I.B.A.
Elizabeth Boultbee
J. R. Burden, AA. Dip., F.R.I.B.A.
P.M.P. Griffiths
Margaret Pope, Librarian
B. Tinsey, M.S.A.A.T.
D. G. Whiteley, AA. Dip., F.R.I.B.A.

Cusdin, Burden and Howitt *are the fifth generation of a continuing practice which was established in 1890 by Edwin T. Hall, MA, VPRIBA. The fourth generation was Easton & Robertson, Cusdin, Preston and Smith. Although widely based, the practice has considerable experience of the design of laboratory buildings for Universities, Hospital Authorities and research establishments both in the UK and abroad. In the UK, the projects undertaken include various laboratories for the Universities of Cambridge, Durham and Reading; Stage II of the New Addenbrooke's Hospital, Cambridge; the Middlesex Hospital Medical School, London; the Medical College of St. Bartholomew's Hospital, London; laboratories and animal houses for the Animal Virus Research Institute, Pirbright; dental school and clinical buildings for the Queens University, Belfast. Overseas projects include work for the Universities of Hong Kong, Malaya and Riyad, Saudi Arabia.*

7 COMPUTER CENTRES

R. F. BRIEN, Cert. Arch. (Natal), F.R.I.B.A.

INTRODUCTION

GENERAL

The object of this section is to assist in the general approach to the problems of designing a computer installation and to provide essential guide-lines for those architects who may be unfamiliar with this type of building.

Computer installations vary considerably in size from subscriber terminals to computer centres, and their composition and complexity tends to be as variable. These notes refer generally to the requirements of larger computers with magnetic storage devices; the requirements for smaller installations will be proportionately simpler.

OBJECTIVES

Definitions of the terms used for a computer installation are as follows:

COMPUTER CENTRE: A building or part of a building designed solely to house a computer and the associated administration, the objective of which is to provide a computing service.

COMPUTER UNIT: An area in which computer equipment is housed, usually part of a building or building complex in which other activities not restricted to computing take place.

A large computer centre will have three basic divisions of accommodation. These consist of:

(a) The computer room and ancillary spaces.
(b) The administration areas.
(c) The plant space.

Even in smaller installations, these divisions will have to be maintained to some degree. It should be borne in mind that in allowing for future expansion the three areas will grow at proportional rates, and particularly in the case of a large centre, it is not possible to extend the computer areas without the essential services back-up of air-conditioning and power requirements.

Because of the sensitivity of electronic devices and integrated circuitry, high-speed large configuration systems will operate satisfactorily only within close tolerances of temperature and humidity. Computer rooms require air conditioning rather more accurately controlled than that provided in buildings designed for humans. It is perhaps fortunate that manufacturers recognise that the working range of the computer must correspond with conditions in which an operator may work comfortably. The operation of these devices produces heat, and the rapid dispersal of this is essential. Whilst the amount of heat produced by a single transistor is minute, the computer cabinets contain many hundreds of thousands of these components.

In smaller installations, it may be permissible to have a simpler form of temperature regulation and to introduce a less sophisticated humidity control; but no general comment can be made in this respect, as the manufacturers of the equipment will state the environmental conditions which are required for their particular installation.

Interconnection of the items of equipment within the computer room and its ancillaries is essential, and this is normally effected by means of cabling in a false floor system. Where the computer is to be installed in an existing building, ramps will be necessary to allow for the changes of level to other areas. For this reason, it is sometimes convenient to extend the false floor beyond the areas in which it is essential to avoid pushing trolleys up and down ramps.

Computer equipment is expensive, and the records stored on cards, tapes and discs are usually of great value. It is important, then, to consider particularly carefully the requirements for the provision of smoke and fire detection. (See CP 95: 1970, 'Fire protection for electronic data processing installations'.) The main concern is to protect the equipment from external hazards rather than the more usual internal causes. In all cases the local fire authority or other qualified adviser should be consulted.

Where the building operates on a 24-hour basis, automatic detection systems (usually smoke-activated) would have repeaters in strategic locations. Serious consideration should be given also to the possibility of a direct private telephone link which would automatically alert the local fire station. Whatever fire detection system is decided upon, the detectors must not be arranged to switch off the power supply to the computer unless it is running unattended.

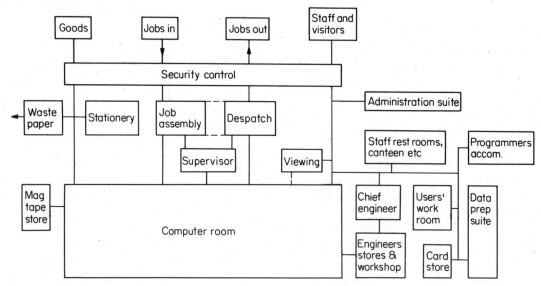

Fig. 7.1 Circulation diagram: computer room and ancillaries

If an automatic extinguishing system is called for, the degree of damage to unaffected equipment must be considered. High pressure water sprays in a computer installation would produce spectacular results, and even flooding the floor plenum with carbon dioxide might have the most serious thermal shock effects on electronic components. It is important, then, that the system provides an early warning to an authorised person who can take quick local action in minimising damage.

The use of halogenated extinguishing agents for full flooding systems should be carefully considered, as there are advantages in storage and use, but disadvantages in lack of cooling and possible danger to personnel in that toxic gases may be formed under fire conditions. The two most useful are BCF (Bromochlorodifluoro methane) and BTM. Both are now approved by FOC (Fire Officers' Committee) and published information should be available shortly. In the USA, scope, development installation and hazards are defined in detail by NFPA International, Boston, USA.

BRIEFING PROGRAMME

The time-scale for both design and constructional work in connection with computers tends to be rather more compressed than for other building. For this reason, it is essential that a clear brief be determined at an early stage. Delays in coping with late changes of mind can be expensive to both the designer and the Client.

SITING

No initial computer installation (see Figs. 7.1 and 7.2) will ever be considered final by the client, and the rapid development, and implementation of new ideas together with constantly improving technology renders it essential to consider expansion at the outset of any design for computer premises. As electronic components and techniques become more sophisticated they tend to reduce in size, but paradoxically the equipment becomes increasingly large, as wider capabilities and greater capacities are demanded by the users.

In choosing a site, the client must study the limiting factors and decide whether they are economically acceptable. The architect's responsibility then, is to ensure that within these limits the maximum provision can be made for future expansion, and that this expansion

(a) can be effected without major disruption to the existing installation,

(b) is acceptable to local planning authorities,

(c) is compatible with existing power supplies and communications facilities, and

(d) is feasible within the finances available.

If a computer unit is to be planned within an existing building there may be additional problems because of restrictions imposed by local authorities or owners, limits on floor loadings, unsuitable floor heights, and fire hazards, including consequential damage by smoke and water from

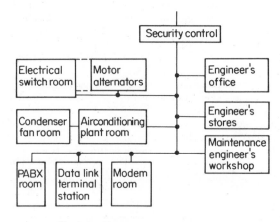

Fig. 7.2 Circulation diagram: plant spaces

other areas in the building. Future expansion may be even more difficult.

Once a site has been selected, various decisions must be made:

(a) *Access*

Security is of prime importance in most computer installations, and the number of access points must be limited (see Fig. 7.1). Provision must be made for work to be brought in and results to be taken away. An entrance for staff and visitors must be provided, and allowance made for the delivery of supplies and equipment and the disposal of waste.

The delivery of the computer itself needs careful consideration. The Central Processing Unit usually arrives as a single large unit which has to be manoeuvred into position, and access doors designed to full storey height will avoid problems involving the temporary removal of doors, frames or partitions.

(b) *Services*

The relationship of service needs with surrounding sites must be considered, and locations found for:

(i) *The air intake*. This should be sited to utilise the cleanest and coolest air available. Avoid intakes over large flat roofs heated by the sun, or near chimneys, or where there is a risk of drawing in fumes or smoke.

(ii) *Grilles for extract fans, cooling towers, or air cooled condenser fans*. Many plants operate at night or over weekends, and great care must be taken to ensure that noise is reduced to an absolute minimum. The effects of an enforced shutdown by a local authority following complaints by nearby residents could be disastrous. The use of acoustic louvres is often advisable (see page **7**–8).

(c) *Standby equipment*

Dependent on the Client's requirements and available finances, if maximum uninterrupted computer availability is to be provided, then consideration must be given to the degree of provision of standby equipment. Duplication of essential mechanical and power supply units will avoid costly delays in the event of subsequent breakdowns (see page **7**–8).

PLANNING

PROGRAMME

In addition to the careful programming requirements of most building planning exercises, the design of a computer centre involves a detailed timetable of operations, to ensure that the delivery of the computer coincides as nearly as possible with the completion of the building. If the computer arrives too early it is virtually impossible to store satisfactorily without deterioration; late delivery will be costly from the Client's viewpoint in terms of lost operating time.

Computer manufacturers provide a service which advises on planning the accommodation and supervises the installation of the computer. This service includes advice on dates to be taken into account in the project timetable.

Because of the timescale of the building work in comparison with the delivery period of the computer, it must be stressed that as much as possible of the planning work for the building and engineering services should be completed before the computer is ordered. A firm date must be agreed with the building contractor by which the accommodation will be ready, cleaned, and with a fully commissioned air-conditioning plant.

Once the computer has been ordered, there should be a full exchange of information between buyer, architect, building contractor and manufacturer's installation engineers, and agreement reached on the layout of equipment, on any outstanding constructional details, and any special requirements for the delivery of the equipment. DTI publication 'Computer installations: accommodation and fire precautions', (HMSO), sets out a detailed schedule of requirements at fixed dates before delivery of the computer is effected, from twelve months before the scheduled installation date (SID) down to the actual day of delivery. It is most important that these by dates are met, particularly the requirement that no further modifications be made to the agreed layout of equipment after SID minus four months.

SECURITY

In all but the smaller installations, a vital factor to be considered at an early stage of planning is security. The number of entry and exit points to the computer suite, at least, must be limited. Provision must also be made for the accommodation of security staff who may be present at all times during which the computer is operational or being maintained.

Particular attention must be paid to the suiting of locks and the limitation of master and sub-master keys, and in some cases a system of double independent locking may be called for. As the computer suite and ancillary rooms are air-conditioned or environmentally controlled to some degree, openable windows are generally not encountered, but these and any accessible fixed windows must be designed to prevent unauthorised entry.

EXPANSION

In order to avoid major disruption to the operation of the computer, a clear policy for the future expansion of the installation must be developed before the work proceeds too far. In most cases, fairly generous accommodation is planned for the computer and its ancillaries, and over a period of a few years, the configuration is slowly modified and added to until ultimately both the accommodation and the services provisions reach their limit. A solution to this problem would be to construct at this stage a duplicate computer room and service unit adjacent to the old, perhaps somewhat smaller than the original, which would house a new computer. Once this is commissioned, the old computer is gradually run down and the expansion of the new machine will correspondingly fill the space vacated.

It is perhaps worth considering that the apparent speed at which a large-scale computer installation attains obsolescence is derived partly from the fact that in operating for 24 hours a day its rate of ageing is increased by a factor of three. This applies not only to the electronic equipment but also to the building itself, a fact which should be recognised when specifying materials and finishes.

The limitation of the size of compartments is a helpful factor in minimising disruption in the event of expansion. In recent years, the miniaturisation of components has meant that each similar-sized package, having an ever-increasing capacity for work, becomes more valuable; and it is not unusual to find in one large computer room several million pounds worth of equipment. Unless control is exercised on the *value* of equipment housed in a space, it will become increasingly difficult for clients to obtain insurance cover for their installations. It appears that 370 m² is perhaps the maximum size for a large computer room.

It goes almost without saying that the use of modular planning will also greatly facilitate expansion. Many of the components associated with computer installations are already provided on a modular basis—flooring units, ceilings etc.; and careful planning will ensure that difficulties associated with this particular aspect are minimised. These remarks apply equally to the computer room and related elements and to plant provisions.

A recommendation for the formation and structure of a Design Team is set out in detail in the section on Research Laboratories (see pages **6**–1 to **6**–4), and information is given on the use of Room Data Sheets which are used as the major tool in the briefing procedure.

At feasibility stage, the architect should be notified of the general requirements of the installation. If the make of the computer has not been settled, it should still be possible to estimate broadly the accommodation required, which would make possible studies for likely sites. A services engineer with experience of air conditioning practice for computer installations should be appointed at an early stage. A programme can then be drawn up which gives key dates in the execution of the project. The planning and construction work may take longer than the delivery period the computer manufacture offers, and so as much as possible of the planning of the building and engineering services should be done before the computer is ordered. However, it will be essential to decide on the manufacturer before detailed planning of the installation can be commenced. (See Examples at the end of this section).

The manufacturer will no doubt issue his Site Installation and Preparation Manual, which will describe in detail the precise conditions, areas, power requirements, etc., he will expect to be provided. It should be stressed that, if in the event of a malfunction of the computer, the manufacturer can prove that these conditions have not been met, then the manufacturer's liability will lapse.

SPACE REQUIREMENTS

GENERAL

The DTI publication 'Computer installations: accommodation and fire precautions', sets out a detailed table listing the various needs to be taken into account in assessing accommodation requirements, and gives the ratio of areas required for different parts of the installation. This information is given in Table 7.1. For convenience, an installation is shown comprising four areas; Area A is made up of rooms for the computer, its peripheral equipment, and the services associated with it. For this area five different examples of installation are quoted. Area B is shown separately, because the amount of data preparation done at the Computer Centre depends upon the nature of the task itself and the organisational need for it to be done at a particular place. Area C, allotted to programmers and stationery storage may also vary widely because of differences in the nature of the work. Area D is frequently underestimated, particularly when computers are used during the night.

The examples are not standards, and each project must be considered separately so that it meets the needs of that application.

DETAILED SPACE REQUIREMENTS

THE COMPUTER ROOM

This is the focal point of the installation, but may take up less than 20% of the total floor area. It will house the Central Processing Unit (CPU) and a series of peripheral devices, such as magnetic tape or disc units, printers and card readers, and the console, from which point the functions of the computer can be initiated, observed and controlled. This equipment is contained in metal cabinets of varying size up to perhaps 2 m high and arranged in suites, the complete layout being known as the configuration.

The interconnection of the units making up the configuration is effected by means of cabling of varying diameters which is accommodated in a false floor space some 200–400 mm deep. It is essential to provide easy access to the cable space, and it is usual to construct the entire computer room floor of removable panels supported on a jack system of corner supports, preferably of a stringerless type in larger systems.

Before delivery of the computer and its peripherals, the manufacturer will provide details of cable entry and airway cut-outs required in the floor panels below equipment. It is important to ascertain that the load-limits on the floor panels are compatible not only with the equipment in its final configuration, but also during delivery and installation. There are a number of proprietary brands of floor panel on the market, usually provided on a supply-and-lay basis. It is seldom advisable to allow the main contractor to produce his own panels, as a proprietary brand will give uniform, interchangeable panels, usually with screw-jacks to provide easy levelling.

The maximum distance between some of the devices may be limited by the manufacturer, and different considerations apply to multi-access equipment having terminals at remote locations and connected either by GPO lines or special links (see page **7**–7: Modem Room).

Several methods of air conditioning the computer suite are available, and the services consultant must consider these and arrive at the optimum solution bearing in mind location and finances. The simplest system of full air conditioning would be effected by direct ductwork with supply and return grilles so spaced in relation to the configuration to give the conditions imposed by the manufacturer.

Table 7.1 ACCOMODATION REQUIREMENTS FOR COMPLETE INSTALLATION*

Description	Approximate area m²
AREA A (1) *The areas given are for installations having a small processor and say up to two magnetic tape units or discs, a printer and punch-card or paper-tape input and output.*	
Computer and peripheral equipment	25–70
Maintenance rooms	10–18
Magnetic tape or disc store (note 1)	up to 18
Power room (where required)	up to 12
Air-conditioning plant room (note 2)	up to 40
AREA A (2) *The areas given are for installations having 3–6 magnetic tape units or discs, a high-speed printer and punched-card or paper-tape input and output.*	
Computer and peripheral equipment	70–150
Maintenance room	18–35
Magnetic tape store and disc (see note 1)	up to 40
Power room (where required)	12–20
Air-conditioning plant room (note 2)	35–75
AREA A (3) *The areas given are for installations having 6–14 magnetic tape units or discs, 1 or 2 high-speed printers and perhaps, 2 card or paper-tape readers and punches.*	
Computer and peripheral equipment	140–240
Maintenance room	24–40
Magnetic tape and disc store (note 1)	35–60
Power room (when required)	12–40
Air-conditioning plant room (note 2)	70–115
AREA A (4) *The areas given are for installations having 10–25 magnetic tape units, several discs, two high-speed printers and several card or paper tape readers and punches and say communications equipment.*	
Computer and peripheral equipment	200–375
Maintenance room	35–60
Magnetic tape and disc store (note 1)	55–75
Power room (when required)	25–50
Air-conditioning plant room (note 2)	100–150
AREA A (5) *The areas quoted are typical for installations having a very powerful processor or more than one processor, large data banks, several input peripherals and printers and control for remote terminals.*	
Computer room and peripherals	400–150 or more This area may include separate rooms for the data banks or printers
Maintenance room	35–80 This area may be divided into workshop, office and storage areas or may be divided between two manufacturers
Magnetic tape and disc store	60–100 It may be desirable to store some items adjacent to the handlers
Power room (when required)	25–80
Air conditioning plant (note 2)	200–600
AREA B *Input data preparation, input assembly, off-line machines and despatch of output, any associated clerical work, working stocks of paper tape, cards and other stationery.*	from 1 to 1½ times Area A
AREA C *Office accommodation for supervisors, programmers and the main stationery stores.*	about 50% to 80% of Area A
AREA D *Corridors, welfare accommodation, cleaners room and miscellaneous.*	This is usually about half Area A

*Table extracted from DTI Publication 'Computer Installations: accommodation and fire precautions'.

Notes : 1. A small number of magnetic tapes and discs might be stored in locked fire resisting cabinets in the computer room.
2. A separate external cooling tower or condenser may be required.

For larger installations, and for greater flexibility, ceiling void or floor void plenum supplies, or a combination of both, might be appropriate. Some systems require air fed from the floor plenum to cool cabinets; others circulate the room air itself. It is therefore most important to establish the type of equipment to be used, before choosing the air conditioning system.

Purpose-built central air conditioning plants are often used, giving say, 90 % recirculated air and the balance made up from a fresh air supply. This type of plant is not easy to extend without disruption, and it may be advantageous to consider more flexible methods.

'Package' room conditioners with their own cooling towers are suitable in this respect, as other units may be added without interference to those already in operation. If used, these units should be sited to one side of the computer suite in a 'corridor' plant room and serve the suite through the floor plenum, to avoid the necessity of changing filter pads within the computer room. This arrangement also has the advantage of reducing the fire hazard to the computer suite.

Cooling of the equipment cabinets is effected by

(a) internal means only, requiring the heat to be dissipated by a chilled water supply from the plant room through the false floor, or

(b) by air circulation, either from the floor plenum, or directly from the computer room air. Fans draw in the air, which is passed over the banks of electronic devices.

If a ceiling or floor plenum is to be used, it is obviously essential to treat all the structural faces or finishes with sealer to prevent dust being blown into the computer room or equipment. Computer manufacturers will lay down air conditioning tolerances, which in some cases are very small. Where the number of units to be housed is large, the degree of variation becomes increasingly difficult to control; and to this end careful consideration must be given to the location of the computer room. Poor U values will subject the air conditioning plant to large additional loads, and if the building is not air and vapour tight the plant may not be able to control room conditions because there will be a considerable moisture loss in winter and gain in summer.

Closely associated with and adjoining the computer room are the following rooms:

(a) *Magnetic tape store*

Magnetic tapes, discs, and other magnetic media are affected by direct sunlight and magnetic fields, and care must be taken to exclude windows and not to route cables carrying large currents through or near this area, e.g. lift machinery, switch gear, transformers, motor alternators and lightning conductors. The temperature and humidity of the store should be the same as in the computer room. The door to the store should allow easy access for trolleys. Metal storage racks carry the tapes and discs, and with conventional racking, 100 tapes or 15 discs may be accommodated per sq.m.

(b) *Job assembly room*

Work arriving for processing will be accepted at a counter and placed on a trolley awaiting the collection of associated material before being wheeled into the computer room. Cards awaiting processing are sometimes held for up to 24 hours in this area, which is controlled at the same temperature and humidity as the computer room, to acclimatise them and avoid causing malfunctions in the sensitive high-speed equipment.

Some card punch machines and card readers are usually located in this room, and for this reason some acoustic treatment is needed to the ceilings and walls. Benches are required around the walls on which work can be assembled, and an adequate level of lighting is important.

A partial extension of the computer room false floor system into this room is useful in cabling up equipment which may feed directly into the computer system. This room can be associated with the job despatch room.

(c) *Engineers' stores and workshop*

The computer manufacturer will specify the accommodation required by his maintenance staff. This space will be used for the maintenance of parts of the equipment brought from the computer room on trolleys, the holding of spares, and the storage of electronic test gear. Smaller installations would require rather less space, and a small computer unit may require only a cupboard in which a few spares, a trolley and an oscilloscope would be kept. In a larger computer centre, it is usual to provide a separate office for the chief engineer.

Workbenches should be provided along the walls, with good lighting and adequate power points, and provision made for cupboards for the storage of spares. Normally the space is air conditioned to the same standard as the computer room except where the equipment has a wider tolerance. A telephone or other means of communication with the plant rooms is important. It is often useful to extend the computer room false floor partly into this area.

(d) *Viewing gallery*

Facilities for visitors to observe the activities within the computer suite are sometimes called for by the Client, and manufacturers generally consider a viewing gallery highly desirable. The gallery should be separated from the computer room by a glazed panel, and entrance effected from a corridor outside the suite. If possible the floor of the gallery should be raised 300–400 mm to improve sightlines.

DATA PREPARATION ROOM

In order to reduce the level of noise from card punch and card reader machines, some form of acoustic treatment is necessary. A modular arrangement of floor socket outlets should be provided to allow the inevitable relocation of equipment from time to time, or better still a false floor space of 100–200 mm which would also allow for cabling.

JOB DESPATCH ROOM

Can be associated with the job assembly room, and requires facilities for holding of completed work pending collection, such as a large pigeon-hole fitting open both sides designed to take standard work-trays.

STATIONERY STORE

Boxed cards are stored in racks arranged to give easy access, both for the replenishment of supplies and for removal for use. The turnover of cards is high, and a large installation not specifically card-orientated may still use 1 million cards in a month. Paper supplies are no longer reliable, and it is advisable to accommodate at least 3 months supply of both cards and paper. The store should be air conditioned to the same temperature and humidity as the computer room, and cards must acclimatise here for a minimum of 24 hours before being used to avoid warping. (See details in BS 4636; 1970.)

The racks supporting the boxed cards should be strong, and attention should be paid to the floor loadings in this area, as well as fire detection and prevention. Where the traffic in cards is considerable, trolleys may be used, and routes must be free of steps with doors allowing easy passage in either direction. Fully automatic doors may be justified for very heavy traffic.

WASTE PAPER STORE

The accumulation of waste paper is rapid and considerable, and storage must be provided in a location which constitutes neither a security risk nor a fire hazard. The store must have easy access for collection, and a doorway to permit the use of trolleys. If the entrance is located externally, it is important to have a lockable door to prevent unauthorised access and possible malicious damage from fire.

PROGRAMMERS' ACCOMMODATION

Requirements may vary considerably, but this area should be divorced from the main computer suite circulation. A small punch room suitably acoustically treated should be provided, and an adjacent conference room is useful both for internal purposes and for briefing parties of visitors.

STAFF ACCOMMODATION

Most large installations will operate on a 24 hour shift basis, and the requirements for staff must not be underestimated. Provision must be made for rest-rooms and facilities for the preparation of light meals and refreshments. These may require duplication if separation of facilities for the computer manufacturer's staff is called for.

MODEM ROOM

Where the computer operates as a central unit providing a service for a number of remote site users, the terminal units are connected by means of either direct lines or the GPO telephone system. In order to render the encoded signal compatible with telephone signal transmission, a device known as a *modem* is used, each remote terminal being equipped with one of these, with a corresponding unit at the computer centre. The number of modem units at the computer centre is determined by the number of incoming connections the centre wishes to handle at one time.

The modem units, usually provided by the GPO, are stacked on metal racks, preferably in a separate room, which must be adequately ventilated to dissipate the heat generated. It is useful to extend the computer room false floor system partially into this area, or to provide floor ducts to allow interconnection of the modem units with the computer. In the former case, care must be taken to anchor the racking firmly to the structural floor below to avoid overturning of the racking when the units are withdrawn on their cantilevered runners for servicing.

AIR LOCKS

Air locks should be provided at entrances to air-conditioned suites, except in the case of smaller installations. These must be long enough to accommodate a person pushing a trolley.

PLANT ACCOMMODATION—POWER

ELECTRICAL SWITCHGEAR

The mains supply will generally be 3-phase 4-wire, and requirements will vary between 5 kVA and several hundred kVA depending on the size of the installation. The air-conditioning plant may require three times the load imposed by the computer, and allowance must be made for future additions to computer ancillary equipment, as well as the computer itself.

For a smaller installation, feeders taken from the main incoming busbars for the building would suffice, while in the case of a large installation a new substation would almost certainly be required. Switchgear tends to be fairly bulky, and with provision for access and future expansion, it will take up a significant proportion of service space. The dissipation of heat generated by this equipment must be carefully considered.

In installations using multiple alternator supplies, Power Factor Correction should be discussed with the local Electricity Supply Board.

MOTOR ALTERNATORS

It is necessary to isolate the computer power supply from the mains feeders, as heavy switching loads in the vicinity will introduce fluctuations in the supply. This can be achieved by the use of alternators driven by the mains supply and producing the necessary steady output.

The alternators are also useful in providing frequencies other than the standard 50 Hz. American equipment, for example requires a 60 Hz supply, and some others 400 Hz. To ensure continuity in the supply during breakdown or maintenance, standby alternators should be provided.

Provision must be made for the starter control panels for the alternators, and once again the heat generated by this equipment must be dissipated by means of a ventilation system. In smaller systems, the use of a Power Supply Regulator to smooth surges in the local supply may be adequate.

POWER DISTRIBUTION

A clearly distinguishable control must be readily accessible in the computer room which will cut off power supplies to the computer in the event of a fire. Other emergency controls must be available to cut off supplies to the air-conditioning plant and power outlets.

Provision of a Brigade Control Switch for the extract system to clear smoke should be considered. This is best located at the main entrance to the Computer Suite.

STANDBY POWER SUPPLY

The power consumption of a large computer installation—the equipment itself together with the air conditioning requirements—is such that the provision of an alternative power supply to be used in the event of the mains failure would not be economically feasible.

It is sometimes possible, however, to make arrangements with the local Supply Board, to use the system of 'looping' the incoming mains, so that in the event of failure of the power supply in one direction an alternative is available. It is of course important to provide in any case an internal emergency lighting system purely from a point of view of safety.

ELECTROMAGNETIC CONTROL GROUNDING OR ARTIFICIAL EARTH

The computer manufacturer will lay down requirements for a 'clean' earth, which may be simply a separate wire from each piece of equipment back to the Supply Board's service earth. Alternatively, he may require the earths to be grouped in a 'star', to a direct external earthing probe or pattern of probes. In larger high-speed systems a complete electromagnetic grounding grid throughout the computer room false floor system may have to be installed, each piece of equipment being separately connected down to this grid.

This earthing (or grounding) system is in no way to be confused with the normal electrical earth wiring. It is advisable to install a device which prevents induction or backflow from the earthing system to the equipment.

PLANT ACCOMMODATION—AIR CONDITIONING

The air conditioning plant for a large installation comprises:
(a) The intake fan and filter system.
(b) Boilers for the heating system.
(c) Compressors for the cooling system.
(d) Cooling towers or condenser fans related to the compressors.
The ductwork associated with the air conditioning tends to be large to reduce the noise usually involved in handling large volumes of air, and care must be taken in planning the plant room to ensure that access to equipment is not impeded by the layout of ductwork.

If the boilers are to be used solely for the computer suite, then these may be of modest size, as the considerable power requirement of both computer and plant has the effect of generating much heat, which should be used if energy wastage is to be avoided. In many cases, electrode boilers are to be desired because of their small size; in any system a standby set of boilers is essential to maintain supplies during routine servicing or breakdown.

The compressors tend to be very noisy, and produce vibration. They must thus be sited so as to cause the minimum disturbance to those inside as well as outside the building, and vibration-free mountings must be employed.

Both cooling towers and condenser fans produce a lesser degree of noise, but as a matter of function they require to be exposed as much as possible to external conditions. The noise generated cannot be ignored if the occupants of adjacent sites are likely to be affected. The use of acoustic louvres or silencers is essential to keep within acceptable limits related to the siting of the building.

TYPICAL DATA

The layout and dimensions for typical equipment used in a computer installation are shown in Figs 7.3 to 7.8. This consists of
  Mobile storage (Fig. 7.3).
  Disc, paper and tape storage (Fig. 7.4).
  Computer room equipment (Fig. 7.5).
  Peripheral equipment (Fig. 7.6).
  Central processing units (Fig. 7.7).
  Equipment racking (Fig. 7.8).

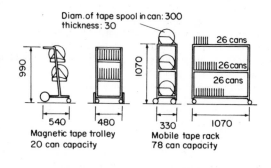

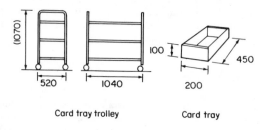

Fig. 7.3   Mobile storage

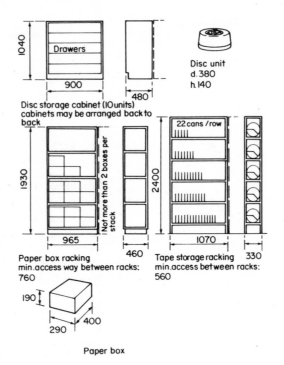

1040

Drawers

900

480

Disc unit
d. 380
h. 140

Disc storage cabinet (10 units)
cabinets may be arranged back to
back

1930

965

Not more than 2 boxes per stack

460

22 cans /row

2400

1070

330

Paper box racking
min.access way between racks:
760

Tape storage racking
min.access between racks:
560

190

400

290

Paper box

Fig. 7.4   Disc, paper and tape storage

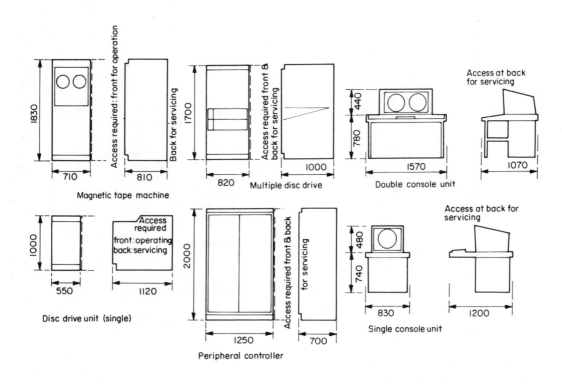

1830

710

810

Access required: front for operation

Back for servicing

Magnetic tape machine

1700

820

1000

Access required front & back for servicing

Multiple disc drive

440

780

1570

Double console unit

Access at back
for servicing

1070

1000

550

1120

Access required
front: operating
back: servicing

Disc drive unit (single)

2000

1250

700

Access required front & back for servicing

Peripheral controller

480

740

830

Single console unit

Access at back for
servicing

1200

Fig. 7.5   Computer room equipment

7–9

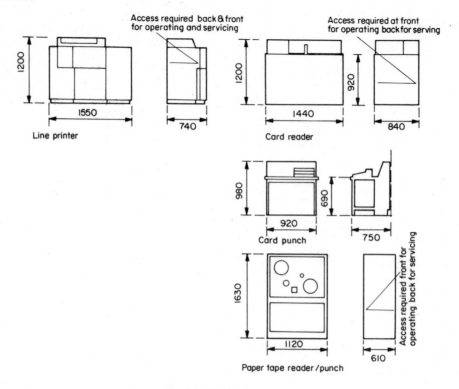

Fig. 7.6   Peripheral equipment

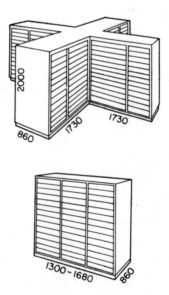

Fig. 7.7   Central processing
units. Note that actual sizes may
vary considerably

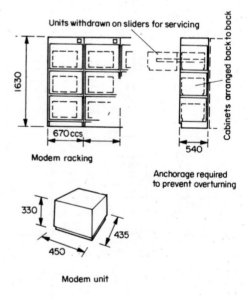

Fig. 7.8   Equipment racking

ACCOMMODATION

Accommodation will be listed under three headings:
1. Computer room and ancillaries.
2. Administration.
3. Plant space.

Detailed information (1) and (3) are given in 5 Space requirements:

1 COMPUTER ROOM AND ANCILLARIES
Computer room
Magnetic tape store
Job Assembly/Despatch
Supervisors' office
Stationery store
Waste paper store
Engineers' stores and workshop
Viewing gallery

2 ADMINISTRATION
Entrance hall/control point
Porters' room
Male and female lavatories
Data preparation room
Offices for managerial staff, secretaries, typists, programmers, etc. *Requirements vary considerably.*
Office for computer manufacturer. *May not be required.*
Library. *Useful location for regularly updated information on computer operations issued by manufacturers.*
Engineers' and operators rest room. *Sited near computer suite.*
Staff canteen, kitchen. *If required, for day use.*
Lecture room or theatre. *Considered vital for briefing staff, visitors, etc.*
Conference room. *Internal meetings, and smaller meetings with visitors.*
Duplicating room
Storage for domestic consumables
Cleaners' stores. *See (c) below 'Finishes and special details'.*
Telephone operators' room

3 PLANT SPACE
Electrical switch room/motor alternators
Transformer chamber. *If required by local Supply Board.*
Air-conditioning plant room
Condenser fan room. *Needed if cooling tower is not used.*
Engineers' office
Engineers' store
Maintenance engineers' workshop
Data link terminal station
PABX room
Modem room

BUILDING TYPE

Accommodation for a computer suite is normally purpose designed, except in the case of smaller installations. Particular consideration must be given to the following points:
(i) Floor loading will be high, particularly in the computer room itself and stationery store. Plant, too, will be heavy, and will require vibration-free mountings.

(ii) Sufficient structural floor heights must be allowed for the false floor construction in the computer room and some ancillaries. (See Detailed space requirements, page 7-4).
(iii) The means of effecting future expansion must be considered, not only for the computer suite but also for the back-up services.
(iv) Insulation is a most important factor. Not only will poor insulation result in unnecessary loading on the heating or cooling system, but because of the close tolerance required in the working environment of the equipment, may adversely effect the operation of the computer in extremes of temperature.

FINISHES AND SPECIAL DETAILS

Within the computer suite, particular care must be taken in specifying materials which do not easily fragment or produce dust or fibrous fragments and which can be easily cleaned.

The actual method of cleaning must be noted and discussed before a final decision is reached. With the relatively clean air produced by the air-conditioning system, walls and ceilings in the computer suite tend not to become dirty quickly, but floors collect dirt from the feet of the occupants, and this becomes a hazard to the equipment. Floor finishes should be carefully chosen to avoid degenerative dusting, and they should have antistatic properties.

Static-treated mats (replaceable on a contract basis) provided in the approaches to the computer suite can help reduce dirt carried in, as can printed and frequently-repeated exhortations to staff and users; but it has to be accepted that dirt will find its way into the computer suite, and efficient means of cleaning must be provided. Suspended floor systems are often covered with pvc sheet, which requires a regular application of sealer. During periodical maintenance of the floor finish, the solvent may penetrate the joints between the floor tiles, which become firmly fixed once the solution dries. There is also the danger of cleansing fluids entering the cavity below and affecting the insulation on cables.

Where carpet tiles are used, ordinary vacuum cleaning is not satisfactory. A horizontally-rotating brush with suction cleaning (commercial-size machine) would suffice, but a more thorough method must be employed from time to time. 'Dry' cleaning may employ either fluids or a powder, both of which could have an adverse effect on the computer environment.

It is important, first to obtain a detailed statement from the flooring manufacturer on cleaning methods, and secondly for the Client to employ either contract or staff cleaners who can be relied upon to follow the manufacturers' instructions implicitly.

LEGISLATION

No special bylaws govern the design of a Computer Centre, which should normally be conditioned by the usual Building Regulations and Means of Escape requirements. A useful check on statutory controls is given in the following publications:

Building Design and Construction.
Guide to Statutory Provisions.
(Department of the Environment: Welsh Office) HMSO.
With regard to fire precautions advice may be sought from the following:
Fire Officers' Committee, Aldermary House, Queen Street, London EC4P 4SD.
NFPA International, 470 Atlantic Avenue, Boston, MA 02201, USA

For authorities within the Public Sector the Department of Trade and Industry, Computers Systems and Electronics Division and the Technical Support Unit of the Civil Service Department are available to give technical advice on accommodation or building requirements.

The following publications provide advice on accommodation and fire precautions:
CP3: Chapters iv, Part 3 (1968) Precautions against fire; Part 3, Office Buildings. (British Standards Institution).
CP95: 1970, Fire precautions for electronic data processing installations. (British Standards Institution).
Computer Installations: Accommodation and fire precautions (Revised edition 1972), Department of Trade and Industry. (HMSO.)

EXAMPLES

Security is always a problem for those who manage computer centres, and they are thus sometimes understandably reluctant to give details of layouts or allow visitors to inspect their installations. There is no doubt, on the other hand, that a well laid-out computer configuration presents an impressive appearance, and to this end viewing galleries are often provided so that visitors may observe the activities within the computer suite without interfering with either the work of the operators or the equipment controls. Stringent precautions are also taken to prevent unauthorised access to power supply controls, which, if operated maliciously, could have a disastrous effect on the entire system.

Computer manufacturers have access to installations in which their equipment has been used, and it is therefore probably better to contact a manufacturer in order to arrange a visit to the type of installation one wishes to see.

A list of some of the more common large computers in current use is appended. The name of the manufacturer is followed by the names and model numbers of the computers concerned, together with a contact required:

Burroughs	B1700, B2700, B3700, B4700, B5700, B6700. All installation queries should be made through the salesman, liaising with the engineering department when necessary.
Control Data	Cyber 172, 173, 174, 175. An installation planner is available to answer queries.
Digital Equipment Corporation	PDP-11/40, PDP-11/45, DEC system 10. Installation queries can be referred to the sales support group.
Honeywell	6000 Series, now being supplanted by Series 60 Levels 61, 62, 64 and 66. Queries can be referred to the engineering department.
I.B.M.	System 370 Models 135, 145, 158, 168, 195. The Local Installation Planning Department will answer queries.
I.C.L.	1900 series from 1903A upwards, System 4 Models 4/50, 4/70, 4/52, 4/72. A new range is being produced. I.C.L. have a subsidiary, Data Space at Newcastle, who can handle installation queries.
Rank Xerox	Sigma 6. Sigma 9 Model 3, Sigma 9. Queries to the Installation and Coordination Manager.
Univac	The Facilities Planning Department is the installation queries contact.

A selection of a few European examples of large computer centres is given below, but it must be stressed that any arrangements for visiting their establishments must be made through the directors or other persons in authority.

England	University of London Computer Centre, 20 Guildford Street, London WC1. University of Manchester Regional Computer Centre, Manchester. Service in Informatics and Analysis, Ebury Gate, 23 Lower Belgrave Street, London SW1.
France	Electricite de France, 17 Avenue de la Liberation, 92 Clanart, Paris.
Holland	The Computer Centre, Philips, Eindhoven.
Switzerland	European Centre for Nuclear Research, Geneva.

BIBLIOGRAPHY

There appears to be a lack of published material in the form of books relating specifically to computer centres, although there have been numerous articles on the subject in the technical press. A valuable source of information for this type of material can be found in:
1. RIBA, Architectural Periodical Index, available from RIBA Publications Ltd., 66 Portland Place, London W.1.
2. The Avery Index to Architectural Periodicals, available from: Columbia University, Central Office, 562 West 113 Street, New York 10025.

Both these indexes can be referred to at the RIBA Library, and for members of the Architectural Association at their Library, 34 Bedford Square, London W.C.1.

ACKNOWLEDGEMENTS

The author wishes to acknowledge with thanks the assistance and encouragement received from the following:
D. G. Campion BA (Arch.), Dip.TP, Cusdin Burden and Howitt, Chartered Architects, London.
D. B. Livingstone, MSAAT, Architect's Dept, Cluttons, Chartered Surveyors, London.
K. D. MacKenzie, B.Sc (Dipl. Ed.), FBCS, University of London Computer Centre, London.

APPENDIX—GLOSSARY OF TERMS

Accumulator. A storage register within the central processor unit of a computer which is used for intermediate storage, logical and arithmetic operations.

Alphanumeric Character. A generic name for numeric digits, alphabetic characters and other special characters.

Analogue Computer. A computer the input and output of which consists of continuously variable information, e.g. electrical waveforms.

Backing store. That part of a computer store which is not contained within the central processor unit.

Binary Digit. A '0' digit or a '1' digit used to represent the binary conditions of a switch which may be either 'off' or 'on'.

Bit. An abbreviation for 'binary digit'.

Card Punch. A device which is used to punch holes in a card in order to record information.

Card Reader. A device which is used to detect the pattern of holes in a punched card.

Central Processor unit. The heart of a computer system containing the 'arithmetic logic' unit and internal store.

Communications Controller. A hardware device for controlling the incoming and outgoing signals to remote peripheral devices.

Compiler. A program used to effect the compilation of one program from another.

Computer System. A central processor unit together with one or more input, output and backing store devices.

Control Typewriter. An electric typewriter which may be used by a person operating a computer in order to control and interrogate the central processor units.

Conversational Mode. A mode of operation where a user is in direct contact with a computer and interaction is possible between man and machine without the being conscious of any language or communication barrier.

Core Store. A form of storage device utilising magnetic cores.

Configuration. The combination of computer hardware used to form a specific computer installation.

Data. A set of information supplied by a computer user for processing by computer. It is also used to refer to both operands and results held within a computer.

Data medium. A medium used to contain data, e.g. punched cards, paper tape.

Data Preparation. The transferring of information to a data medium.

Data Processing. The overall operation of receiving data and manipulating it so as to produce certain results.

Data tape. A length of paper tape on which data is represented by particular patterns of holes. The information on the data tape is input to the computer under the control of a program while the latter is being executed.

Digital Computer. A computer, the input and output of which consists of alphanumeric information which takes the form of sequences of binary digits. Different types of input and output devices are used to interpret information in the forms in which it passes between a user and the computer; by this means the user is enabled to supply and receive information in the form in which it is most meaningful to him, e.g. drawing on a cathode-ray display.

Digital plotter. A form of output device allowing information from a computer to be presented in graphical form, e.g. line drawings. This device may take the form of either a 'drum plotter' or a 'flat-bed plotter'; information is normally plotted as a series of incremental steps.

Disc Store. A backing store device taking the form of magnetic discs.

Flat-bed plotter. See digital plotter.

Flow diagram. A form of diagram using both written information and graphical symbols to indicate the flow operations required to solve a particular problem.

Graphical display Unit. A television-like screen for the display of text and/or graphical information output by the computer.

Hardware. A term used to indicate physical items of computer equipment, e.g. the central processor unit, backing store devices, input and output devices.

Immediate access Store. The form of storage provided within the central processor unit.

Input. A term used to indicate either the method or the means for transferring information into a computer.

Input Device. A device used for transferring information from a data medium into the central processor unit of a computer.

Input/output. A multiple term used to refer to the processes of both input and output of information.

Instruction. A means by which a computer is instructed to execute a particular operation; a computer program consists of a series of instructions.

Internal Store. The part of the computer's store which is contained within the central processor unit.

Key Punch. A tape or card punching device with an alphanumeric or numeric keyboard.

Language. The basic language of a digital computer takes the form of a binary code; this is used as the means of communication and storage inside a computer. A programmer writes the instructions forming a particular computer program in what is referred to as a computer programming language; this allows the programmer to use a form of everyday English language instead of the computer's binary language.

Lineprinter. A form of output device for the presentation of typewritten information; a complete line of print is output at a time. A form of continuous stationery is moved past the printing mechanism.

Light Pen. A form of input device which is used in connection with a CRT display. The light pen is used to detect the presence of information displayed on the graphical display screen.

Liveware. The people involved with the operation of a computer.

Modem. A hardware device for linking terminal equipment to private or shared telephone lines.

Magnetic Disc store. A backing store device taking the form of magnetic discs on which information may be recorded and retrieved when required.

Magnetic Drum store. A backing store device taking the form of a magnetic drum.

Magnetic tape Unit. A backing store device enabling information to be recorded and retrieved from magnetic tape; the tape is contained on spools which may be loaded on to, and removed from, the tape handler unit as required by an operator.

Main store. The part of a computer store which is contained within the central processor unit: this normally takes the form of an immediate access core store.

Memory. A term used to refer to computer's store.

Multi-Programming. A term used to imply that a particular computer is capable of containing more than one program in its internal store at the same time, and is capable of executing more than one concurrently, or more than one in such a way that parts of different programs are executed in a selected sequence.

Multiplexor. A hardware device for collecting the incoming data from many remote terminals and linking them into the computer.

Microfilm Unit. A hardware device for recording computer output on microfilm (com); also covers microfiche.

Off-Line. A process carried out by a device which is not directly connected to the central processor unit of a computer.

On-line. A process carried out by a device which is connected to, and controlled by, the central processor unit of a computer.

Operator. A human computer operator, or the symbols used in a written computer program to designate particular mathematical operations such as addition and subtraction, etc.

Output. The process, or the result, of transferring information from the central processor unit to an output device where it is then intelligible to the user.

Output Device. A computer peripheral device which enables information inside a computer to be displayed in a form which is intelligible to a user.

Paper tape. A medium used for transferring information into digital form. A form of pencil is used to trace out graphical information, which may take the medium as a set of two-dimensional co-ordinates.

Peripheral Device. Any device which is attached to the central processor unit of a computer, i.e. an input device, output device or a backing store.

Pencil Follower. A device for transferring graphical information into digital form. A form of pencil is used to trace out graphical information, which may take the form of a drawing, and the relevant information is transferred to some data medium as a set of two-dimensional co-ordinates.

Plotter Tape. A small reel of magnetic tape, often containing 600 ft of tape, used for the temporary storage of computer output which is then transferred to an off-line plotter for producing drawings.

Printer. An output device used to print information.

Program. The information which is necessary for the solution of a problem. A source computer program consists of information written by the programmer; an object computer program consists of the same information converted into internal language of a particular computer. A program consists of a series of instructions, each of which will cause the computer to carry out a specific operation, and any other information which is required for the solution of the particular problem.

Reader. A form of input device which enables information on a particular data medium to be transferred into a computer, e.g. a tape reader, a card reader or an optical reader.

Real-time Operation. A term used to refer to the method of operating a computer whereby there is interactive communication between a user and the computer, e.g. using a CRT display and a light pen, or an on-line typewriter, allowing two-way communication between man and machine.

Register. A special-purpose form of storage location in a central processor unit which allows operations to be carried out on the information contained in it.

Reserve Accumulator. An auxiliary storage register allied to the main accumulator in a central processor unit.

Remote Terminal. See *Terminal.*

Software. The means by which the operation of a computer is controlled; software is the name given to the programs that cause a computer to carry out particular processing operations.

Source Language. The programming language used by a computer programmer when writing a source program, e.g. ALGOL, FORTRAN, COBOL, etc.

Source Program. A computer program in the format required by a source language. A source program may exist either in written form or on some data medium such as paper tape.

Standard Interface. A standard physical means by which all peripheral devices are connected to the central processor unit, i.e. a standard form of plug and socket.

Storage Device. A device used for storing information inside a computer, e.g. core store, tape store, disc store, drum store, etc.

Systems Programs. Programs provided by a computer manufacturer in order to relieve the user from many programming chores, e.g. control of input devices, output devices and storage devices, and various diagnostic aids used in program testing, etc.

Tape Reader. An input device used for transferring information from paper tape into the central processor unit of a computer.

Terminal. A configuration of computer hardware connected to a larger remotely-situated computer via a communication link; a terminal may typically consist of:

1. A teletypewriter.
2. A VDU.
3. A card reader/line printer with VDU.
4. A complete mini-computer.

Time-Sharing. A method of operation whereby a computer automatically shares its central processor with one or more input devices, output devices and storage devices so as to make the optimum use of the central processor unit. Since the peripheral devices operate relatively slowly compared with the speed of the central processor unit, this mode of operation allows the latter to keep the peripheral devices busy while still having spare time itself to carry out other parts of the current program which do not require the use of the peripheral devices, the effect is that many operations are able to proceed in parallel.

Visual Display unit (VDU). A television-like screen for the display of information output by the computer; an alpha-numeric VDU handles textual information while a graphical VDU handles information in the form of drawings.

Word. A computer word consists of the information stored to a set of binary digits in a single location in the computer's store. Different computers are designed to handle different lengths of computer word, e.g. 18, 24, 39, 48 binary digits.

Brien, Robert Frank, *Cert. in Arch. (Natal), FRIBA. (Principal Associate of Cusdin, Burden and Howitt). Awarded Edwin Swales Scholarship in 1946, and attended University of Natal School of Architecture. Joined Easton and Robertson, Cusdin Preston and Smith in 1961 and continued with Cusdin Burden and Howitt as Associate on formation of new practice in 1965. Specialist subjects include hospitals; wards and theatres; burns treatment units; residential accommodation and hostels. Job architect for many hospitals and accommodation including the Astor College for the Middlesex Hospital Medical School, London; residences, Nurses Training School and Staff Health Centre for Addenbrooke's Hospital, Cambridge; Computer Centre for the University of London and the Royal Victoria Hospital Development, Belfast.*

8 STUDIOS—RECORDING, RADIO & TV

SANDY BROWN, D.A., F.R.I.B.A.
Sandy Brown Associates

INTRODUCTION

The range in scale and complexity of studios is enormous. At one end of the range is to be found the small 'demo' (or demonstration) recording studio whose purpose is solely to produce a recording of sufficient quality to convince a recording company that the material is worth exploiting in a commercial manner; in short, a 'dry-run' studio with undemanding standards of quality. At the top end of the range is the TV/Radio Complex which, by its nature, will also include recording facilities (both video and audio) of the highest quality.

This section outlines the use for which studios may be required and states in simple terms various activities.

RADIO STUDIOS

(a) SYMPHONIC MUSIC

In broadcasting Symphonic music, an attempt is made to achieve a 'realistic' simulation at the receive of the sound of the music in the studio. Engineers recognise, of course, that 'true' realism is not attainable in listening conditions imposed by the dimensions and acoustics of a domestic living room (or a saloon car) but the effort is nevertheless made.

Many symphonic and operatic broadcasts are made in stereo (itself a misnomer as its derivation implies depth rather than biophony) in order to enhance the impression of reality. There is little doubt that well engineered stereo does just this, but the techniques used are no more than loosely based on placing two mikes as if they were ears (model heads are not used in practice in radio broadcasting). One seldom finds less than 4 or 5 microphones in service.

Symphonic music studios of the best quality do not need to approach the internal volume of a concert auditorium, but it is difficult to achieve first class results with a 100 piece orchestra if the studio has a volume of less than 10 000 m³. Other essential acoustic attributes are described later in this section.

Further reverberation is occasionally added to some forms of symphonic music. This can be achieved either by real reverberation from an echo (or reverberation) chamber or increasingly by artificial reverberation. In the latter case the electro-acoustic device most favoured is the echo (or reverberation) plate originally devised by W. Kuhl in 1958. One must bear in mind, therefore, that nowadays the interface between electronics and building even in the most 'real' domain of broadcasting is dynamic and moving towards electronic or electro-acoustic solutions.

(b) LIGHT ORCHESTRAL/DANCE MUSIC

The great majority of the Classical Symphonic and Operatic repertoire was written for performance in a natural acoustic environment and this was also once true of Light Orchestral Music. As an example, it is not exceptional to hear broadcast arrangements for Light Orchestra with a flute lead over 5 or 6 open brass.

In a concert hall the flute, being a quiet instrument, would be inaudible in these circumstances, so a microphone is brought close to the flute and its sound is electronically amplified. As the same situation could be applied to any quiet instrument, this has led to what is called the 'close microphone technique'.

The balance between the instruments is obtained by the engineer in the control room not the conductor in the studio and the broadcast sound is quite different to the 'real' sound in the studio. This means, in consequence, that the less intrusive the studio acoustics are, the better. (By 'intrusive' we can, by simplifying the definition somewhat, substitute 'reflective').

The studio should therefore be rather absorbent, but nowadays light-orchestral musicians throughout the world (mostly symphonic-trained) are unprepared to accept an acoustic environment as dead as that which is accepted by jazz and pop musicians. The designed reverberation time for a light orchestral studio should thus be below that for symphonic music and above that for jazz and pop studios.

From a volumetric criterion we can to some extent move to an area criterion. Assuming a maximum light orchestral complement of 70 players, the area required should be the area allowed for one 'symphonic' musician (1.1 m) $\times$ number of players = 770 m²). For reverberation, and other reasons, the height need not exceed 6 m so the volumetric maximum can be approximately 4600 m³. For a light orchestral/dance studio accommodating 35 players the appropriate area would be 385 m² and the volume 2300 m³. All these figures should be multiplied by a factor of $\times 1.5$ in the special case of light orchestral music: this for reasons to do with storage of screens, equipment and access.

(c) JAZZ AND OTHER ETHNIC MUSIC

Jazz shares with other ethnic music two important aspects:
(a) The tradition dates from a pre-electronic age.
(b) The number of musicians is usually small (1–16).
The consequences of (a) are that the musicians are used to hearing each other, with or without electro-acoustic aids and that some of the instrumentalists' techniques are based on purely acoustic phenomena. With (b) the area allocated can be small.

In the latter instance it is also true to say that jazz and other ethnic music players do not always demand the space normally allocated to symphonic players. The range of space allocation can, however, approach that for symphonic players where instruments are large (vibraphone, electric or electronic organ, drums). In other cases it can be reduced to 1.0 m per player and in all cases the multiplication factor can be $\times 1.30$: again for storage of screens, equipment and access. These are very crowded conditions indeed, but they have been totally successful.

(d) POP MUSIC

Pop music depends entirely upon electronic techniques. Almost none of it is completely 'live', even in a broadcasting situation. This means that the space allocation in a control room must be increased in order to accommodate more sophisticated control equipment.

On the other hand the studio space can be reduced, because 'over-dubbing' (a pejorative word where trade unions are concerned) is involved. This is simply a method of laying one or more solo tracks on top of others in order to build up a 'performance'. An example from the recording media may suffice to demonstrate this. The Beatles' Revolver Album took nine continuous weeks of usage in Trident Studios, London. Many later pop releases took much longer. A jazz album usually takes one day.

Pop studios are also inhabited by unamplified string players, often symphonic musicians, but only rudimentary measures are taken to 'match' symphonic conditions. In the great majority of cases the only concession is to provide approximately 30 % of the floor with removable, as opposed, to fixed carpeting; the surface under the removable carpet is reflective.

Although the increase in real reverberation time is small, an area of local reflection is very helpful to symphonic players in an alien acoustic environment. In a small number of cases 'variable' acoustic treatments are provided. The technical advantage of this technique is dubious and it has a serious disadvantage in that all mechanical forms of variable acoustics are frequency conscious: there are no ways, short of actually adding or removing absorption, which can achieve similarly shaped reverberation curves

with differing average values. Where mechanically variable acoustics are provided, it is usual, after an initial period of experimental use, to find that an optimum position is chosen and permanently adopted.

Various forms of electronic aids are employed to vary the electro-acoustic response of Pop studios, but these need not concern the designer. A satisfactory floor area for a fully flexible Pop studio is 150 m². A minimum volume, for this floor area, is 500 m³. The acoustic separation provided by screens can approach 15 dB average but as this value is too low to give an adequate level difference at the microphone between a full brass section remote from the microphone and a quiet local source such as a singer, a separate booth should have a floor area sufficient for eight singers. A normal size would be 20 m² floor area. The acoustic separation from the studio need not exceed 30 dB average.

(e) DRAMA

Radio studios for drama are normally designed to a 'live-end/dead-end' specification. The reverberation time of the whole studio is considered first, and subsequently, a large preponderance of the acoustic treatment is concentrated in the dead end. The calculated reverberation time of this part of the studio is normally 0.20–0.30 sec. It has been found that these values are always exceeded but the subjective difference between the two ends is marked. The reverberation time is never the whole story and this is particularly the case in a 'live-end/dead-end' condition.

The two halves of the studio are separated by a drawable double skin curtain extending, in the closed position, the full height and width of the studio. On the dead side, the curtain material should be absorbent (velour or similar) and on the live side, as reflective as possible (artificial close-weave fabric or similar). The volumes or such studios range from 600–850 m³ depending on the degree of sophistication required. At the top end of the range approximately 25 % of the available floor space is occupied by devices for acoustic effects (stairs with differing tread materials, booths, etc.).

The most sophisticated drama studios include a separate 'dead' and 'live' or 'echo' room. The 'dead' room must be near-anechoic; the walls and ceilings therefore require treatment with absorbing porous wedges of a total depth not less than 660 mm, and preferably 1.2 m. A plan-form addition to user requirements of 2.4 m in both horizontal dimensions is therefore likely. The 'live' room should have hard reflecting surfaces and be well protected from extraneous noise.

(f) ENTERTAINMENT

These studios require an audience and currently are invariably converted theatres or cinemas. Volumes range from 2800–8500 m³. New studios for this purpose should be of similar size. Reverberation times are designed to accommodate speech rather than music, although music is an integral requirement.

(g) GENERAL PURPOSE STUDIOS

Volumes range between 85 m³ and 850 m³, mostly at the lower end of the scale. Reverberation times are designed for speech rather than music.

(h) ANNOUNCERS(CONTINUITY)DISC-JOCKEY/TALKS

These studios range in volume from 50 m² (DJ's and announcers) to 200 m³ and reverberation times are designed for speech.

(i) SUMMARY

Extreme care should be exercised by the designer in defining the brief very closely in terms of usage. The appropriate design solutions are very different as will be apparent later in this guide.

TV STUDIOS

GENERAL

In all parts of the world, the uses of TV studios have now become multi-purpose. Previous decades had discriminated between music and drama. Economic pressures and the increasing acceptance of acoustically 'dead' conditions by musicians have combined to erode this distinction. Increasing use of zoom lenses rather than camera tracking has led to boom microphones being located further away from performers in extreme situations and this, in turn, has meant that reverberation times must be extremely low even in large TV studios.

Although all TV studios are now 'general purpose' in character, the smallest variety are normally used for presentation or news purposes. The absolute minimum floor area for such studios is 60 m² and an absolute minimum height, dictated by lighting, is 4 m.

(b) MAIN GENERAL PURPOSE STUDIOS

The horizontal dimensions of these studios are not critical but should give a clear floor area of 560 m² with a length to breadth ratio of approximately 1·15–1·25. The height to the ceiling grid should not be less than 11 m. Above the grid there should be a clear height of 2·5 m.

This is at variance with most TV studios in the USA, but it should be noted that the great majority of American TV productions, apart from news and chat shows, are filmed either on location or in normal film studios which have high ceilings. The height requirement is in respect of lighting and increasing usage of zoom techniques. It's also acknowledged that studios in the USA with low ceiling heights (5 m or so) impose production constraints which are not generally acceptable even by the users of such studios.

All TV studios which utilise mobile cameras, a category which includes all but the smallest examples, have reflecting floors with stringent level difference specifications. The maximum acceptable level change is 3 mm within a 3 m radius. In order to achieve the required low reverberation times (see Fig. 8.1) it is necessary to treat the entire wall and ceiling areas acoustically and, for this purpose, 400 mm should be added to each horizontal dimension and 200 mm to the vertical dimension in order to ensure the clear areas needed.

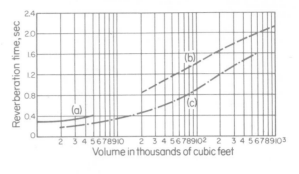

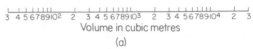

Fig. 8.1(a) *Optimum reverberation time of sound studios. Values represent maximum reverberation time in the frequency range 500–2000 Hz. (a) Studios for speech. (b) Music studios. (c) Other studios*

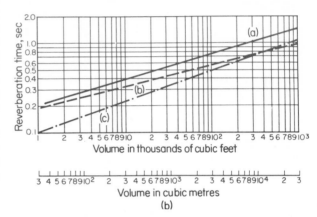

Fig. 8.1(b) *Optimum reverberation time of TV studios. Values represent maximum reverberation time in the frequency range 500–2000 Hz (a) Highest acceptable reverberation time. (b) Optimum reverberation time. (c) Lowest practicable reverberation time*

Lighting galleries at a height of approximately 4·5 m above studio floor level are required on all four walls of the studio. This level can be varied, locally, to avoid obstruction of doorways (scenery access) or observation windows (see later under 'control areas'). The lighting galleries should be a minimum of 1·25 m wide.

Within the area defined by the width of the lighting galleries, a cyclorama track is required. It is normal to have this track at a height no greater than 1 m below that of the lighting grid. This means that a cyclorama may obscure the view through the observation window, if there is one (see 'control areas').

RECORDING STUDIOS

POP/GENERAL PURPOSE

This is the main category in recording studio design and in general terms it conforms to the standards as laid down for radio studios. As the recording equipment is very often, though not always, more extensive than that for radio pop studios (where separate adjacent recording rooms are normal and accommodation in the control room must be made for record producers and other clients without either upsetting the acoustics or the sound balance engineer) the control room floor area must be larger than that for the radio version.

A normal control room size would for pop/general purpose be 50 m² floor area.

FILM DUBBING

This category resembles pop in some respects, but the control apparatus is normally in the studio itself. A further narrator's booth, 10 m² in floor area, is required and projection facilities are also needed. The vocalists booth can be omitted.

The projection facilities must be located over and behind the control desk in the studio thus generating a minimum ceiling height of 4 m. If the functions of pop/general purpose and film dubbing are combined, not an infrequent occurrence, the control room must be reinstated together with the vocalists booth. The projection room is thus inevitably located above the control room and the studio ceiling height will therefore be 6 m minimum. It should be remembered that in this configuration the control desk *inside* the studio must be retained so that *two* control desks are needed. Fig. 8.2 gives a typical diagrammatic combined arrangement.

It is usual for a film dubbing studio to occasionally assume the role of a film or Videotape preview·theatre. The extra requirement has no material consequence on design or planning of the studio or any ancillary accommodation except that dimmers (preferably thyristor) are mandatory on all lighting circuits. These are, in any case, desirable in' pop/general purpose and film dubbing studios.

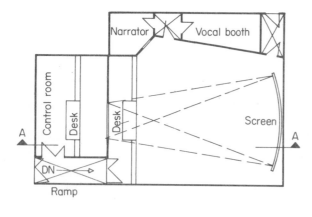

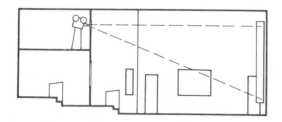

Fig. 8.2   Combined pop/general purpose and film dubbing studio

CONTROL AREAS

Every studio of any kind must have a control facility between the output from the studio and the final transmission or recording chain. The individual circumstances vary a great deal and are dealt with separately below.

LOCAL RADIO STATIONS CONTROL/STUDIO AREAS

Whether Local Radio Stations are State controlled, Corporation controlled, or Commercial is irrelevant. It is normal for the planning of each station to be dictated by the apportionment of programme material throughout the schedules. As this varies enormously (from exclusively news to exclusively pop output) uniformity cannot be expected. An added complexity to logical design is that, even when the output quotas in broadcasting schedules are more-or-less identical, there remains a diversity of opinion among Chief Engineers as to the best solutions.

It should also be remembered that nearly all local radio stations are situated in central urban areas and occupy relatively small floor areas (average 1000 m² plus ancillary office and other spaces) so that invariably the location is an existing building, with the consequent design constraints.

Some guidance about the choice of suitable existing buildings is essential:

(i) A clear floor to ceiling height of less than 3·7 m poses difficult technical problems both in terms of acoustics and routing of ventilation ductwork.

(ii) Timber floors and/or ceilings should be avoided where possible.

(iii) Basement areas present less problems than areas on other floors.

The control areas in Local Radio Stations are normally shared and must therefore, to some extent, be interchangeable. The fundamental requirement, however, is that there *must* be a Master Control Room which acts as the last link from the station in the transmission chain. There will be other Control Rooms which can be switched, through the Master Control Room, to monitor *any* of the studios whether they overlook them through observation windows or not. The dimensions of the Master Control Room will be dictated by the amount of equipment to be housed. Those of other Control Rooms should conform, as closely as possible, to those recommended for normal radio broadcasting studios, but some reduction in size (and therefore quality) is normally acceptable.

Where recorded pop music comprises a large proportion of the station output, the reduction can be as much as 30% of the floor area. Other parameters are provided in the following subsection.

RADIO BROADCASTING CONTROL AREAS

An acceptable minimum floor area for these areas is 30 m² with a minimum ceiling height of 3 m. If the recording equipment is contained in the room, the dimensions may have to be increased for functional reasons. An observation window is required between the control room and the studio controlled by it. This. like the wall between the areas, should provide a sound insulation value of at least 50 dB. A typical detail is shown in Fig. 8.3. A lower value would be acceptable where monitoring is *never* undertaken off magnetic tape.

68										
41	78	ORCHESTRAL/MULTIPURPOSE STUDIO								
75	1									
72		57								
45	82	37	69	DRAMA STUDIO						
75	1	90	1.4							
68		54		50						
41	78	34	66	—	58	TALKS/CONTINUITY/NARRATORS STUDIO				
75	1	90	1.4	—	1.4					
68		72		68		68				
41	78	45	82	41	78	36	73	LIGHT ENTERTAINMENT STUDIO		
75	1	75	1	75	1	75	1			
47		54		48		60				
37	62	34	66	28	56	35	70	CONTROL CUBICLE (Same programme in adjacent areas)		
125	2.8	90	1.4	90	1	90	1			
68		57		54		68		46		
41	78	41	65	34	66	41	78	—	56	CONTROL CUBICLE/MIXER (Other programmes in adjacent areas)
75	1	125	1	90	1.4	75	1	—	2	

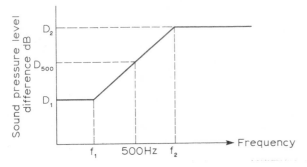

Sound pressure level difference at 500 Hz (dB)	
D_1 (dB)	D_2 (dB)
f_1 (Hz)	f_2 (Hz)

Fig. 8.3   Transmission loss between rooms.

Exclusively 'direct' monitoring is extremely rare and is likely to disappear altogether.

When studio sound is monitored from tape there is a time delay caused by the distance between the recording and play-back heads on the tape machine. Usually this delay is one fifth of a second. In speech, such a delay is disastrous as can be demonstrated by playing one's voice back on a recorder, even at a very low level. The psycho-acoustic effect is to induce stuttering and dyslexia.

Where circumstances allow, a sound cut-off lobby should be introduced between areas which require a specified sound insulation separation of more than 30 dB average (see under TV ancillaries later in this section). The sound cut-off lobby need not exceed 3·5 m² in floor area.

TV BROADCASTING CONTROL AREAS

(i) *Location*

No firm consensus has yet been reached as to whether TV Control Rooms should overlook the studios which they monitor or not. The tendency appears to incline towards the view that they should not, for the following reasons.

The cyclorama track and studio scenery are likely to interfere with the producer's view to an extent that the whole basis of direct visual contact is questionable. Where colour TV is concerned, an adjustment to an observation window, in terms of chroma, is required, in order to conform with the colours reproduced by the TV monitors. This distinction applies whichever system of colour TV transduction is employed. There are no commercially available tinted glazing systems which can cope with that problem, and an applied, tinted, finish is needed: all such finishes are friable, with a 'half-life' of approximately one year. Producers are inclining to the view that production decisions should be made by examining the picture on monitor screens. Furthermore, the disadvantage of immediate same-level access to the studio floor being unavailable to production staff if it must be overlooked from a higher level, can be obviated in the planning of the complex.

It is less easy to define the arguments against 'no-direct-

vision' control rooms for TV studios in cogent terms. That
this is true should not sway designers: arguments which are
easily marshalled may often be suspect simply because they
are so easily marshalled. Arguments against are less amend-
able to rush logic. They can be summarised by noting that
the Producer—ultimately responsible for the programme
content—has no un-electronic visual contact either with his
floor manager or with the performers. All the more important that the brief should be agreed by the Client, having
given both alternatives to him in a simple description. This
should, in all cases, be accompanied by an assessment of
the comparative costs. Conditions will dictate costs, but the
direct visual contact (overlooking the studio) situation is
normally more expensive by a large margin.

(ii) Plan-form

In major TV studio control areas it is normal to include three
elements: Lighting and Vision, Sound and Production, in
one connected area with approximately 25 dB average
separation between each and with visual contact. The
Lighting and Vision control and the Sound control should
have a minimum floor area of 30 m². The Production
Control room—which should always be central—should
have a minimum floor area of 40 m². A normal minimum
ceiling height would be 3·5 m. Acoustically, the Production
and Lighting and Vision Control Rooms should be as dead
as possible, disregarding the shape of the reverberation curve
related to frequency. The acoustics of the Sound Control
room should be designed to a *level* curve of approximately
0·35 sec.

(iii) Internal layout

No element changes more rapidly than electronic gadgetry.
Amortization over a period of 5 years is not unusual. Designers
can only take heart from the realisation that equipment has,
without exception, reduced in physical dimensions over the
years. This has been an invariable rule but it follows no
linear pattern.

Moreover, new gadgets appear and are either necessary or
desired by clients, so that the overall dimensions of control
areas have not significantly diminished in the last 20 years.
On the other hand, the overall dimensions have not increased. The reasonable conclusion to draw is that a space
allocated in the mid-1970's will be adequate for future
changes.

While these comments are the result of extrapolation,
(informed guesswork if you like), the same is not true of the
Production Control room. In this room there must be space
for at least eight TV monitors, possibly on two levels, one
above the other, and these are not subject to changes
wrought by electronics but to the sensitivity of the human
eye-brain system which operates no faster than the evolu-
tionary scale. It would therefore be wise for the designer to
concentrate on this part of the brief in order to acquire clear
instructions from the client on what is required. If in doubt,
add 20 % in floor area and fully identify the reasons for
doing so to the client.

SOUND INSULATION AND VIBRATION
PRIMARY DESIGN INFORMATION
The importance of giving all design team members, main
contractors and subcontractors, identical and compre-
hensible information cannot be over emphasised. Typical
examples of:
(a) Maximum permissible noise levels from all sources;
(b) Noise criterion curves;
(c) Typical 35 dB sound insulating door detail and,
(d) Typical 50 dB insulation observation window detail.
are given in the appendices. Vibration, in the sense that it
concerns stability of the structure, is within the province and
responsibility of the structural engineer. Where it concerns
noise levels in studios or technical areas, the responsibility
should be identified. If not, it will be thrust on the shoulders
of the architect unless an absolution clause can be written
into the Memorandum of Agreement or other approved
Contract with the client. The appropriate Code of Practice
would appear to be the Code of Practice for Composite
Construction rule 117 which was not designed for this
purpose, but it serves well to identify a crucial and difficult
matter which defies simple analysis. In the BS note, designers
are warned against the possibility of encountering induced
vibrations which coincide with the natural frequency of
the structure. As the latter is not, in the majority of cases,
calculable within reasonable certainty, designers are being
asked, as a matter of law, to provide a service which is not
capable of solution where a redundant structure is involved.
It would be extremely unwise for any Professional to enter
this area without either (a) a full explanation to, and
indemnity from, the Client, or (b), expert advice on the
subject.

In short: any elastic structure will vibrate if driven by
any form of energy. 'Undesirable' vibrations will jeopardise
Professionals in the Courts. As 'undesirable' has not, in the
mid-70's, been defined by the Courts, it seems sensible to
eschew unknown legal implications particularly where
acoustic parameters are concerned.

It is certainly not enough to provide anti-vibration
mountings to machinery without giving close consideration
to the frequency components involved in the machinery,
the anti-vibration mountings *and* the structure itself.

In cases where studios or other 'noise-protected' technical
areas are located in steel or concrete frame buildings, and
where the floors of these areas are not in direct and continuous
contact with the solum under the building, it is essential to
'float' the studios. There are a number of suitable methods
available: steel springs, rubber carpet mountings and re-
newable anti-vibration mountings. The advantage of the
latter (replaceability) is not great unless some major future
change in the floor loading is foreseen. In all cases the
maximum natural frequency should not exceed 7–10 Hz.
This frequency should also be considered in conjunction with
some assessment of the natural frequency of the structure
upon which the floated areas rest. As stated earlier it is not
possible to assess this with a degree of accuracy that would
obviate possible adverse coincidences between harmonics of
the fundamental resonances.

SPECIAL CASES
(i) TV Scenery doors

These doors must be large enough to accommodate the

largest TV scenery and props. The clear opening should be 4·3 m × 3 m. They are normally electrically operated on the 'lift-and-slide' principle so that the weight of the door seals on all edges, including the threshold. This last is important because a raised threshold, or any similar impediment to camera dollies or trollies of any description, is unacceptable.

It should also be noted that as a sound insulation value of 50 dB average is required from the door, and a manoeuvrable lightweight construction is required, it is not possible to design a door which would also satisfy fire codes in most parts of the world. This occurs for reasons which are too complex to explain here, but they are well supported and logical. At least one, and possibly two, fire shutters are required in series to the scenery doors.

(ii) *Electric and electronic trunking*

It is essential that trunking be provided between areas connected in programming. In a number of cases the trunking cannot readily be made airtight. The most extreme example is that of TV coaxial cables, which can accommodate a radius no tighter than 0·5 m. Any 90° turn will therefore demand this tolerance, and, as the turns tend to coincide with penetration of walls, floors and/or ceilings, this is a problem which deserves special attention.

The normal way to achieve the most acceptable results is to partition the holes through the structure in a direction parallel to the cable and if possible, normal to the partition. The compartments should extend to 1 m in toto and internally should be packed tight with bags of heavy density mineral wool. Externally they should be grouted into the structure and the cracks or interstices plugged with non-hardening mastic. The compartments can be constructed in any suitable building material such as reinforced concrete, steel, or, if fire codes allow, timber.

(iii) *Smoke-outlets*

These are not always required, and when they are, only for TV Studios. They should be designed as a sound cut-off lobby rotated through 90° and *both* sets of doors should be activated by a fusible link. Consult the local fire codes.

(iv) *Location*

Every location must be treated as a special case. The ambient and foreseeable noise levels will vary. In each case a full one-third octave band, site noise level survey must be carried out and the enclosing structure designed accordingly.

It should be borne in mind that a sound insulation value, using a homogeneous partition, can never exceed 65 dB average within reasonably economic bounds. Nor, in some types of ambient noise environment with a large low-frequency content, can a double or triple leaf lightweight structure help to reduce the residual low-frequency component of the noise in sensitive areas.

TV ANCILLARIES

There are a burgeoning number of these which will be identified in any brief. The major concern will be with VTR/Telecine Areas.

This is happily much more simple and amenable to solution than the portenteous title would imply. Although Video-Tape-Recording and telecine (a TV camera that looks at a film) are very different articles, their planning requirements are practically indistinguishable. It is not important to keep the background noise level below that which would be suitable for open-plan offices. What *is* important is that the operator of each machine should be able to hear cues through a small, average quality, loudspeaker, above the noise of other cues nearby and the ambient noise in the room. A very satisfactory solution is to house each machine, whether VTR or Telecine, in cubicles separated with heavily acoustically treated walls and ceilings. Doors to these cubicles are undesirable but an acoustically treated valance, draped to door-head level, is worthwhile. All the cubicles should be under the surveillance of a central control position.

Last link from station. A master switch/Control Room is always required. This will be defined in the brief and can be treated acoustically as an open-plan office environment.

TV SCENERY

Resistance should be offered to long-term storage of TV scenery in central urban areas. If this advice is accepted, it should also be recognised that deliveries present other problems to do with traffic and urban planning.

MECHANICAL SERVICES

Previously this has been considered as a design problem specific to TV/Radio Broadcasting and Recording Complexes, but this is not so. The heatloads should be calculated on the current available data in the normal way. No other considerations need be examined. As electronic aids become more sensitive pro rata of power (and therefore heat) output, less compass is expected of the air handling and cooling system. Of course, this results, eventually, in over-design, but no certain means of predicting advances in electronics exists. To essay it might mean a longish period of discomfort and inefficiency for the Client.

APPENDICES

Anything outside the extraordinary world of studio complexes described above is within the competence and scope of a professional architect. Armed with this information he should not take fright but do his normal work in reasonable confidence. It would not, be sensible however to undertake it without advice. There are a number of firms who will provide such advice and their names are available from the professional architectural organisations. Studio planning is a special sphere between architecture, engineering physics and law. The difficulties are formidable but not insuperable, as you can witness on your radios, TV screens and Hi-Fi sets. Useful data is given in Appendices 1–4.

Noise Rating Curves

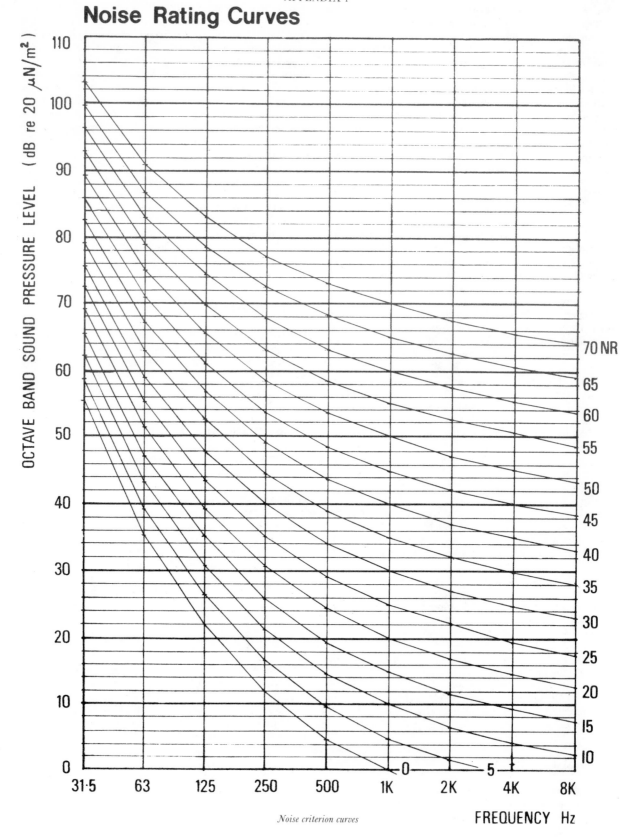

Noise criterion curves

APPENDIX 2

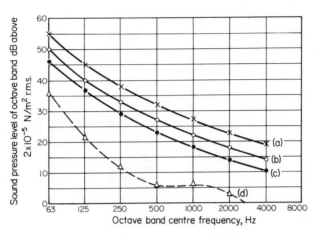

(a) RADIO STUDIOS,
    LIGHT ENTERTAINMENT
(b) TV STUDIOS
(c) RADIO DRAMA
(d) THRESHOLD OF HEARING FOR
    CONTINUOUS SPECTRUM NOISE

Permissible background noise levels in studios for radio and TV

APPENDIX 3

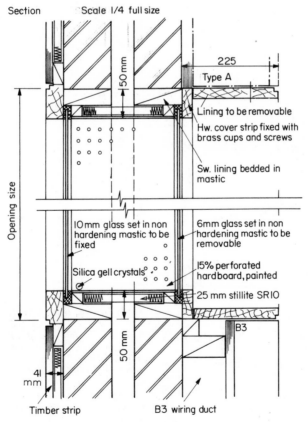

Typical double-glazed observation window

APPENDIX 4

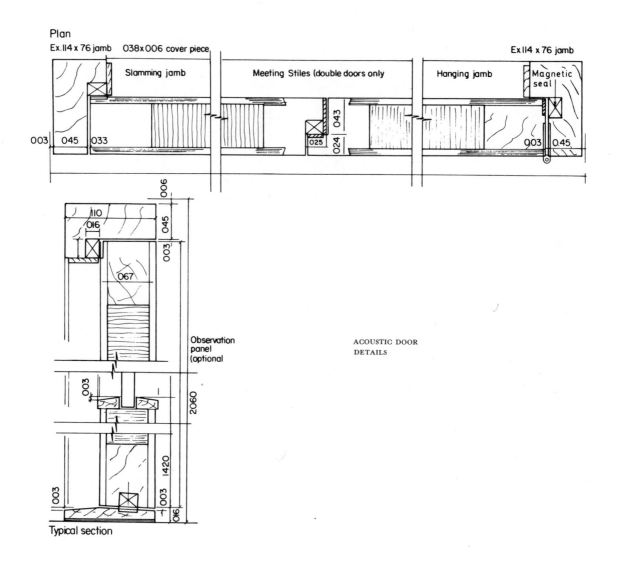

Plan

Ex.114 x 76 jamb   038x006 cover piece

Slamming jamb   Meeting Stiles (double doors only   Hanging jamb   Magnetic seal   Ex 114 x 76 jamb

003 | 045 | 033   025 | 024 | 043   003 | 0.45

006

110
016
003
045
003

067

Observation panel (optional

003

2060

1420

003   003

016

Typical section

ACOUSTIC DOOR
DETAILS

BIBLIOGRAPHY

Burd, A. N., Gifford, C. L. S. and Spring, N. S., *Data for the acoustic design of studios* (1966).
Brown, S., 'Recording studios for popular music', *Proc. 5th Int. Congress on Acoustics*, Liege (1965).
Gifford, C. L. S., *Acoustics for Radio and TV studios*, IEE Monograph Series (II) (1972).
Sabine, W. C., *Collected papers on acoustics*, Harvard University Press (1972).

Sandy Brown, *D.A., R.I.B.A. Founder of Sandy Brown Associates in 1968. Studied at Edinburgh University and Edinburgh College. Acoustic expert, for 16 years head of BBC Acoustic Department. Sandy Brown Associates are consultants to London Weekend Television, the Kings Reach Scheme, Usher Hall Edinburgh and the Edinburgh Opera House as well as the designer of radio and recording studios in England and many other parts of the world.*

Sandy Brown was a jazz musician of world wide reputation (voted Europe's best clarinetist from 1960–72). He was also a writer with a regular jazz column in ' The Listener' and several T.V. scripts to his credit. He died in March 1975 aged 46, but the practice is continuing under the same name.

INDEX

1

INDEX